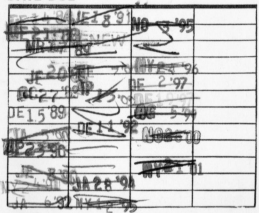

Race and Schooling in the City

Race and Schooling in the City

EDITED BY

Adam Yarmolinsky
Lance Liebman
and
Corinne S. Schelling

HARVARD UNIVERSITY PRESS

Cambridge, Massachusetts, and London, England · 1981

Library of Congress Cataloging in Publication Data

Main entry under title:
Race and schooling in the city.
   Bibliography: p.
   Includes index.
      1. School integration—United States.
2. Discrimination in education—Law and legislation
—United States. I. Yarmolinsky, Adam.
II. Liebman, Lance. III. Schelling, Corinne Saposs.
LC214.2.R32   370.19'342   80-20424
ISBN 0-674-74577-9

*This collection of essays was prepared under the auspices
of the American Academy of Arts and Sciences.*

Contents

Part Three / Approaches for the 1980s

Part Four / An Overview

Preface

During the Boston school busing controversy of the late 1970s I found myself in a state of considerable frustration. As a participant in one of the advisory bodies established by the Court, I was close enough to the situation to be aware of most of the obstinate difficulties in the way of progress, but not close enough to do anything about them—even if I could figure out what ought to be done.

It occurred to me that it might be worthwhile to try an approach that in the past had yielded some modest successes in dealing with problems almost as intractable as this one. The approach called for assembling a small group of people who were already sensitized to the problem, but not actively embroiled in it, and asking them to try over several day-long meetings to find ways out of existing dilemmas. Their deliberations would be stimulated by papers prepared for the meetings, and might in turn stimulate new ways of dealing with the problem.

The American Academy of Arts and Sciences agreed to sponsor the study group. With the encouragement of its executive officer, John Voss, and generous support from the Ford Foundation, the George Gund Foundation, and the Charles F. Kettering Foundation (and later from the New World Foundation), we invited some two dozen people to commit themselves for three day-and-a-half meetings over a period of a year. Surprisingly, almost everyone invited agreed to take part, and several others asked to join. As it worked out, the process did not altogether meet the original prescription. The study group included several activists who were willing to take time off to speculate about what they were doing; and, on an issue so sensitive and already so thoroughly explored, it was inevitable that a good deal of time would be taken up reiterating preconceptions and defending previously established positions. It was also predictable that no common conclusions or recommendations would be reached for a problem with so many ramifications. But during the sessions the group explored many ideas, opinions, and policy suggestions that the Academy and the study group organizers felt should be made available to a wider audience. The papers published here are among those commissioned for the meetings, extensively revised in the light of discussion. They reflect the wide range of issues and viewpoints examined in the three study group sessions.

The proliferation of issues under the rubric of urban school desegregation was dramatized by the 1979 reopening of the landmark case of *Brown* v. *Board of Education*, twenty-five years after it had been decided by the United States Supreme Court. The case was reopened on the initiative of the next generation of parents in Topeka, Kansas, including the daughter of the plaintiff in the original lawsuit. The issues in the reopened case include the substantial disparities between proportions of black and white students attending individual Topeka schools (which vary widely in both directions from the percentage of black and white students in the entire school system). There is also a separate lawsuit by a white parent attacking the school district's long-range facilities plan, and another private suit by a student claiming that she had received inferior education because of school desegregation, as well as a dispute between the continuing authority of the court and that of the federal Department of Health, Education, and Welfare. The situation in Topeka today is atypical only in the relatively low proportion of black students in the system, and in the apparent absence of controversy about the role of black teachers and administrators.

Without attempting to attribute conclusions or recommendations to the Academy study group, as a participant-observer I can at least describe how my own perceptions of the problem were changed as a result of the deliberations, and how I now view the prospects for constructive change. As I saw it, two perhaps obvious conclusions emerged almost immediately from the discussions:

(1) The urban school desegregation problem has been radically transformed since the 1950s. It is no longer a matter of disestablishing formally separate systems, but rather of attempts (admittedly not always in the best of faith) to mitigate the external influences that tend to reinforce segregation.

(2) The resegregation of the inner city is—or appears to be—a more intractable problem than the problem of breaking down the original dual school systems. Yet it is no less important to resolve, in a society that sees easy association among members of different ethnic groups as a prerequisite for equality of opportunity, as well as a virtue in itself.

There was surprisingly little discussion in the study group of the great issue of busing. Perhaps the arguments pro and con had been rehearsed too often, but I prefer to believe that the absence of discussion was the result of an unspoken agreement that busing is a generally necessary but never sufficient instrument for desegregation, and that it is best, therefore, to concentrate on those issues that will suggest additional elements that must be added to a comprehensive program.

The study group meetings revealed basic disagreements about both the underlying facts and the hierarchy of values on which policy should be based. Revision of the original papers has not perceptibly narrowed the range of disagreement. In the face of the clash of views on remedies, and even on the nature of the problem, two observations emerge. First, we are still at the stage where we need to apply a changing combination of approaches, since individual measures seem to generate resistance proportional to their potential for effectiveness. And second, one can distill from the group discussions, and equally from the chapters in this book, a continuing conviction that we cannot afford to abandon the search for solutions. At a minimum we can adopt the formulation of William of Orange that "it is not necessary to hope in order to attempt nor to succeed in order to persevere." Or we might choose the slightly more encouraging formulation offered in Chapter 5 by Harold Isaacs, in his quotation from William Morris: "Men fight and lose the battle, and the thing they fought for comes about in spite of their defeat and when it comes it turns out to be not what they meant, and other men have to fight for what they meant, under another name."

Adam Yarmolinsky

Race and Schooling in the City

Introduction

American public affairs have been bedeviled in recent years by our inability to decide what we know. Committing vast resources to social research, we have swung between two extremes: that knowledge would soon offer solutions to complex problems, and that all intelligence is contingent and therefore irrelevant to decision on any question that matters.

The issue of school integration illustrates this problem. On the one hand, we have explored in great detail every statistical correlation that can be built upon twenty-five years of post-*Brown* educational experience. On the other hand, we have too often made public decisions as if information, experience, thought, and prediction cannot advance policy, cannot even narrow the range of disagreement among persons whose values differ or who rank differently the relevant goals.

The American Academy study group began in 1977, as the country approached the twenty-fifth anniversary of *Brown* v. *Board of Education* and as Boston began to implement its court-ordered desegregation plan. The meetings were explicitly based on the assumption that we had learned from the experience of recent years, and could make better choices if we attended to what we had learned. Our premise was not that research compels policy, only that it can structure choices; we also felt that informed debate about goals and values is desirable, for its own sake and as a guide to action.

When in 1954 the Supreme Court, in *Brown* v. *Board of Education of Topeka*, declared that racially segregated schools violated the constitutional rights of black children, the Court was finally beginning the long and difficult process of ending America's caste system, of extending true citizenship to blacks and other nonwhite persons. But the Court was also saying important things about public education: that racially separate schools are educationally harmful to all students; that separation stigma-

1

tizes blacks and whites, that racial discrimination cannot be an *educational* policy. Step by step, the courts and the other branches of government have had to deal with questions of fact and value unanswered by *Brown*: What of freedom-of-choice plans that do not achieve integration? What of neighborhood schools that mirror the segregation of the neighborhoods? What of municipal boundaries that are in fact color bars? What of heavily black cities, and cities of diverse nonwhite populations?

The chapters of this book present their authors' evaluations and proposals on these and other unresolved issues. In doing so, they offer instruction on the relevance of fact to value and the forms of rational argument on a controversial subject. Particularly interesting are the questions the authors choose to address. To ask whether racial integration has improved the reading scores of black children is one sort of question. To ask whether it has improved race relations, or affected the racial composition of cities or schools, or made bilingual education impossible —each is its own kind of question, asked because of an attitude to education and to justice, calling for data of a different kind. It is one kind of inquiry to ask whether integration as we have sought it has aggravated tension or contributed to so-called white flight. It is another to ask whether that flight is morally justified, or whether it leaves the city unintegrable. And it is an entirely different inquiry to ask what strategies, if pursued by political and educational leaders, make integration more or less successful, and by what measure of success.

For all the conflicting answers to conflicting questions that arise from conflicting values, a great deal is known about school integration, and should be recognized as known by those (emphatically including citizens) who make policy on education and on race relations. For example:

• Racial and economic integration by themselves do not seem to change school performance greatly. Student self-perception and teacher perception of students are vital and can be affected by positive strategies in the home, the educational system, and the polity. But substantial evidence supports the proposition that integration alone will neither teach children to read nor prevent their learning.

• The process of integration can be an occasion for altering ongoing routines in a large school system. Public bureaucracies are hard to change at all, and especially hard to change for the better. Integration can occur in ways that are generally desirable for the educational process, or it can become an experience in uncreative disorientation. Preparation and leadership matter.

• Schools are part of the urban political process. They teach children, but they also socialize children and supply jobs to adults. Integration is a piece of the fabric of political authority, a significant component in a landscape of expanding minority populations, disharmony among racial and ethnic minorities, and what the English call "gentrification"— middle-class urban resettlement.

• American communities vary. Big cities are complex social enterprises, difficult places in which to carry out managed change. Integration has been accomplished far more satisfactorily in middle-sized cities than in the nation's twenty or so giant metropolises.

• Voluntary behavior can be more effective than coerced action. That suggests incentives. But if the basic undertaking is moral or constitutional, it is hard to explain why incentives, rather than binding orders, are appropriate. Is it not unfair to seek integration by methods (financial incentives) that will attract compliance chiefly from those without the financial means to refuse? In any event, a period of perceived shortage of public funds is a difficult time for enactment of noncoercive schemes.

• School integration will come more easily when there is integration of neighborhood housing arrangements. Yet housing separation may persist until economic opportunities are shared more equally among the races— that is, until there is integration on the job. And given the correlation between place in the labor market and length and status of education, we may indeed face a circular problem: we must have integrated schools before we can have integrated jobs before we can have integrated housing before we can have integrated schools. It is at least one theoretical solution to this trilemma to say, as a few of the contributors to this book do, that quality predominantly minority schools will lead to jobs and eventually to integrated housing and schools.

Aware of these considerations, knowledgeable about the variety of America's community situations, actively involved in the issues in different ways, from different points of leverage, the participants in these meetings and authors of these chapters do not see the future with clarity and consensus. Indeed, they sometimes seem as divided, confused, ambivalent, and unimaginative as the general population. Yet all are convinced that the country has vital decisions to make, that those decisions will shape our society, that they can only be made based upon a realistic assessment of facts and satisfactory explication of values, and that facts and values can be improved by consideration and communication.

The first part of the book reviews what has happened since *Brown*.

Diane Ravitch describes the tension between two opposing commitments, each encouraged by legislation of the 1960s, brought into conflict by the idea and especially by the implementation of desegregation. These are the commitments to equality of opportunity and to community control. Ravitch also discusses recent big-city demographic trends that bring into question not only the possibility of achieving desegregation but even the very definition of racial balance. Gary Orfield traces the southern desegregation experience, identifying the factors that were critical to its success and that are now lacking in the North. To be successful, desegregation plans must be tailored to local conditions and must be backed by clear administrative and legal commitments that have not existed since urban desegregation efforts were introduced in the North. The legal complexities and confusions central to the history of desegregation are analyzed by Frank Goodman, who concludes that the Supreme Court has not managed to achieve satisfactory doctrine about the nature of the desegregation duty or the relation between violation and remedy. Nancy St. John reports on the effect of desegregation, where it has taken place, on the academic achievement, self-concept, and racial attitudes of children. She reviews social science research results through 1977 and concludes that mere mixing will be neither beneficial nor detrimental, but that we are learning about the conditions under which integration brings positive results.

Part II analyzes some of the major changes in circumstances and attitudes since the *Brown* decision, changes that help explain the differences in the extent of the national commitment to desegregation. Harold Isaacs is concerned that the values of cultural pluralism have become so strong that they are eroding the cohesion of the national social fabric; he asserts that special efforts are required to halt this fragmentation. Indeed, the issues Isaacs raises appear in one form or another in almost every chapter (as community control, for example, in Ravitch; as black perspective in Barbara Jackson; as bilingualism in Linda Hanten). Charles Willie questions the generally accepted view that there is a "shortage" of white students in urban areas. He sees equal benefits from racial mixing for whites and for blacks and says that if a system is unitary it does not matter whether the majority of pupils are white or black. Willie also predicts the adoption of new educational goals, stressing truth and honesty as well as "communication and calculation skills," in school systems that are heavily black and brown. Finally, Nathan Glazer examines the continued and intensified housing segregation by race and class in urban areas, which he feels is in large part a result of personal preference. All the authors agree that this segregation, whatever its cause, contributes greatly to the difficulty of desegregating schools. Glazer concludes that integration in the economic, political, and cultural spheres must precede housing desegregation; only then will school desegregation take place.

The third part of the book outlines policy approaches for the 1980s. On the basis of a review of recent social science research (especially subsequent to that summarized by St. John), Willis Hawley outlines the policies schools must adopt to make desegregation effective. He believes that these programs can and should be implemented; others disagree with him. It is not always clear whether that is because they do not accept his interpretation of the research evidence or because they do not believe it is possible to implement such policies without seriously infringing on values they rank ahead of racially integrated schools. Questions of political feasibility as well as of value differences underlie the disagreements between Thomas Pettigrew and some of the other contributors. Pettigrew presents the case for official metropolitanization plans. James Coleman also would like to see metropolitanization, but only as a consequence of individual choice. He writes about the role of incentives, reminding the reader of the ineffectiveness of public policies that do not have the support of those whom they most affect.

The ostensible beneficiaries of policies that flow from *Brown*, black schoolchildren, are the prime concern of Derrick Bell. He sees current programs as damaging to academic achievement, and recommends court action directed toward improving education rather than toward increasing racial mixing. His position is echoed by Barbara Jackson, who describes the court-sponsored Atlanta Settlement Plan as one designed to achieve the best possible education for black children. In addition, a first-rate black urban school system, she says, may ultimately lead to integration if it attracts whites back to the city. It should be noted that where Jackson sees potential success in Atlanta, Orfield remains skeptical about this substitute for integration. This difference stems from varying interpretations of the evidence or the facts. Where Jackson says first-rate education in all-black systems is possible, Orfield and some of the other contributors would clearly disagree. This disagreement reflects a difference of opinion about the social goals of education, especially the independent value of racial mixing. That issue is also touched by Linda Hanten's chapter on bilingualism, the most interesting and difficult context for considering cultural pluralism. Finally, David Kirp describes a very different approach to racial policy and the schools, the British official policy of "inexplicitness," which contrasts sharply with our own interventionist policy.

Additional issues raised throughout this book include the role of the courts in making social policy, the function of different branches and levels of government, the complex connections between schools and other sectors of society, and above all the ways in which a fragmented society moves to meet new circumstances without creating profoundly damaging conflict and disorganization. In the final chapter Lance Liebman faces these questions and asks what are the implications of pursuing some of the values discussed earlier, and which of them should become constitutional values, formulated and implemented judicially.

The following chapters, then, are not offered as coherent policy; they are far from that. Rather they are presented as points of view held by concerned and knowledgeable persons at the start of the 1980s, in the hope that they may provoke the reader's thoughts and challenge his assumptions about these complicated questions.

Lance Liebman
Corinne S. Schelling

PART ONE

Since *Brown*

1   The Evolution of School Desegregation Policy, 1964-1979

DIANE RAVITCH

The context in which school desegregation takes place has been substantially altered by the legal, political, demographic, and cultural changes of the past fifteen years. A time-traveler from the early 1960s would be astonished to discover that by the end of the 1970s Americans had become relatively blase about events that only a few years ago would have seemed impossible. At the time this chapter was written, in 1979, the time-traveler would have observed extensive signs of change in the position of blacks in American society, such as: active black political participation in states that had fought since Reconstruction to keep blacks disenfranchised; black mayors in major cities, including Los Angeles, Detroit, Newark, Atlanta, and New Orleans; a black spokesman for the United States at the United Nations; a black Solicitor General of the United States and a black director of the Civil Rights Division of the Justice Department; black politicians working with George Wallace, the one-time symbol of white opposition to racial equality; Lester Maddox, formerly a symbol of redneck racism, parodying himself in a nightclub act with a black partner; the conviction of a Klansman in Birmingham for the 1963 bombing of a church in which four black children were killed, a verdict sought by a native white southern prosecutor and delivered by a racially mixed jury; replacement of the word *Negro* by the word *black*; the new popularity among blacks, especially the young, of natural appearance at the expense of hair straighteners and skin lighteners; black actors on television programs and commercials; and the success of black plays and movies. In a remarkably brief time the legal, political, and institutional supports for racism have been dismantled. We are too close to the period to know with certainty how the various personalities, events,

This chapter was published previously in *History of Education* 7(1978):229-236 and appears here, in revised form, by permission of Taylor and Francis, Ltd.

and trends of the recent past interacted to produce particular changes. But one thing seems clear, and that is that the pace of change has been faster than anyone would have dared to predict in January of 1964.

I contend that there have been two major themes in the domestic political and social arena during the past fifteen years: the pursuit of equality and the pursuit of community. These two goals have often clashed; indeed, such conflicts are inevitable, given the nature of the goals—the one universalistic, the other particularistic. Those who pursue equality demand the right to be treated the same as everyone else; those who pursue community demand the right to be different. Learning to live with these conflicts without sacrificing either equality or community may be the new American dilemma.

The period from 1964 to 1979 has been marked by intense controversy and by the emergence of new values. If one were writing a history of these fifteen years from the perspective of the pursuit of equality, the logical starting point would be the passage of the Civil Rights Act of 1964, which was the first comprehensive legislation of its kind since the Reconstruction era and which firmly added the power of the executive branch to the fight against discrimination. If one were writing a history from the perspective of the pursuit of community, the place to begin would be the passage of the Economic Opportunity Act of 1964, which launched not just the antipoverty program but also a debate about the nature of community and about the relation of group life to individual well-being.

Obviously history is not divided into neat boxes for the convenience of future readers, and it would be a gross distortion to apply tunnel vision from one perspective or the other. Nonetheless, it is ironic that these laws, passed in the same year by the same coalitions, both in response to the demands of the civil rights movement, ultimately had implications that were quite dissimilar. Although no one recognized it at the time, the two laws legitimized opposing ideas and commitments that continue to lend ambiguity to the meaning and direction of desegregation. The Civil Rights Act was a watershed for the civil rights movement and a culmination of decades of activity on behalf of racial equality. The Economic Opportunity Act, most particularly the community action program, set in motion new forces in minority communities by giving political power and recognition to those who were primarily interested in local control of jobs and programs. The one gave legal sanction to those who made desegregation their first priority, the other gave organizational impetus to those whose chief concern was community development. The Civil

Rights Act made a value of negating local control (which was identified with bigotry), the poverty program made a value of encouraging individual participation and decentralized control against bureaucratic imposition (which was identified as the establishment or power structure). The conflict in means and ends was not apparent in 1964; it only became apparent when the tensions between community and equality were revealed in particular controversies.

The importance of the Civil Rights Act of 1964 in the implementation of school desegregation cannot be overstated. The key section was Title VI, which empowered the federal government to cut off federal funds to districts that were guilty of racial discrimination. In 1964 this was not an especially controversial item, because there still was no general program of federal aid to local schools; threatening to cut off federal funds, therefore, did not appear to be a very potent weapon. Furthermore, northern concerns that the act might be used to bring about racial balance in northern school districts were assuaged in Title IV of the Civil Rights Act by an explicit prohibition of efforts to impose racial balance: " 'Desegregation' means the assignment of students to public schools and within such schools without regard to their race, color, religion, or national origin, but 'desegregation' shall not mean the assignment of students to public schools in order to overcome racial imbalance." Nonetheless, the enactment of Title VI as an enforcement mechanism for school desegregation was of great significance, particularly because the decade since the *Brown* decision had demonstrated the effectiveness of the southern strategy of massive resistance to desegregation: whereas 58 percent of black children in the border states were in biracial schools by 1964-65, only 2 percent of black students in the Deep South attended school with whites (*Southern Education Report*, 1966, p. 29).

If a fund cut-off provision was of limited utility in 1964, it became an instrument of great power in 1965, with the passage of the Elementary and Secondary Education Act (ESEA). Since the 1880s Congress had tried and failed to pass a general aid-to-education bill; federal assistance had always been blocked by concerns about religion, race, and local control. Some public-school supporters insisted that public money should go only to public schools; Catholic groups were equally adamant against federal aid that excluded nonpublic schools. Some groups opposed federal aid if it went to segregated schools; other opposed it if it could not go to segregated schools. And still other pressure groups worried that federal aid would erode local control and bring about standardization and federal control. The religious issue had undermined President John F.

Kennedy's attempt to gain approval for federal aid to education in 1961, and some observers at the time thought such a bill would not pass for many years. But Lyndon Johnson, swept into office in a great landslide and abetted by lopsided Democratic majorities in both houses of Congress, made the passage of federal aid to education one of his top priorities in 1965. The President's education aides worked out an acceptable compromise between major groups on the issue of aid to nonpublic schools, settling the religious question; the existence of Title VI of the Civil Rights Act of 1964 foreclosed the race issue, since it was already illegal to grant funds to segregated schools. And the size of the Democratic majorities in Congress simply overwhelmed those who were concerned about the intrusion of federal control into local affairs (Meranto, 1976).

Thus Title VI and the ESEA had a mutual feedback effect: the existence of Title VI cleared the way for ESEA by eliminating the customary fight over the racial issue, and the federal funds of ESEA made Title VI a powerful weapon in the enforcement of school desegregation. Between 1966 and 1974, Title VI cut-off proceedings were started against 634 school districts, and another 646 school districts in southern and border states were placed under federal court order to desegregate (U.S. Department of Health, Education, and Welfare, 1974, pp. 2-3). Gary Orfield, in *The Reconstruction of Southern Education*, has showed how the United States Office of Education and the Office for Civil Rights employed Title VI to desegregate southern school districts by abrogating local control (Orfield, 1969). According to the Office for Civil Rights, by 1972, because of compliance agreements and court orders, 46.3 percent of all southern black pupils were in schools that were more than 50 percent white; only 24.5 percent were in schools that were more than 90 percent minority. Indeed, by 1972 the South was more desegregated than any other region of the nation, since in that year 39.2 percent of black pupils in the North and West were in schools that were more than 90 percent minority. By 1972 60 percent of all black children who were in schools that were 80 to 100 percent minority were attending schools in twenty-one cities (New York, Los Angeles, Chicago, Philadelphia, Detroit, Miami, Houston, Baltimore, Dallas, Cleveland, Washington, Ft. Lauderdale, Milwaukee, St. Louis, New Orleans, Atlanta, Newark, Oakland, Kansas City, Birmingham, and Gary); these twenty-one cities had one-third of the total black public-school enrollment in the nation (HEW, 1974, table 1).

The authority of the executive branch to enforce desegregation orders was steadily augmented by a series of Supreme Court decisions during the same period. Until 1968, most lower courts in the South had adhered closely to the view expressed in 1955 in *Briggs* v. *Eliott* that "the Constitution . . . does not require integration. It merely forbids discrimination." With this dictum as their standard, many southern districts constructed freedom-of-choice plans or other arrangements that either maintained total segregation or permitted only token desegregation. However, in 1968 the Supreme Court struck down a freedom-of-choice plan in the landmark *Green* v. *County School Board* decision. New Kent County, Virginia, had two schools, one white and one black, and no residential segregation. Under its freedom-of-choice plan, 15 percent of the blacks attended the formerly white school, but no whites chose to go to the black school. The Supreme Court required the local school board to develop a plan that "promises realistically to work now," one that would produce "a system without a 'white' school and a 'Negro' school, but just schools."

The import of the *Green* case was that it declared that desegregation remedies must be judged by their effectiveness; thus, a racially neutral plan like freedom-of-choice was not acceptable if it did not actually eliminate discrimination. This principle was extended in the *Swann* v. *Charlotte-Mecklenburg* decision in 1971. Because the Charlotte-Mecklenburg (North Carolina) area was residentially segregated, its racially neutral neighborhood school policy produced many racially identifiable schools. The Supreme Court, following *Green*, directed lower courts to "make every effort to achieve the greatest possible degree of actual desegregation," which was to be measured by how many blacks and whites were in the same schools. Local officials were instructed to do whatever was necessary—including the use of racial quotas (as "a starting point in the process of shaping a remedy, rather than an inflexible requirement"), the gerrymandering of districts, busing, and the creation of noncontiguous attendance zones—in order to redistribute white and black pupils into the same schools. Although the *Swann* decision provided explicit support for busing and racial balancing, the decision contained two sentences that enabled the Court, several years later, to modify the integrationist thrust of *Swann*: first, "As with any equity case, the nature of the violation determines the scope of the remedy," and second, "The constitutional command to desegregate schools does not mean that every school in every community must always reflect the racial composition of the school system as a whole."

But the process of modification (some would call it backtracking) had not yet begun, and in 1973 the Court ruled in *Keyes* v. *Denver School District No. 1* that "state-imposed segregation in a substantial portion of the district will suffice to support a finding by the trial court of the existence of a dual system." This case was of particular moment because Denver had never mandated or permitted racial segregation. It appeared that the Supreme Court was creating a standard for desegregation that would obliterate the distinction between de jure and de facto segregation and would ultimately require the elimination of racial isolation wherever it existed. Since only a single dissent was registered in the *Keyes* case, there was every reason to believe that the future decisions of the Court would follow the clear path delineated in *Green*, *Swann*, and *Keyes*.

Whereas the Supreme Court seemed at the time to be moving inexorably toward the goal of school integration, events in the world of affairs reflected contrary currents. Just as the civil rights movement was savoring its greatest political triumphs in 1964 and 1965—the Civil Rights Act, the Economic Opportunity Act, the Voting Rights Act, the establishment of Headstart programs—urban black communities began to explode in riots and disorders that traditional leaders neither provoked nor controlled. Black activists in these communities abandoned the civil rights movement's commitment to nonviolence, self-discipline, Christian love, and integration. A new black consciousness emerged, formed in part by the concept of "maximum feasible participation" of poor people in the poverty program, by the apostles of Black Power, by reaction to the assassination of black leaders, and by a newly articulated sense of racial identity and solidarity. Its spokesmen had no reluctance about endorsing violent tactics and separatist goals and spoke openly of their anger and hatred of whites and Uncle Toms. The poverty program was one important source of the new mood because it required the involvement and participation of local residents and it paid staff to work with the local community, determine its grievances, and organize residents to fight for their demands. In effect, the federal government subsidized, legitimatized, and organized the expression of discontent. Community organizers, reaching into the lower depths of impoverished communities, frequently touched feelings that found expression in the urban riots.

Along with the new mood in urban black communities came a new mood in society as a whole. Increasingly after 1965 the antiwar movement challenged the authority of the government and urged citizen participation in protest rallies. Furthermore, the rise of the counterculture, with its explicit rejection of all sorts of authority, changed styles of behavior and spread the message to "do your own thing." Community groups, encouraged in some instances by poverty workers or emulating their example, became more vociferous in demanding greater participation in official decisions that affected them, whether it was the construction of a new highway in their neighborhood or the choice of a new school principal. Community action programs and antiwar protesters shared many ideological bonds, including hostility to authority—be it that of Washington, "city hall," or "the bureaucracy"—and shared a commitment to participation and decentralization of decision making. With the appearance of the Black Power movement in 1966, these issues became politicized along racial lines.

The Black Power movement and the poverty program contributed to the emergence of the community control movement, which rejected outright many of the tenets of the civil rights movement. While in one sense the community control movement grew out of the failure of big cities to bring about integration, its ideas represented an explicit loss of faith in integration as a remedy for black problems. The leading theoretician of the community control movement, Preston Wilcox, denounced assimilationist policies that would undermine black culture and black self-consciousness. The issues were joined most forcefully around the militant Ocean Hill-Brownsville district of New York City, which in 1968-69 became locked in a power struggle with the overwhelmingly white teachers' union. The Ocean Hill-Brownsville experimental school district, supported by Ford Foundation funds, attempted to secede from the New York City school system and establish a black-controlled program. In an effort to demonstrate its authority over teachers, the district ousted several union leaders, which led to a three-month teachers' strike against the entire city school system. After an intensive struggle in the legislature and on the streets the city school system was decentralized, but the Ocean Hill-Brownsville district was dismantled and absorbed in a larger community school district. The final defeat of the district was not a triumph for integration, but a rebuff of the black nationalist ideology associated with the district's spokesmen. While the political movement for community control foundered, many of the values that it espoused or provoked to the level of consciousness survived.

The black consciousness movement was like a rock dropped into a still lake, producing ripples that continue to stir the surface long afterward. From it came demands for black studies programs, black role models in the classroom and the media, and other manifestations of heightened black awareness. It aroused too the ethnic consciousness of other groups that had long accepted, or at least paid lip service to, the melting-pot ideal. A "new ethnicity" appeared on the American scene, and there was suddenly revitalized interest in asserting the bonds of fellowship and common memory among Italians, Slavs, Jews, Hispanics, and others. Non-English-speaking groups began to resist the pace of assimilation and to demand bilingual programs.

In the area of bilingual education, the tension between equality and community leads to contradictory interpretations: school authorities usually see bilingualism as a way to improve school performance and hasten assimilation, while Hispanic leaders generally see it in terms of biculturalism and language maintenance. While both the Supreme Court (in *Lau* v. *Nichols*) and the Congress have endorsed bilingual education, this inconsistency in its purpose persists. Will it be used for cultural preservation, or as a bridge out of cultural isolation and into the mainstream of American life? Can it be both? While Hispanic children are often lumped together with black children in desegregation cases, their needs are not identical. The requirements of bilingual programs present new problems that have received inadequate attention; for instance, is a bilingual classroom for Hispanic children segregated? Again, there is an unresolved clash between the needs of the community (the bilingual program and the requirements of equality (integration of different racial groups in the same classroom). And this is not mere theoretical speculation: precisely this situation arose in 1977 in New York City when the federal Office for Civil Rights identified a number of bilingual classrooms as segregated because they consisted entirely of Hispanic children.

Even as the federal government and the courts have forged the tools to bring about racial balance in schools in the North and South, urban demography has been shifting at a rapid pace. Whites began moving out of the major cities as early as the 1950s, and their exodus was joined by middle-class blacks in the 1970s. Enormous complications resulted for urban schools because in many cities there were no longer enough whites to make every school majority-white. This mattered because both the Coleman report in 1966 and the United States Commission on Civil Rights in 1967 expressed strong support for the value of integration in a majority-white setting; the latter particularly recommended the Massachusetts definition of racial imbalance as any school where enrollment was more than 50 percent black. The scale of white-enrollment decline in many major cities meant that this kind of integration would not be possible for most urban schools. When the distinguished sociologist James Coleman, long an advocate of desegregation, concluded in 1975 that court-ordered busing led to white migration from city schools, a controversy erupted that called attention to the phenomenon of "white flight." His critics went so far in denouncing him as to suggest that the seriousness of white flight had been exaggerated. But, in fact, white flight has been continuing and significant in every major city; the fact that it was as great in cities that were not under court order as in cities that were does not detract from the magnitude of the phenomenon (see Table 1 and Coleman, Kelly, and Moore, 1975; Rossell, 1975; Ravitch, 1978).

An additional demographic complication in the biggest cities was the concentration in inner-city schools of very poor children. In New York City, for example, 52 percent of its one million pupils in 1975-76 were poor enough to be eligible for free lunches, and fully one-third were on welfare (Gifford, 1977, p. 19). Furthermore, the movement of blacks into central cities in the 1950s and 1960s corresponded with changes in the family structure: from 1965 to 1975 the proportion of black female-headed families grew from 23.7 to 35.3 percent, and the rate of black illegitimacy rose from 26.3 percent in 1965 to 48.8 percent in 1975 (U.S. Department of Commerce, 1974, p. 107; U.S. National Center for Health Statistics, 1976). Whether these trends are correlated with urbanization or some other factor is not clear. Whatever their causes, the statistics are important not simply as a matter of lifestyle or middle-class standards, but because it is among female-headed families that poverty is concentrated. Black family income in 1974 was only 58 percent of white family income, compared to 54 percent in 1964. But poverty was not spread randomly among the black population; it was most pronounced among female-headed families, which comprised *two-thirds* of all poor black families in 1974. By contrast, young black families in the North and West, those in which both husband and wife are employed, had incomes that were 99 percent of the income of equivalent white families; even in the South, where black earnings were lowest, these families earned 87 percent of the income of corresponding white families (U.S. Department of Commerce, 1974, p. 37; Farley, 1977).

Perhaps the most dramatic trend of the recent past is the advance of minority youth in educational attainment. Between 1965 and 1976 the number of black college students nearly quadrupled, from 274,000 to 1,062,000 (during the same period, white college enrollment was up by 61.5 percent). By 1976 blacks were 10.7 percent of all college students, slightly less than the proportion of blacks in the population as a whole. The Hispanic college enrollment has also grown quickly, from 155,000 in 1970 to 427,000 in 1976, increasing the proportion of Hispanics to 4.3 percent of the total college population (as compared to their 5.3 percent

Table 1 Racial change in urban public schools, 1968 to 1976.

City[a]	Year	Total pupils	Whites (%)	Minorities[b] (%)	White loss (%)	Total loss (%)
New York	1968	1,063,787	467,365 (43.9)	596,422 (56.1)		
	1976	1,077,190	328,065 (30.5)	749,125 (69.5)	139,300 (29.8)	—
Los Angeles	1968	653,549	350,909 (53.7)	302,640 (46.3)		
	1976	592,931	219,359 (37.0)	373,572 (63.0)	131,550 (37.5)	60,618 (9.3)
Chicago	1968	582,274	219,478 (37.7)	362,796 (62.3)		
	1976	524,221	130,785 (25.0)	393,436 (75.0)	88,693 (40.4)	58,053 (10.0)
Houston	1968	246,098	131,099 (53.3)	114,999 (46.7)		
	1976	210,025	71,794 (34.2)	138,231 (65.8)	59,305 (45.2)	36,073 (14.7)
Detroit	1968	296,097	116,250 (39.3)	179,847 (60.7)		
	1976	239,214	44,614 (18.7)	194,600 (81.3)	71,636 (61.6)	56,883 (19.2)
Philadelphia	1968	282,617	109,512 (38.7)	173,105 (61.3)		
	1976	257,942	82,010 (31.8)	175,932 (68.2)	27,502 (25.1)	24,675 (8.7)
Miami	1968	232,465	135,598 (58.3)	96,867 (41.7)		
	1976	239,994	98,362 (41.0)	141,632 (59.0)	37,236 (27.5)	+7,529 (+3.2)
Baltimore	1968	192,171	66,997 (34.9)	125,174 (65.1)		
	1976	160,121	38,992 (24.4)	121,129 (75.6)	28,005 (41.8)	32,050 (16.7)
Dallas	1968	159,924	97,888 (61.2)	62,036 (38.8)		
	1976	139,080	53,008 (38.1)	86,072 (61.9)	44,880 (45.8)	20,844 (13.0)
Cleveland	1968	156,054	66,324 (42.5)	89,730 (57.5)		
	1976	122,706	46,383 (37.8)	76,323 (62.2)	19,941 (30.1)	33,348 (21.4)
Washington	1968	148,725	8,280 (5.6)	140,445 (94.4)		
	1976	126,587	4,484 (3.5)	122,103 (96.5)	3,796 (45.8)	22,138 (14.9)
Milwaukee	1968	130,445	95,161 (73.0)	35,284 (27.0)		
	1976	109,565	61,738 (56.3)	47,827 (43.7)	33,423 (35.1)	20,880 (16.0)
Memphis	1968	125,813	58,271 (46.3)	67,542 (53.7)		
	1976	117,496	33,848 (28.8)	83,648 (71.2)	24,423 (41.9)	8,317 (6.6)
Jacksonville	1968	122,637	87,999 (71.8)	34,638 (28.2)		
	1976	110,707	73,730 (66.6)	36,977 (33.4)	14,269 (16.2)	11,930 (9.7)
St. Louis	1968	115,582	42,174 (36.5)	73,408 (63.5)		

City	Year					
Columbus, Ohio	1976	93,364	17,933 (19.2)	75,431 (80.8)	16,740 (48.3)	17,419 (15.7)
	1968	110,699	81,655 (73.8)	29,044 (26.2)		
Indianapolis	1976	96,372	64,657 (67.1)	31,715 (32.9)	16,998 (20.8)	14,327 (12.9)
	1968	108,587	72,010 (66.3)	36,577 (33.7)		
Atlanta	1976	82,002	45,187 (55.1)	36,815 (44.9)	26,823 (37.2)	26,585 (24.5)
	1968	111,227	42,506 (38.2)	68,721 (61.8)		
San Diego	1976	82,480	9,231 (11.2)	73,199 (88.8)	33,275 (78.3)	28,747 (25.8)
	1968	128,414	98,163 (76.1)	30,751 (23.9)		
Denver	1976	121,423	80,153 (66.0)	41,270 (34.0)	18,010 (18.3)	7,491 (5.8)
	1968	96,577	63,398 (65.6)	33,179 (34.4)		
Boston	1976	75,237	36,539 (48.6)	38,698 (51.4)	26,859 (42.4)	21,340 (22.1)
	1968	94,174	64,500 (68.5)	29,674 (31.5)		
San Francisco	1976	76,889	34,561 (45.0)	42,328 (55.0)	29,939 (46.4)	17,285 (18.4)
	1968	94,154	38,824 (41.2)	55,330 (58.8)		
Seattle	1976	65,255	14,958 (22.9)	50,297 (77.1)	23,866 (61.5)	28,899 (30.7)
	1968	94,025	77,293 (82.2)	16,732 (17.8)		
Nashville	1976	61,819	41,623 (67.3)	20,196 (32.7)	35,670 (46.1)	32,206 (34.3)
	1968	93,720	71,039 (75.8)	22,681 (24.2)		
Cincinnati	1976	77,998	54,522 (69.9)	23,476 (30.1)	16,517 (23.3)	15,722 (16.8)
	1968	86,807	49,231 (56.7)	37,576 (43.3)		
San Antonio	1976	65,635	30,697 (46.8)	34,938 (53.2)	18,534 (37.6)	21,172 (24.4)
	1968	79,353	21,310 (26.9)	58,042 (73.1)		
Pittsburgh	1976	65,712	9,962 (15.1)	55,750 (84.9)	11,348 (53.3)	13,641 (17.2)
	1968	76,628	46,005 (60.3)	30,263 (39.7)		
Kansas City	1976	59,022	31,954 (54.1)	27,068 (45.9)	14,051 (30.5)	17,606 (23.0)
	1968	74,202	39,510 (53.2)	34,692 (46.8)		
	1976	51,047	17,560 (34.4)	33,487 (65.6)	21,950 (44.4)	23,155 (31.2)

SOURCE: Prepared by the author from materials made available by the HEW Office for Civil Rights and by individual districts.

a. Two big cities—Phoenix and San Jose—are not included because both have numerous districts that are not coextensive with the city's boundaries; both are predominantly white.

b. "Minorities" include blacks, Hispanics, Asians, and Native Americans.

proportion of the total population). Because of these gains, the disparity in educational attainment among racial groups has been sharply reduced; among whites from 22 to 24 years old, the median number of school years completed is 12.9, for blacks the comparable figure is 12.5, and for Hispanics it is 12.3. The scale of change can be measured by noting the disparity of educational attainment among persons 25 years and older: whites, 12.3 years completed; blacks, 10.9 years; Hispanics, 9.6 years (U.S. Department of Commerce, 1977a and b). The narrowing of the educational gap and the rapid movement of minority youth into the upper reaches of the educational system is a significant development, since there continues to be a strong relationship among education, income, and occupation.

Richard Freeman, in a report for the Carnegie Commission on Higher Education, *Black Elite: The New Market for Highly Educated Black Americans*, has documented the educational and occupational gains of blacks since the passage of the 1964 Civil Rights Act. His central finding is that blacks have made remarkable strides in income, occupation, and education. The most dramatic progress has been made by young college graduates, who have achieved full economic equality with their white peers. Freeman found that the occupational profile of black workers in general has begun to converge with that of whites, as black women move out of domestic jobs and into factory and clerical work, and as black men move increasingly into professional, craft, and managerial jobs. Among college graduates the convergence has been even more pronounced, as young blacks move into fields that had been traditionally closed to them—like law, management, engineering, accounting, and medicine. And for the first time in history, young black professionals have begun their careers on an equal footing with whites. According to Freeman,

> Census statistics on income, special survey data from southern black colleges . . . and interviews with college placement directors at those institutions reveal a collapse in labor market discrimination against starting black male graduates in the late 1960s, which, if continued, marks the end of discrimination in high-level labor markets.

Certain traditional patterns were reversed during this period, according to Freeman: (1) as late as 1964, most black students attended predominantly black colleges; but by 1970, three-quarters of black college students were in predominantly white colleges; (2) in the past, because of discrimination, the difference between white and black incomes grew larger with increasing levels of education, but this pattern was shattered in the late 1960s; (3) because of discrimination nearly half of all black professionals customarily went into teaching, but by 1975 the career plans of black college students and graduates were very similar to those of whites (only about 10 percent planned to go into education) (Freeman, 1977, pp. 27-47).

Thus the years from 1964 to 1979 were a time of paradox. From the perspective of the occupational and educational status of blacks, it was a time of substantial progress. But from the perspective of big-city school desegregation, the prospects were limited by demographic change. Only nine of the largest thirty cities had white majorities in public school in the 1976-77 school year, and three of these were fast approaching the time when they too would be majority-nonwhite.

Two events occurred in 1974 that brought the new urban demographics into sharp focus: school busing began in Boston, and the Supreme Court declined to order metropolitan desegregation in Detroit (the *Milliken* decision). The turmoil in Boston rekindled the national debate about busing and clearly pitted the demands of the community (in this case, the Irish and Italians) against the requirements of equality. It was not really a contest, however, because the power of the federal court superseded any resistance that Boston's white ethnics could muster; what the ethnics did have, though, was the power to withdraw—and many did. The Boston public schools, 61 percent white when the busing order was issued, became majority-nonwhite because of the departure of some 20,000 white pupils (about one-third of the white enrollment). The Boston decision demonstrated that the power of the federal court to impose remedies was broad and could not be deterred by protest or white flight. The *Milliken* decision showed, however, that the school bus could not cross the city line unless both the city and the suburbs were guilty of constitutional violations. Since the number of white students in every major American city was diminishing, the *Milliken* decision decisively affected the outlook for urban school desegregation.

The shift away from the *Green-Swann-Keyes* approach became even more evident in a series of decisions that began with the *Washington* v. *Davis* case (1976), in which the Court refused to invalidate a civil service examination for police officers, even though it had a racially disproportionate impact (four times as many blacks as whites failed the test). The reason given was that there had been no showing of "discriminatory purpose." The Court referred to the *Washington* v. *Davis* ruling in rejecting lower-court desegregation orders in Austin, Texas; Pasadena, California;

and Dayton, Ohio. Lower courts understandably may be confused about
whether to base their decisions on the broad remedies authorized by
Green-Swann-Keyes or to rely instead on the more narrowly construed
warnings since 1976 to show "discriminatory purpose" and to tailor the
scope of the remedy to the nature of the violation. As if in response to
this confusion, the Supreme Court approved system-wide busing plans
for Dayton and Columbus, Ohio, in 1979. While the Court's approval of
broad racial balancing was heartening to civil rights lawyers, the relevance of this strategy for cities with majority black and Hispanic enrollments was not clear, nor was it clear what would be remedied by racial
balancing in those circumstances.

A central problem in thinking about urban school desegregation, if it is
not to involve city-suburban mergers, is that we do not have a reasonable
theoretical basis on which to define what we are talking about and what
we expect to accomplish. What does desegregation mean in a city like
Detroit, which is now 80 percent nonwhite, or Chicago, 75 percent nonwhite? Is it schools where at least 10 percent of the enrollment is of the
other race? Is it a racially balanced system in which no school deviates by
more than 10 or 15 percent from the system-wide average? Then wouldn't
this latter definition mean that a school in Detroit that was 50 percent
white and 50 percent black was "segregated"? Does it mean the elimination of white enclaves? Or does it mean that no school should remain
majority-white in a majority-nonwhite system? In an urban setting, and
particularly in what is now a typical urban system with a nonwhite majority, there is no present understanding of what desegregation is or
ought to be.

Even though some cities have erupted in angry protests against busing,
the principle of desegregation enjoys broad popular support. The difficulty is that particular remedies provoke conflicts between competing
values. Were there no racial hostility whatever, there would still be concern among white, black, and Hispanic parents about the relation of the
school to the parents and the local community. We have to begin to think
about desegregation in terms that go beyond the stereotypes of the past.
Mores and values have changed significantly; race relations are light
years away from the bitterness of the 1960s or the caste patterns that pre-
dominated before then. White and nonwhite professionals can and do
meet as equals, and so too do white and nonwhite workers. Racist behavior and expressions are as publicly unacceptable today as they were acceptable less than twenty years ago; indeed, when a public figure makes a
remark that disparages blacks, it is cause for a news story and cause even

for a member of the President's cabinet to be drummed out of office. No politician, even in an overwhelmingly white district, would campaign on a racist appeal and expect to be taken seriously; the once-dreaded Ku Klux Klan was hooted out of town in the Deep South and in the industrial North in the late 1970s. American society has changed, and the change is real. The dilemma remains: Can we continue to pursue equality without sacrificing community? Can we pursue community without compromising equality?

References

Coleman, James S., Sara D. Kelly, and John Moore. 1975. *Recent Trends in School Integration*. Washington, D.C.: Urban Institute.

Farley, Reynolds. 1977. Trends in racial inequalities: have the gains of the 1960s disappeared in the 1970s? *American Sociological Review* 42:189-207.

Freeman, Richard B. 1977. *Black Elite: The New Market for Highly Educated Black Americans*. New York: McGraw Hill.

Gifford, B. R. 1977. *School Profiles, 1975-76*. New York: City Board of Education.

Meranto, Philip. 1967. *The Politics of Federal Aid to Education in 1965: A Study in Political Innovation*. Syracuse, New York: Syracuse University Press.

Orfield, Gary. 1969. *The Reconstruction of Southern Education*. New York: John Wiley.

Ravitch, Diane. 1978. The "white flight" controversy. *Public Interest* 51:135-149.

Rossell, Christine. 1975. School desegregation and white flight. *Political Science Quarterly* 90(4):675-695.

Southern Education Report. 1966. 1(4), January-February.

U.S. Department of Commerce, Bureau of the Census. 1974. *The Social and Economic Status of the Black Population in the United States*. Washington, D.C.: Government Printing Office.

———. 1977a. *Current Population Reports*, ser. P-20, no. 295, Educational attainment in the United States: March 1975. Washington, D.C.: Government Printing Office.

———. 1977b. *Current Population Reports*, ser. P-20, no. 309, The school enrollment—social and economic characteristics of students: October 1976. Washington, D.C.: Government Printing Office.

U.S. Department of Health, Education, and Welfare, Office for Civil Rights. 1974. Title VI of the Civil Rights Acts of 1964—ten years later. Washington, D.C.: Government Printing Office.

U.S. National Center for Health Statistics. 1976. Monthly Vital Statistics Report, 24, no. 10, December 30. Washington, D.C.: Government Printing Office.

2 Why It Worked in Dixie: Southern School Desegregation and Its Implications for the North

GARY ORFIELD

A quarter-century ago, when the Supreme Court decided *Brown*, the North assumed that only the South was guilty. For almost two decades, while the dual school systems of the South were dismantled step by step, the Court said nothing about northern segregation. Southerners today often express their puzzlement about the bad behavior of their northern counterparts now that judicial attention has swung to the other side of the Mason-Dixon line. As northern cities and states go through the cycle of mass movements to avoid court-ordered schooling assignments, the politics of racial polarization, and the enactment of state and local laws designed to preserve segregation, history seems to repeat itself. There is a sense of déjà vu as residents of peacefully integrated cities in the Deep South read about the antibusing amendments to state constitutions recently adopted in the states of California and Washington. The North, seemingly unaware that the South has passed through many of the same stages, appears unwilling to learn anything from that experience.

When paratroopers occupied Little Rock in 1957 to protect the right of nine black children to attend Central High School, the screaming mobs and the soaring popularity of Arkansas's segregationist governor, Orval Faubus, promised unending resistance. Northerners supporting the action of the President and the Supreme Court against the raw racism found in even this relatively moderate part of the South could never have guessed that a generation later integrated education would be a peacefully accepted norm in most of Dixie, but a bitterly resisted policy in the North. Who could have guessed that Boston would become the leading symbol of racial antagonism and that many scholars and political leaders would gravely announce that real desegregation was unwise or even impossible in the North? Obviously the issues have evolved in the last twenty-five years, and there are important differences between North and South. Nonetheless, the profound ironies of the situation are unfailingly noted in the South.

The desegregation of much of southern education is one of the most important government-imposed social changes in American history. Now efforts to overcome the intense segregation of the huge and spreading ghettos and barrios of the metropolitan North have raised our most bitter social and political issues. What ideas does the southern experience provide about the prerequisites for successful desegregation that may help illuminate the northern dilemma? Failure to act successfully may make the North of the future like the South of the past.

In some ways we know very little about what happened in the South. The battle was too intense and too controversial to measure or even recall accurately. Educational research, if any, in most southern communities was poor and very narrowly defined.[1] This chapter therefore deals with the question of "success" only in terms of two easily observable, yet fundamental changes—actual movement of children into biracial schools and the ending of overt political controversy over and active organized resistance to desegregated schools. Peaceful acceptance of schools with black and white children sitting next to one another does not mean that the integration process is over. The years of effort within individual schools, building true integration, can only begin after desegregation has taken place.

The changes in the South, both in racial composition of schools and in political climate, have been astonishing. During the 1962-63 school year, 99 of every 100 southern black children were in all-black schools. Only 14 of every 100 were in all-black schools in 1974-75. (Thirty-two percent of black students in the Northeast, and 45 percent in the Midwest, were in schools with virtually no whites in 1974-75.) During 1974-75, 44 percent of southern black children attended predominantly white schools, compared with less than a fifth of their counterparts in the Northeast and Midwest and about a fourth in the West (*Congressional Record*, June 18, 1976). Calculations by the Department of Health, Education, and Welfare (HEW) based on 1976 enrollment statistics found that blacks in the Northeast were more than twice as likely to be segregated as those in the South. According to the HEW Office for Civil Rights, in the Midwest the situation was even worse: blacks were more than three times as likely to be segregated (*Washington Post*, September 12, 1978).

The transformation of the school issue has been equally remarkable. The issue that made the careers of the "massive resisters" who dominated much of southern politics in the fifties and sixties has now disappeared in much of the region. Even the busing issue, which enabled George Wallace to dominate major parts of the South in 1972, is rapidly receding. Wallace himself, who became nationally known for his "segregation forever" speech when he was inaugurated governor of Alabama, endorsed school integration (although assailing busing) during the 1976 campaign. Senator Strom Thurmond, whose anti-civil rights credentials are second to none and who was a powerful influence in shaping Richard Nixon's "southern strategy" against school desegregation, has now found it politically wise to enroll his young daughter in a half-black South Carolina school. Recent southern governors conferences have avoided the busing issue completely. Network film crews seeking dramatic footage of racial confrontations as schools open lately have had to travel outside the Old Confederacy.

The change in the politics of the school issue was dramatically apparent in the 1976 southern campaigns. Hubert Humphrey had carried only one southern state after the 1968 campaign, in which both Wallace and Nixon assailed federal school desegregation policy and Nixon in a southern regional television appearance attacked HEW enforcement and endorsed "free choice" (Synon, 1968; *Washington Post*, September 13, 1968). In 1972 the moderate Democratic candidates were badly damaged by the Florida primary victory of George Wallace, whose campaign was built around an attack on the county-wide busing plans recently implemented in much of the state.[2] Four years later Wallace tried the same approach. The Florida vote was again decisive in 1976, but the message was very different. Wallace found that after several years of metropolitan desegregation the issue had lost much of its electoral intensity. Jimmy Carter's successful campaign, which made him the South's politician and the favorite for the Democratic nomination, included an attack on Senator Henry Jackson's antibusing plan as "a basically negative, emotional issue which has connotations of racism" (Witcover, 1977). Although Carter said his personal preference was for voluntary desegregation plans, he pledged to enforce the law and to oppose the proposed constitutional amendment to curb busing. Many factors contributed to Carter's victory and the end of Wallace's domination of southern politics: one was the decline of the busing issue. Although only 28 percent of Florida Democrats *favored* busing (*Miami Herald*, March 10, 1976), integrated schools had become a well-established fact of life. Enrollments had stabilized and the issue had receded.

The busing issue was raised in 1976 in some of the southern Republican primaries: Ronald Reagan supported an antibusing constitutional amendment, and President Gerald Ford attacked the courts and called for legislation and Justice Department intervention to limit busing. But busing virtually disappeared from the election campaign. Despite the fact that the GOP platform called for changing the Constitution, in contrast to Democratic support of busing as a "judicial tool of last resort",[3] the issue did not become salient and Ford did little to develop it. Attention had turned to other questions. The South was living peacefully with desegregated schools. But very little desegregation was occurring in the North.

Although the South as a whole is far more desegregated than other regions, there are major exceptions. Older cities with overwhelmingly black enrollments, like New Orleans, Atlanta, and Richmond, which have been unable to devise effective desegregation plans, are experiencing rapid ghetto expansion and white flight as in the North. Both Richmond and Atlanta were at one time involved in long and futile litigation over metropolitan plans for desegregation. The Atlanta case is still under appeal. The two largest southern districts, Dade County (Miami), Florida, and Houston, Texas, have only partial plans, which rely primarily on "desegregating" black children by integrating them with Hispanic children, thus pooling two minority groups. Some plans, like the one in Memphis, permit retention of large numbers of all-black schools.[4] There is rapidly diminishing political conflict in the border-state cities of Louisville, where the first metropolitan merger plan was implemented in 1976, and Wilmington, which implemented a metropolitan plan in 1978.

The changing character of the issue was evident in the comments of two southern senators during a debate in 1976 on an amendment intended to restrain the Justice Department's school desegregation actions. Dale Bumpers of Arkansas and Robert Morgan of North Carolina opposed the amendment, describing it as a misleading political ploy and an effort to stop in the North a change that had already been accomplished in the South (*Congressional Record*, June 24, 1976). In fact, during the seventies most of the antibusing moves in Congress were initiated by northern members.

Is the Southern Experience Relevant to the North?

During the '50s and the early '60s the media and the intellectual world generally treated the South as a special case—as a part of the country where common decency could not be expected because of its intense racism and irresponsible segregationist politics. This stimulated the movement for strong federal intervention in the form of the 1964 Civil Rights Act and the 1965 Voting Rights Act, laws to force "them" to behave like "us."

Now that the South has made such progress in desegregation and the North is immersed in intense debate over urban segregation, a new stereotype of the South has gained currency. The North cannot duplicate the South's achievements, we are told, because the South is a special case. The old segregation battles obscured the fact that southern blacks and whites were really much more comfortable with one another than their counterparts in the North because they shared many basic cultural values. This argument even became a significant theme in discussions of Jimmy Carter's phenomenal success with black voters in 1976.

In retrospect it does seem clear that the South had some advantages in achieving school desegregation. Its cities are smaller and, until recently, the region has experienced substantial white in-migration and black out-migration. There are no urban complexes on the scale of New York, Chicago, and Los Angeles, though the region does contain many of the nation's largest school districts. Northern cities have to deal with much more complex patterns of ethnic and religious division. Except in Texas and southern Florida, most southern communities do not have the large enrollments of Hispanic children that make complex three-way desegregation plans necessary in many cities outside Dixie. Furthermore, the decline of older cities and suburbanization are more advanced in the North, although the South is catching up.[5]

The advantages, however, were more than balanced by special problems. The South entered the transitional period with a public far more opposed to integration than the northern public and with many elected leaders who had built careers on resistance (Sarratt, 1966). The South faced the problem of three hundred black belt counties where the white minority had long maintained a rigid system of political and economic control and where any desegregation challenged an entire way of life. The South started with total segregation, whereas there has long been some integration and some experience with desegregated settings in the North. Many southern systems provided no significant training to teachers and administrators entering a desegregated setting for the first time in their lives, and many lost an invaluable resource for successful integration by firing or downgrading black teachers and administrators (U.S. Department of HEW, 1972; Hall, 1974, pp. 5-14). Northern school districts usually do better on these fronts.

The record of continuing segregation in the North while the South de-segregated is not the result of cultural or educational differences. Segregation is largely the consequence of the failure of public authorities to devise and enforce a clear, consistent, and workable policy. None of the following prerequisites for rapid and basic change evident in the South are yet present in the North:

(1) Clear legal requirements, requiring actual desegregation, consistently applied by the courts;
(2) Active enforcement by administrative agencies supported by elected officials;
(3) Plans that will produce lasting integration, given local demographics.

Legal Requirements in the South.

For more than a decade after *Brown* v. *Board of Education* the goal of the desegregation process remained uncertain. The prevailing southern theory was that the Constitution would permit continued operation of separate black and white schools as long as black children were offered a formal opportunity to transfer. This policy of "freedom of choice" left the degree of segregation little changed in almost all of the many hundreds of districts where it was tried. Ninety-eight percent of black children remained in all-black schools after the 1964 Civil Rights Act was signed.[6]

During the next five years HEW and the courts worked together to develop requirements for prompt and thorough desegregation. At first free-choice plans were permitted, but only on the condition that they move a substantial number of black students into white schools each year. The courts became increasingly insistent and impatient with further delays, particularly after a unanimous Supreme Court in 1968 endorsed prompt merger of racially identifiable schools.[7] The following year, when the Nixon administration undermined the HEW enforcement process and sent the Justice Department into court to urge further delays in Mississippi, a unanimous Supreme Court angrily rejected the tactic and in the next months issued a number of orders requiring immediate compliance in all cases.[8] By 1970 the requirement for the rural South had become unambiguous—immediate and complete merger of the separate black and white schools.

In the urban South, where blacks and whites lived apart, the problem was more difficult. Legal requirements remained unclear until 1971, as the courts and HEW struggled with the question. Finally, in the *Swann* decision, the Supreme Court sustained a county-wide busing plan in a large urban district, authorizing lower courts to do whatever was necessary to produce actual desegregation in cities with a history of de jure segregation.[9] Since there was no need to prove that history in the South and since courts were continuing to supervise existing urban plans, it was possible for civil rights groups to accomplish a great deal through relatively simple proceedings asking that court orders be updated to comply with *Swann*. Looking at the unanimous decision that granted sweeping powers to the lower courts and considering the "presumption" the Court had established against substantially imbalanced schools, many judges ordered rapid district-wide plans to integrate virtually all schools. Thus the 1971-72 period brought dozens of urban court orders.[10]

From 1968 to 1972 the strong and consistent decisions of the Supreme Court were extremely important in creating a belief that desegregation was inevitable in the South. This was critical in sustaining the momentum created by earlier HEW enforcement and countering some of the attacks on desegregation from the Nixon White House, the Justice Department, and Congress. Until 1973 every major decision was unanimous.

Although in retrospect commentators have spoken of the greater support for desegregation among southern than northern whites and the less abrasive political climate of the South, in fact there was almost monolithic opposition to the change, with no responsible elected or high appointive official endorsing desegregation and with continual attacks in much of the press (Gates, 1964; Muse, 1964; Sarratt, 1966). In the black belt the resistance was bitter and sometimes brutal. For example, a significant fraction of the black parents who chose free-choice transfers found themselves victims of economic intimidation or even terrorist shootings at their homes (U.S. Commission on Civil Rights, 1967). The Ku Klux Klan (KKK) had a major revival in parts of the South in the mid-sixties as the change was taking place.[11] In 1964 and 1968 the region abandoned its Democratic political affiliations of many generations, primarily over the race issue. Outside of Boston there has been nothing in the North to equal the level of opposition often faced in the South. Desegregation was not welcomed—it was imposed.

Administrative Commitment

Without support from the executive branch of the federal government or from state government agencies, the entire burden of enforcing school desegration rests on private civil rights groups. Often they face elaborate and endless legal maneuvers, requests for delays, and appeals. It is commonplace for a district to pay more for legal battles, which have virtually no chance of ultimate success, than for preparations to make desegregation work. Civil rights groups simply lacked the resources to bring all the southern systems into court, counter all the opposition tactics, pursue appeals when the district court did not provide an adequate remedy, and oversee compliance with the final court orders. Therefore, as early as 1955, the National Association for the Advancement of Colored People (NAACP) began to work for legislation to empower HEW and the Justice Department to enforce desegregation requirements.[12]

When the 1964 Civil Rights Act required HEW to withhold federal aid from discriminatory school systems and authorized the Justice Department to intervene in school cases, it soon became clear that the NAACP had been right. The sanctions, the bureaucratic resources, and the influence of the executive branch weighed heavily in the process. Desegregation plans multiplied, the rate of change within individual districts soared, and federal lawyers took the lead in proving that freedom of choice would not work and in moving the courts toward policies requiring root-and-branch reshaping of the dual school system (Orfield, 1969). During the four years of active HEW enforcement (1965 to 1968) all rural southern districts began desegregation and most completed the process. The schools of the rural South became the country's most integrated.

When the executive branch was playing its role effectively, one of the principal weaknesses of the judiciary was taken care of: even after the Supreme Court announces new constitutional requirements, nothing happens in individual school districts until legal action requiring more desegregation is filed and processed. After a major decision such as the 1968 *Green* ruling against freedom of choice, however, HEW was able to send out letters requiring changes in hundreds of districts. The Justice Department used its resources to file motions in courts across the South to update earlier plans.

Even during the Nixon administration there were brief periods when the executive branch hastened desegregation. After the administration's position was rejected by the Supreme Court in the *Swann* decision, for instance, HEW designed desegregation plans for some cities and warned others of the possibility that their federal funds would be cut off if they did not comply (Brown, 1971; Pottinger, 1971). Although the White House reversed the policy later in the year, the assistance was useful at a very important time. Federal courts subsequently found HEW guilty of intentionally ending enforcement of the law and ordered the agency to resume its efforts to implement *Swann*.¹³ The modest executive branch contribution to desegregating southern cities helps explain the incompleteness of the urban effort.

Workable Plans

The design of a desegregation plan and its relation to the social composition of a community can help precipitate local reactions ranging from a concerted community-wide effort to make things work, on the one hand, to accelerated ghetto expansion and neighborhood transition, on the other. If a plan reaches only one part of a community and excludes the rest, it may reinforce the expectation that blacks will become increasingly dominant in the affected sections and that whites will flee to the excluded areas. If a plan places the burden of desegregation on low-income whites or linguistic minorities, it will probably have little educational value for black children and will create community resentments. If a plan reaches all groups in the community, however, the success of the local school system requires the success of desegregation—and all groups will have an interest in that outcome.

Developing workable plans usually was not difficult in the rural South, where there are few school buildings and relatively little residential segregation. Simple plans could often put all children in integrated, predominantly white schools, sometimes with less busing than before desegregation, since duplicate coverage of the same regions by black and white buses could be ended (Gendron, 1972, pp. 3-5; U.S. Commission on Civil Rights, 1972, p. 14). There were difficult problems in some districts with large black majorities, where a simple desegregation plan would have meant that all children would attend black-dominated schools. A few of these districts encountered almost total white abandonment of the public schools, and in many there was a significant movement into the new private "segregation academies" (all-white schools created at the time of desegregation).

The urban South presented far more difficult challenges. Where blacks (and Hispanics) made up a relatively small share of a district's enrollment, or where there were county-wide school districts that permitted full integration of entire metropolitan areas under the principles of *Swann*, the results of desegregation were stable, allowing local leaders to turn to the long-range issues of building educational quality in an integrated setting.¹⁴ The problem came when desegregation orders were superimposed on an existing process of very rapid white suburbanization and limited to all or part of a central city. The dilemmas involved in ordering desegregation in a setting where well-established trends showed that it would be temporary and perhaps even counterproductive produced three kinds of response: (1) some courts simply applied the *Swann* principles to county-wide plans; (2) in some cases, including Atlanta, the court refused to order full desegregation; and (3) in one important decision a federal district court in Richmond ordered a city-suburban merger, but the court of appeals overturned the decision and the Supreme Court's 4-4 vote let the appellate decision stand.[15] The dominant tendency in recent decisions has been to issue geographically limited orders, leaving considerable segregation in cities with white-student minorities.

Most of the nation's experience with urban desegregation has been in the South. Since a significant number of large districts can be observed eight or nine years *after* the desegregation crisis and since a wide variety of plans have been tried, we have an unusual opportunity for studying the southern experience as plans are made for the North. The evidence suggests strongly that metropolitan plans are feasible and necessary for stable desegregation in large cities.

The Nature and Stability of Plans in Various Southern Cities

Research in the large southern cities suggests that no one has yet found a good "separate but equal" solution, and that including as much as possible of the metropolitan area within the plan has a powerful impact on the long-term viability and stability of desegregated education. A careful comparison of the experiences in Charlotte, Richmond, and Nashville found by far the greatest stability in Charlotte, where the plan included virtually the entire metropolitan area, and the least stability in Richmond, which has a central-city-only plan after the Supreme Court deadlocked in the Richmond metropolitan-area case. Nashville, where the plan included part of the suburbs, but excluded others, had an intermediate record. Between 1970 and 1976 Charlotte enrollment dropped 9.8 percent, Nashville 21.8 percent, and Richmond 26.1 percent, even though the degree of desegregation was greatest in Charlotte (Lord and Catau, 1978). A study of eight county-wide desegregation plans in Florida found little initial white loss and great stability after the first year (Giles, Gatlin, and Cataldo, 1976). Even prominent scholarly critics of urban desegregation plans, including James Coleman and David Armor, report the greatest stability in the southern metropolitan plans (Coleman, Kelly, and Moore, 1975; Armor, 1978).

Atlanta and Charlotte offer an opportunity to compare the impact after several years of fundamentally different approaches. Frequently praised by President Carter as having an ideal solution, Atlanta is the only major city in the South where the local civil rights group agreed to drop a lawsuit demanding city-wide desegregation in exchange for increasing the number of blacks in key administrative jobs. In a school district with a rapidly shrinking white minority, the federal courts accepted this compromise. They were supported by Carter, then governor, and Federal District Judge Griffin Bell, Carter's future attorney general, in spite of the appeals of the national NAACP.[16]

In an analysis of the results of the compromise, researchers at Atlanta's Clark College reported that the jobs were provided but the basic problems remained. Total school enrollment in 1976 was about half that of a decade earlier, and by the 1978-79 school year the system was 90 percent black. All but five of the elementary schools had heavy concentrations of poor children. The researchers from the black college found a "low level of community involvement" and a lack of interest in city schools by business leaders. Even under black administrators the one region that retained a number of predominantly white schools had the smallest class size, the highest per-student expenditures, and by far the highest achievement scores. (All the schools in two of the three other administrative regions were operating below the national achievement norm; see Hadden et al., 1979.) Black control, obviously, had brought neither stability of enrollment nor rapid educational transformation. A metropolitan desegregation case based on housing violations was rejected by the Supreme Court in May 1980.[17]

While Atlanta was trying a compromise, Charlotte became the first key test of metropolitan-wide desegregation in the United States. The community had bitterly resisted the busing plan, President Nixon had denounced the court decision, and his Justice Department had fought the case to the Supreme Court, which first sustained district-wide busing as a remedy in the 1971 Charlotte case. Since the district covered the entire county, suburban families were included and residential flight was virtually impossible.

After a difficult transition, in which widespread resentment culminated in riots in some high schools, Charlotte community leaders helped redesign the plan and active resistance declined sharply. Aware that they would have to redraw boundaries to deal with the spread of residential segregation, school officials pressed authorities for scattered-site public housing. The city council unanimously adopted the idea in 1979, partly on the grounds that it would be a step toward less busing and more "natural'' integration. When the Department of Housing and Urban Development refused to finance acquisition of sites in the most prosperous white areas because of their high costs, city funds were provided. During 1979 the city won permission from the state legislature to adopt a broad fair-housing ordinance. A large school bond issue was passed in 1979, and leading school officials report that the strong reputation of Charlotte schools was a key element in winning the transfer of a large IBM installation to the rapidly growing community.[18] The president of the school board at the time was a prominent black realtor.

Charlotte has not, of course, solved all the problems of desegregation and Atlanta is not, of course, without its successes. Yet even a brief comparison is enough to suggest that there is a feasible approach to urban school desegregation through community-wide integration efforts and that there is no magic effect of changing the color of the administrators as an alternative to desegregation.

Legal Requirements in the North

In the years since the *Brown* decision there has never been a clear and unambiguous set of principles of northern desegregation law. Most policy makers assumed that since northern segregation was innocent and accidental, there was no obligation to desegregate. Even in states like Indiana, where state law had permitted openly segregated schools until shortly before the *Brown* decision and school boards had often followed overtly segregationist practices, no action was expected (Weinberg, 1968).

The Supreme Court did not even decide a major northern urban case until 1973. In its *Keyes* decision the Court did not dismiss the de facto argument, but only adopted a presumption that made it easier to obtain a city-wide desegregation plan once civil rights lawyers proved that a substantial part of a city had been segregated as a result of official actions.[19] Many observers thought that this might be intended as an indirect way of holding all segregation to be de jure, thus authorizing broad remedies similar to the *Swann* model. During the following years, however, the Court succeeded in undermining this analysis and thoroughly confusing lawyers and policy makers across the country.

The Supreme Court never said what was needed to prove de jure segregation in the North, but in Denver it accepted evidence of the intentional creation of one segregated school as critical. If such evidence could trigger city-wide desegregation on the assumption that the misdeeds influenced a wide range of housing choices, it was reasonable to assume that any significant proof of segregation would justify a city-wide order anywhere. Some scholars and some courts reached exactly this conclusion, as did the dissenting justice, William Rehnquist. Many concluded that the Court had abandoned the theory that some segregation could be innocent, without ever quite saying so.

At a time when the Supreme Court was taking increasingly cautious positions in many other areas, such a dramatic innovation on the most controversial domestic issue seemed improbable. It was not long, in fact, before the Court's other civil rights decisions began to raise doubts about the meaning of the school ruling. In cases involving job discrimination and suburban exclusion, the Court moved away from looking at the racial impact of government action toward a more constrictive standard —one assuming the validity of actions unless there was proof of a segregationist intent.[20] There was also a disturbing note in the Supreme Court's 1974 decision rejecting metropolitan desegregation in Detroit— an argument that the reach of the remedy should be limited to repairing damage clearly resulting from discriminatory policies.[21]

From 1976 to 1978 the Supreme Court took a series of actions that deepened confusion in the lower federal courts and often increased the burden of proof imposed on civil rights groups. The Court required reconsideration of a number of urban cases decided earlier, and language in its important *Dayton I* decision suggested that the lower courts could limit desegregation plans to the particular schools and neighborhoods directly affected by proved violations of the Constitution.[22] Pressed to its logical extreme, this "incremental segregative effect" doctrine could have required separate consideration of each of the hundreds of individual schools in a big city and created a burden of proof no civil rights group could meet. During the fall of 1978 Justice Rehnquist increased the impression of uncertainty by suspending implementation of the Columbus, Ohio, desegregation plan days before school opened. Civil rights groups were required to devote their resources to defense of earlier victories as school boards returned to court asking elimination of existing plans.

Only after the Supreme Court acted in mid-1979 with strong decisions sustaining city-wide plans in Columbus and Dayton did it become clear that civil rights groups and federal agencies could continue to obtain comprehensive plans within a city.[23] The metropolitan issue remained unsettled, with all the metropolitan plans, including the consolidation orders in Louisville and Wilmington, limited to the southern and border states. In 1980 the Supreme Court made matters more ambiguous by first approving the metropolitan Wilmington case on a split vote and then, weeks later, rejecting a metropolitan approach for Atlanta without a hearing or an opinion. In the meantime, a Court of Appeals decision upheld a metropolitan approach in Indianapolis. Indeed, the law is muddled. The practical difficulties of obtaining even a central-city plan remain great, with most northern cases continuing year after year in the courts and costing hundreds of thousands of dollars to litigate.

Administrative Enforcement

In the 1970s, during the first years of large-scale urban school desegregation, the relationship between the courts and the elected branches of national government was far worse than during the drive to desegregate the South in the 1950s and 1960s. Although President Dwight Eisenhower professed personal neutrality toward the *Brown* decision, his Justice Department had supported desegregation in arguments before the Court and he did eventually act, in Little Rock, to end direct defiance of court orders. The Kennedy Justice Department attempted unsuccessfully to intervene on behalf of desegregation in some pending cases and proposed legislation to greatly increase federal enforcement powers. The Johnson administration was the high point of support for integration, winning enactment of the 1964 Civil Rights Act and enforcing it in the South.

After the Supreme Court authorized city-wide desegregation plans in 1971, however, HEW did very little to enforce the law, and the Justice Department, which fought the *Swann* decision, has often argued for more limited remedies and more demanding standards of proof (Orfield, 1978, ch. 10). President Nixon threatened to fire any federal official who supported busing, and he appealed to Congress for antibusing legislation (Panetta and Gall, 1971; *Congressional Quarterly*, August 28, 1971, pp. 1829-30).

The Carter administration brought a significant change, at least in tone. The President himself has had virtually nothing to say about school integration, but the administration is no longer hostile to desegregation. Executive agencies have stopped attacking the courts, and the administration has proposed no antibusing legislation. In some cases the Justice Department has filed supportive briefs.[24] There was even a brief attempt to revive enforcement of the fund cut-off provisions of the 1964 Civil Rights Act, an attempt that only stimulated Congress to enact new limitations on HEW (*Congressional Record*, June 28, 1977, pp. 10918-19; and

September 27, 1978, p. 16311). Some officials, particularly in HEW, have actively pursued controversial cases like the Chicago school segregation controversy, which HEW referred to the Department of Justice for possible litigation in the fall of 1979. The administration endorsed a modest bill to strengthen fair-housing enforcement, but the measure has languished in Congress. HUD has been applying more and more pressure on suburbs to build subsidized housing, but the small number of family units actually constructed are often occupied by local whites. Even though the administration is no longer an opponent of the civil rights groups and many of its officials are sympathetic, there are no signs of the kind of coordinated policy or political priority required for successful urban integration strategies.

Workable Plans in the North

Perhaps the greatest handicap to more rapid progress in the North is the failure of the courts to develop policies that promise to produce lasting, reasonably stable desegregation. Because of major differences between North and South in economic base, historical migration patterns, religious traditions, and local government structure, there are special problems in the North. Before the issue of urban desegregation ever arose, northern blacks were far more concentrated in a few areas than in the South, far more likely to be central-city residents, far more likely to live in a city where many of the white children attend Catholic schools, and far more likely to live in an old city whose growth has long since been cut off by the incorporation of independent suburbs (Orfield, 1978). Rapid white suburbanization and in-migration of another minority, the Hispanics, have magnified the problems.

Simple projections of existing enrollment patterns in the early '60s showed that there was little hope for lasting desegregation in many central cities unless the demographic trends reversed themselves. They did not. The result is that a number of the cities that have faced or will face desegregation begin with a student enrollment already dominated by minority groups and a school system already perceived as a minority institution. A continuation of the demographic trends means less and less integration and a narrower and narrower sector of the white public involved in any urban-desegregation plans as the years pass. The dominant reaction of middle-class white families in these situations is not to try to make desegregation work, but to follow the well-established path outward to white middle-class areas. Eventually middle-class minority families also abandon city schools, leaving them segregated by class as well as by race. This process of black suburbanization (in segregated suburbs) is far advanced in Washington, St. Louis, Cleveland, and elsewhere.

The Supreme Court's 1974 rejection of the Detroit metropolitan plan is the principal constraint on private enforcement of the law in the urban North. It is difficult to produce enthusiastic commitment to a plan that would, for example, make each Chicago school almost 80 percent minority in a metropolitan area where two-thirds of the students are white.[25] Desegregated schools with large nonwhite majorities are commonly perceived by whites as minority schools, not integrated schools; and surveys show far more white resistance to predominantly black than to half-black schools. There is also substantial evidence that blacks do not approve busing their children to largely minority "desegregated" schools. Much of the logic of the desegregation movement rests on the premise that schools that reflect the overall (largely white) society will be treated better by, and serve as more effective ports of entry into, the dominant (largely white) institutions of society. There is no reason to think that schools with only a few whites will be treated or perceived in this fashion.

If plans are limited to a central-city district and do not follow a racial balance approach, other problems emerge. After the Eighth Circuit Court of Appeals ruled in the 1980 St. Louis case that desegregated schools should have 30 to 50 percent blacks—in a city with 75 percent black students—the school board developed a plan that desegregated about half the schools and left most black children in segregated schools.[26] Similar plans are under consideration in Chicago and Los Angeles. In these plans many minority children with a right to desegregation receive no remedy. Within the central city the courts face a cruel choice between a meaningless remedy and one that openly excludes many students.

Trends

At a time when all three of the preconditions for successful big-city integration in the North are lacking, the prognosis is discouraging. The law has ignored the metro scale of segregation. While many smaller northern communities can be stably *and fully* desegregated under existing law, most of the big cities cannot. HEW enforcement powers have been cut back. In the Carter administration there has been little effort to develop a new commitment to the goal of integrated schools.[27] The plans that are emerging from the courts after years of waiting often fail to make any provision for the demographic changes that seem likely to produce re-segregation.

Projecting the existing trends in our city schools and in some of the inner suburban communities in large metropolitan areas, it is apparent that we are heading toward ghettoized education on a vast scale. Central-city desegregation plans in cities with few white students will provide only a brief detour in this development. Intellectuals do not have the power to reverse this trend, but they surely have the responsibility to examine closely the experience of the South in search of workable policies. How many Americans realize that nine of our fifty largest school systems have been operating metropolitan-wide school desegregation plans for years? How many know that the busing cost is usually only 1 or 2 percent of the local school budget (U.S. Senate Select Committee, 1972, pp. 208-209)? Who has even explored the relation of integrated schools to the moderation of racial attitudes in the South, keeping in mind that school desegregation was the only substantial racial change imposed on most southern communities outside the six states covered by the Voting Rights Act?[28]

It is strange but true that the most dramatic increase in support for integrated education has come from the public of the very region that fought it most fiercely. Perhaps this happened because it is the only region that has had much experience with integrated schools in recent years. Table 2 shows the change in southern attitudes.

In the country as a whole, the present debate is squarely focused on the wrong issue—the amount of busing. There is no evidence to show that busing has any educational effect, that people dislike busing when it is separated from desegregation, or that desegregation plans that minimize busing are more successful or more acceptable than those that employ it on a large scale. The real issue is whether peaceful, stable integration is

Table 2 Trend in attitudes of southern white parents toward school integration (percent objecting to schools of various racial compositions).

Level of black enrollment in schools	1959	1963	1965	1966	1969	1970	1973	1975
Few	72	61	37	24	21	16	16	15
Half	83	78	68	49	46	43	36	38
Majority	86	86	78	62	64	69	69	61

possible. The southern experience shows that it is and also strongly suggests the necessary preconditions. At a time when the dominant mode in social analysis is the "nothing works" approach, it is odd how little attention has been devoted to the remarkable successes of civil rights policy in many parts of the South. The courts, our policy makers, and the public deserve a much better analysis both of the feasibility of integration and of the consequences of doing nothing in the face of existing patterns of urban racial change. The failure to learn from the successes of the South will doom the North to a future of growing racial and class separation in our schools.

Notes

1. An important exception is the study of 550 southern schools by Robert Crain and his associates: *Southern Schools: An Evaluation of the Effects of the Emergency School Assistance Program and of School Desegregation* (Chicago: National Opinion Research Center, 1973).

2. Because of its county-wide school systems and a very active program to bring them rapidly into compliance with the *Swann* decision, Florida had the most extensive desegregation plans of any state. In most of the major metropolitan areas there was city-suburban desegregation with substantial busing. The plans went far beyond anything ever implemented in the North. The 1972 primary came when the programs were only a few months old in some systems and the threat of new plans still dominated community discussion in others. For an account of the 1972 Florida primary see Ernest R. May and Janet Fraser, eds., *Campaign '72: The Managers Speak* (Cambridge, Massachusetts: Harvard University Press, 1973), pp. 9-10, 101-102, 296.

3. The Democratic party's reluctant acceptance of busing when there was no alternative, and its pledge to support successful school integration, produced no dissent at the convention.

4. For Dade County and Houston, see Ross v. Eckels, 434 F.2d 1140 (5th Cir. 1970); Pate v. Dade County School Bd., 434 F.2d 1151 (5th Cir. 1970). For Memphis, see Northcross v. Board of Educ., 466 F.2d 890 (6th Cir. 1972). A federal district court in Houston ordered the Texas Education Agency to report on the possibility of metropolitan integration in 1980.

5. The South became predominantly urban about forty years later than the remainder of the country, and a far higher proportion of its cities retained power to annex suburbs.

6. The problems of the freedom-of-choice system, even under very strict procedural standards and strong pressure for annual progress from HEW, are spelled out in U.S. Commission on Civil Rights, *Southern School Desegregation 1966-67*, 1967, pp. 5-9, 45-69.

7. Green v. County School Bd., 391 U.S. 430 (1968).

8. Alexander v. Holmes County Bd. of Educ., 396 U.S. 19 (1969).

9. Swann v. Charlotte-Mecklenburg Bd. of Educ., 402 U.S. 1 (1971).

10. During the 1971-72 school year 154 school districts implemented new desegregation plans. All but five of these districts were in southern and border states. School Busing: Hearings Before Subcomm. No. 5 of the House Comm. on the Judiciary, 92d Cong., 2d Sess. 1226-34 (1972) (insertion into statement of Elliot L. Richardson, Sec'y. of HEW).

11. The KKK revival was most rapid in the mid-sixties in the black-majority counties of southside Virginia and eastern North Carolina. In several other southern states the White Citizen's Council pursued similar objectives. For one report on council activities, see *Mississippi Black Paper* (New York: Random House, 1965). See also Sarratt, 1966, ch. 12.

12. The Powell amendment, first introduced in 1955 by Harlem congressman Adam Clayton Powell in response to a demand by the NAACP to deny federal aid to school systems violating the Constitution, was a focal point in battles over education legislation in the fifties. See James L. Sundquist, *Politics and Policy: The Eisenhower, Kennedy, and Johnson Years* (Washington, D.C.: Brookings Institution, 1968).

13. Adams v. Richardson, 356 F. Supp. 92 (D.D.C. 1973) was the first of a series of federal district court and court of appeals decisions in this case.

14. Research in Mississippi suggested that the level at which white enrollment stabilized after desegregation was closely related to the proportion of the local population that was black. See Luther Munford, "Desegregation and private schools," *Social Policy* (January-February 1976), 42-45. The following is an excellent account of the evolution of issues and attitudes in Charlotte by the city's school superintendent: Rolland W. Jones, "Thoughts on integration," reprinted in *Congressional Record*, May 21, 1976, pp. S7776-77.

15. See also Bradley v. School Bd., 416 U.S. 696 (1974).

16. Calhoun v. Cook, 332 F. Supp. 804 (N.D. Ga. 1971); "NAACP suspends Atlanta unit: repudiates school agreement," *Crisis* (May 1973), 168-69.

17. A three-judge court rejected a metropolitan remedy in September 1979, and the Atlanta American Civil Liberties Union promised further appeals (*Atlanta Constitution*, September 25, 1979, p. 1); the Supreme Court, however, summarily affirmed the lower-court decision. Armour v. Nix, 48 U.S.L.W. 3732 (May 12, 1980).

18. Jerry Shinn, "Housing plans would end lip service to integration," *Charlotte Observer*, February 19, 1975; "Scattered sites near completion," Charlotte Housing Authority, *Communicator*, October 1979, p. 1; interview with Donald Carroll, Jr., Charlotte city councilman, November 8, 1979; interview with Jack Bullard, Community Relations Commission of Mecklenburg County, November 8, 1979; interview with John Phillips, deputy superintendent, Charlotte-Mecklenburg School District, November 8, 1979.

19. Keyes v. School Dist. No. 1, Denver, 413 U.S. 189 (1973).

20. Washington v. Davis, 426 U.S. 229 (1976); Arlington Heights v. Metropolitan Hous. Dev. Corp., 429 U.S. 252 (1977).

21. Milliken v. Bradley (Milliken I), 418 U.S. 717 (1974).

22. Dayton Bd. of Educ. v. Brinkman (Dayton I), 433 U.S. 406 (1977).

23. Columbus Bd. of Educ. v. Penick, 443 U.S. 449 (1979); Dayton Bd. of Educ. v. Brinkman (Dayton II), 443 U.S. 526 (1979).

24. For example, Brief for the United States as Amicus Curiae, Dayton Bd. of Educ. v. Brinkman (Dayton I), 433 U.S. 406 (1977).

25. Current Illinois State Board of Education guidelines, if applied without modification, would require such desegregation in Chicago. Civil rights litigants in some big-city cases are pressing for city-wide orders on this model.

26. See Liddell v. Bd. of Educ. of St. Louis, 469 F. Supp. 1304 (E.D. Mo. 1979), *aff'd*, F.2d (8th Cir. 1980).

27. The Carter urban policy devised in 1978, for example, has no strategy for urban desegregation and does not even mention the relation of urban school desegregation to urban social and residential patterns.

28. Many commentators on the transformation of the South emphasize the central importance of the Voting Rights Act. They seldom note, however, that the act applied only to six states among the seventeen southern and border states and that there had been substantial black voting for some time in much of the remainder of the South. No doubt voting was extremely important in ending the overtly racist tone of politics in the Deep South and in permitting the election of moderate governors and members of Congress, but it is hardly a full explanation of the vast changes in the entire region.

References

Armor, David. 1978. *White Flight, Demographic Transition, and the Future of School Desegregation*. Santa Monica, California: Rand Corporation.

Brown, Cynthia. 1971. Nixon administration desegregation. *Inequality in Education* 9:11-16.

Coleman, James, Sara Kelly, and John Moore. 1975. *Trends in School Integration, 1968-1973*. Washington, D.C.: Urban Institute.

Gates, Robbin. 1964. *The Making of Massive Resistance: Virginia's Politics of School Desegregation, 1954-1956*. Chapel Hill: University of North Carolina Press.

Gendron, Eldridge J. 1972. Busing in Florida: before and after. *Integrated Education* 10 (2):3-7.

Giles, Michael W., Douglas Gatlin, and Everett F. Cataldo. 1976. Determinants of resegregation. Unpublished report submitted to the National Science Foundation.

Hadden, Susan G., et al. 1979. *Consensus in Politics in Atlanta: School Board Decision-Making, 1974-1978*. Atlanta: Southern Center for Studies in Public Policy.

Hall, Leon. 1974. School desegregation: a (hollow?) victory. *Inequality in Education* 17:5-14.

Lord, J. Dennis, and John Catau. 1978. The desegregation-resegregation scenario in urban school districts of the South. Unpublished.

Muse, Benjamin. 1964. *Ten Years of Prelude: the Story of Integration since the Supreme Court's 1954 Decision*. New York: Viking.

Orfield, Gary. 1969. *The Reconstruction of Southern Education: The Schools and the 1964 Civil Rights Act*. New York: John Wiley.

——— 1978. *Must We Bus? Segregated Schools and National Policy.* Washington, D.C.: Brookings Institution.

Panetta, Leon, and Peter Gall. 1971. *Bring Us Together.* Philadelphia: Lippincott.

Pottinger, Stanley H. 1971. HEW enforcement of *Swann. Inequality in Education* 9:6-10.

Sarratt, Reed. 1966. *The Ordeal of Desegregation.* New York: Harper & Row.

Synon, John J. 1968. *George Wallace: Profile of a Presidential Candidate.* Wilmarnock, Virginia: Manuscripts, Inc.

U.S. Commission on Civil Rights. 1967. *Southern School Desegregation 1966-1967.* Washington, D.C.: Government Printing Office.

——— 1972. *Your Child and Busing.* Washington, D.C.: Government Printing Office.

U.S. Department of Health, Education, and Welfare, Office of Equal Educational Opportunity. 1972. *Displacement of Black Educators in Desegregating Public Schools.* Washington, D.C.: Government Printing Office.

U.S. Senate Select Committee on Equal Educational Opportunity. 1972. *Toward Equal Educational Opportunity.* Washington, D.C.: Government Printing Office.

Weinberg, Meyer. 1968. *Race and Place: A Legal History of the Neighborhood School.* Washington, D.C.: Government Printing Office.

Witcover, Jules. 1977. *Marathon: The Pursuit of the Presidency, 1972-1976.* New York: Viking.

3 Some Reflections on the Supreme Court and School Desegregation

FRANK GOODMAN

More than a quarter of a century has passed since the Supreme Court first declared school segregation unconstitutional, and more than a decade since it began to shape affirmative-action remedies designed to achieve racial balance. Throughout that period fundamental questions about the nature of the wrong and the appropriateness of the prescribed remedies have persisted. Recent decisions of the Court have somewhat clarified the basic principles. At the same time they have brought to the forefront new problems of application.

These developments, or aspects of them, are the subject of the present chapter. It is divided into three parts. The first deals with the distinction, now constitutionally critical, between permissible de facto and impermissible de jure segregation; the second evaluates the theory underlying the Court's remedial decisions; and the third comments briefly on the problems of metropolitan or multidistrict desegregation.

The Scope of the Wrong

In *Dayton Board of Education* v. *Brinkman*,[1] known as *Dayton I*, the Supreme Court finally laid to rest a long-standing issue concerning the very nature of the constitutional violation defined in *Brown*. It held that racial imbalance does not violate the Fourteenth Amendment "in the absence of a showing that this condition resulted from intentionally segregative actions on the part of the Board"; de facto segregation, in short, is not unconstitutional.[2] Many courts and commentators had thought otherwise, not altogether without reason. Certain language in the *Brown* opinion[3] could be read to imply that segregation, though particularly harmful when sanctioned by law, was sufficiently harmful to be unconstitutional even when not so sanctioned. This interpretation seemed to be reinforced by the Court's remedial decisions holding that a *Brown* violation must be corrected by affirmative racial balancing, not mere color-blindness—a requirement most easily explained by the theory that racial imbalance per se is the violation to be remedied.

The question was complicated, moreover, by confusion about the precise meaning of the terms de facto and de jure. Many assumed that the distinction hinged not on the presence or absence of segregative intent but on the presence or absence of "state action." Segregation, it was thought, is de jure when "imposed by law," de facto when it results from private decisions or other circumstances in which the state plays no part. On that premise, those who favored the broader prohibition could argue unanswerably that all school segregation is de jure, since it is the state—indeed the state alone—that decides which children are to attend which schools.

It is fair to say, however, that the weight of authority above the district court level has always supported the more limited view of the constitutional wrong. By the mid-1960s, at least three courts of appeals had held that de facto segregation is not unconstitutional.[4] In 1972 the Supreme Court affirmed, without opinion, a state-court decision so holding.[5] And although it skirted the issue a year later in *Keyes*,[6] it did make clear that "the differentiating factor between de jure segregation and so-called de facto segregation . . . is *purpose* or *intent* to segregate,"[7] thus rejecting the definition upon which the broader prohibition had sometimes been predicated. From *Keyes* it was a short step to the resolution of the question in *Dayton I.*

There are signs, however, that the de facto-de jure distinction, now firmly established in principle, may come to very little in practice. Segregative intent is not hard to prove. For one thing, it need not be proven directly; it can be, and usually must be, inferred from objective circumstances, often little more than the fact of racial imbalance plus the failure to correct it. As long as the district judge is careful to make an explicit finding of segregative intent, rather than treating racial imbalance as itself the ultimate fact, that finding is unlikely to be disturbed on appeal. Indeed, some courts of appeals have attempted to smooth the path by holding that "a presumption of segregative intent arises once it is established that school authorities have engaged in acts or omissions, the natural, probable, and foreseeable consequence of which is to bring about or maintain segregation."[8] The burden then shifts to school authorities to prove the purity of their motives. This prima facie showing could be made in virtually every case, since the segregative effects produced by school-assignment policies are almost always clearly predictable at the time of action. To be sure, there are many instances in which schools were originally built and attendance-area boundaries fixed long before the emergence of the segregation issue or the advent of blacks in significant numbers; but even in those cases the decision to retain existing boundaries and feeder patterns can be viewed as a continuing stream of annual acts (or at least omissions) foreseeably resulting in continued or increasing racial imbalance. The Supreme Court has not endorsed this burden-shifting rule; indeed it has by implication rejected it.[9] But although the plaintiff may have the burden of proof, district judges inclined to be skeptical of official motives or convinced that even de facto segregation should be outlawed will have little difficulty finding violations.

Moreover, the Supreme Court itself established in *Keyes* another burden-shifting principle only slightly less helpful to plaintiffs than the one it rejected: "[A] finding of intentionally segregative school board actions in a meaningful portion of a school system . . . creates a presumption that other segregated schooling within the system is not adventitious. It establishes, in other words, a prima facie case of unlawful segregative design on the part of school authorities, and shifts to these authorities the burden of proving that other segregated schools within the system are not also the result of intentionally segregative actions."[10] In *Keyes* itself, the district court's findings of intentionally segregative actions in the 1960s in one rather small section of Denver (Park Hill) triggered a presumption of segregative intent everywhere else in the district, including the core-city area in which schools were already heavily black decades earlier.

But the fragility of the de facto-de jure distinction goes beyond problems of proof; it lies also in the elusiveness of the very concept of segregative intent. For some legal purposes *intent* means nothing more than foreknowledge of consequences. Such a definition would virtually obliterate the conceptual distinction between de facto and de jure segregation and lead to the classification of nearly all segregation as de jure. It is clear that in the area of school segregation, if not of racial discrimination generally, the Supreme Court means to employ a definition of intent more in keeping with ordinary usage—one that demands not mere knowledge but purpose or desire to bring about the forbidden segregative effects. On the other hand, this state of mind need not involve malice, racial prejudice, or other wicked thoughts—only a purpose, for whatever reason, to cause or keep the racial distribution deemed unacceptable by the courts.

Having said this, one immediately becomes aware of how razor thin the de facto-de jure distinction can be, both factually and morally, in a great many instances. A school board that hews to a neighborhood-assignment policy strictly for nonracial reasons—economy, convenience, safety, or conservation—acts constitutionally even though it knows full well, and cares not a whit, that its policy will produce segregation. The resultant racial distribution is deemed an incidental side effect. Let that same school board take that same action for those same reasons plus one other—fear that desegregation will trigger white flight—and it may well find itself on the wrong side of the constitutional line. The segregative effects are no longer merely incidental; they are the very effects the school board aimed to produce, albeit only as a means to ulterior, nonracial, ends.

The distinction becomes still narrower when it is noted that segregative intent need not be the sole or dominant motive for the state's action; indeed, there is some question that it need even be a sine qua non. In *Keyes* the Court indicated that de jure segregation is established whenever the action of school authorities is motivated "to any degree"[11] by segregative intent—whenever segregative intent is "among the factors"[12] that motivate the action. On the other hand, in two later cases not involving school desegregation the Court stated that proof that official action was motivated in part by a racially discriminatory purpose merely shifted to the state the burden of showing that the same action would have been taken anyway.[13] Even on this latter view, defendants will have great difficulty carrying the burden of proof. A school board that fails to convince a district judge that its actions were not racially motivated is unlikely to convince him that the racial motivation was superfluous.

The moral near-equivalence of de facto and de jure segregation appears not only when we compare individual acts or omissions on both sides of this conceptual line, but also when we compare overall patterns of action. One board may adopt a conscious (albeit undeclared) general policy of segregation and carry it out on a system-wide basis. Another, without adopting such a policy even covertly, may nevertheless take segregative action in those specific instances in which it seems both necessary and feasible, while refraining from such action in other situations where demography makes it superfluous or futile. On these facts, the first board would be held subject to a system-wide desegregation order, whereas the second would be required merely to undo the limited effects of its local violations. One wonders whether the moral difference between the two is great enough to warrant the difference in treatment. Here, too, it may be that the *Keyes* presumption, and the readiness of district judges to use it to convert cases of the second type into cases of the first, may reflect an implicit judgment that the two cases ought not be treated differently even when factually distinguishable.

The artificiality of the conceptual distinction, at least in the marginal cases, together with the vagaries of proof previously discussed, raises serious questions about the wisdom of hinging so much upon so little. Obviously the distinction puts enormous power in the hands of the trial judge. District judges making identical findings based on the objective facts can and do reach different conclusions about the existence of a constitutional violation, either because of greater or lesser willingness to infer segregative intent or because of unarticulated differences in their understanding of what segregative intent means. Even if one could be confident that outcome differences reflected true factual distinctions from case to case, one would still wonder whether those factual differences have any real moral significance, or enough moral significance to justify the enormous legal consequences attached to them. Can it really be supposed that the two school boards in the previous example deserve to be treated as differently as they well might be, the one having no remedial duty at all, the other a duty of massive busing?

The Problem of Remedy

In the first *Brown* opinion the Court did not prescribe a remedy for the newly defined wrong; in the second, a year later, it addressed the problem in the barest generalities. Offending school districts were directed to move, with "all deliberate speed," toward a "racially nondiscriminatory system," a system of public-school assignment on a "nonracial basis." Many, if not most, observers assumed that this requirement would be satisfied by a colorblind assignment policy based on freedom of choice or, as in most northern communities, geographical zoning. In 1968, in *Green* v. *School Board of New Kent County*,[14] the Court rejected that view, holding that freedom-of-choice plans would not satisfy the duty of school boards to disestablish dual systems unless they actually produced a satisfactory racial distribution. Desegregation plans were to be judged not by intentions but by results, the school racial compositions actually achieved. A "nonracial" system was defined for the first time as one in which schools were not identifiably black or white but were racially mixed—and mixed, presumably, in proportions not greatly differing from that of the district at large. The duty to convert "dual" into "unitary" systems demanded not colorblind assignment but color-conscious assignment to achieve the desired balance.

The nature of this "affirmative duty" was further elaborated by *Swann* v. *Charlotte-Mecklenburg Board of Education,* [15] in which the Court held that a neutral neighborhood-assignment plan provided too little racial balance and had to be replaced by an extensive busing plan, and by *Keyes* v. *School District No. 1, Denver, Colorado,* [16] holding that racial gerrymandering and other unconstitutional acts of segregation in one part of a school system create a duty to desegregate schools throughout the system.

Critics have argued that the racial-balance decisions stood *Brown* on its head, commanding the very practice—pupil assignment based on race —that *Brown* condemned (Graglia, 1976). This objection is misguided. Racial assignment for the purpose of integration is very different from racial assignment for the purpose of segregation. The former, unlike the latter, is designed to promote a clearly legitimate, indeed a compelling, public interest. Furthermore, since the purpose and effect of racial balancing are to place all children, black and white, in classrooms and schools of uniform racial composition, it cannot be described in any meaningful sense as discriminating "against" any person or group; the aim is to treat everyone alike. The latter point may explain why even those who oppose "benign" racial quotas in employment or graduate-school admission as discriminatory against whites rarely make that charge against racial-balance plans in the schools. All of this undercuts the contention that the racial assignment compelled by *Green* and *Swann* violates the very principle for which *Brown* stands.

To say that racial balancing is constitutionally permissible, however, is a far cry from saying that it is constitutionally mandatory, even as a remedy for past wrongs. It is not self-evident why a colorblind residential-assignment policy—elsewhere not unconstitutional despite its predictable segregative effects—should be outlawed in those, and only those, school systems in which de jure violations historically occurred.

Several reasons might be offered. First racial balancing could perhaps be justified as a prophylactic measure, a means of satisfying the courts, the black community, and the society as a whole that purposeful segregation is not continuing under the cloak of a racially neutral neighborhood-assignment policy. Second, this drastic remedy might be thought of as a deterrent, impressing upon potential offenders, as a mere cease-and-desist order would not, that segregation does not pay. Third, racial balancing may be thought necessary in order to deprive the wrongdoer of that which he sought unlawfully to achieve; it may reflect a judgment that it is morally unfitting for a school board that, in violation of the

Constitution, purposefully established a racially segregated system to be permitted to continue operating that system on the plea, however factually justified, that demography alone is now to blame for it.

The Supreme Court has never explicitly adopted any of these grounds. Its own rationale for racial balancing is a different one. A court of equity has the power and the duty to "render a decree which will . . . eliminate the discriminatory effects of the past."[17] Hence, the objective of the desegregation remedy is to "eliminate from the public schools all vestiges of state-imposed segregation."[18] Just what were these "vestiges" and why was busing thought necessary to eliminate them? The Court's answer was that current racial imbalance in schools may itself be a consequence of past and present de jure violations through the influence of those violations on residential patterns and on the size and location of schools. In *Swann* the Court explained that a neutral, geographically based assignment plan "may fail to counteract the continuing effects of past school segregation resulting from discriminatory location of school sites or distortion of school size in order to achieve or maintain an artificial racial separation."[19] It observed that "people gravitate toward school facilities, just as schools are located in response to the needs of the people. The location of schools may thus influence the patterns of residential development of a metropolitan area and have important impact on the composition of inner-city neighborhoods."[20] Racially motivated siting and zoning decisions "may well promote segregated residential patterns which, when combined with 'neighborhood zoning,' further lock the school system into the mold of separation of the races."[21]

The Question of Causation

The Court did not suggest, however, that causation was to be a subject of particularized factual inquiry in each case or that by negating causation the authorities could substantially limit their liability. To be sure, the Court conceded that a few single-race schools might temporarily be tolerated if their racial compositions were shown not to be the result of discriminatory official action;[22] but that very exception, carefully guarded as it was, implied that schools would not be exempted wholesale no matter what the causal showing. Disproof of causation was to be a necessary but not a sufficient condition for limitation of liability. In effect, the duty to eliminate racial imbalance from the statutory dual systems of the South was predicated in *Swann* on a virtually conclusive presumption of causal relationship between this racial imbalance and past unconstitutional state action.

In *Keyes* the Court applied the same analysis to the segregation problem in the North, where de jure violations typically take the form of
gerrymandering and other covert administrative practices rather than explicit statutes. In Denver such violations occurred during the 1960s, in
the formerly white Park Hill section east of Colorado Boulevard, as
blacks began moving into that area from the core-city ghetto farther
west. The Court held that the violations, though confined to Park Hill,
could justify a system-wide desegregation remedy by virtue of their
causal impact on the system as a whole. Returning to the theme it had
earlier sounded in *Swann*, the Court noted that a variety of racially motivated assignment, transfer, and construction policies, all having the clear
effect of "earmarking" schools according to their racial composition,
may have a "profound reciprocal effect on the racial composition of residential neighborhoods within a metropolitan area, thereby causing further racial concentration within the schools."[23]

Here, however, in contrast to the southern statutory situation, the
Court was prepared to submit the issue of causation to case-by-case inquiry. It granted that there may be rare cases "in which the geographical
structure of, or the natural boundaries within, a school district may have
the effect of dividing the district into separate, identifiable and unrelated
units,"[24] and it instructed the district court on remand to consider
whether Colorado Boulevard is "the type of barrier that of itself could
confine the impact of the Board's action to an identifiable area."[25] In the
absence of such a finding of geographic separateness, "proof of state-
imposed segregation in a substantial portion of the district will suffice to
support a finding by the trial court of the existence of a dual system";
and "where that finding is made, as in cases involving statutory dual systems, the school authorities have an affirmative duty to effectuate a
transition to a racially nondiscriminatory school system."[26]

It is not altogether clear whether the Court meant simply to equate
geographic separateness with causal insularity[27]—in which case defendants could rarely hope to carry their burden—or whether the two questions, geography and causation, were to be answered separately and seri-
atim. Even on the latter assumption it was clear that the presumption of
system-wide segregative impact would be strong and the burden of proof,
resting squarely on the school authorities, would be heavy.

In the mid-1970s the Court seemed for a time to be moving away from
its previous approach to causation. In *Milliken* v. *Bradley*[28] it held that
desegregation decrees embracing more than one district are proper only
upon an affirmative showing that the underlying violations have pro-

duced "interdistrict effects"—for example, that violations within a city system have contributed to the racial polarity between city and suburban districts. No longer, it seemed, was the Court willing simply to presume the existence of the critical causal relationship; it demanded specific proof.

Three years later, in *Dayton I,*[29] the Court appeared to extend the proof-of-causation requirement to the single-district situation as well. Overturning a court of appeals decision that had imposed a system-wide desegregation remedy based on district court findings of isolated de jure violations, the Court stated that the proper procedure was to determine "how much incremental segregative effect these violations had on the racial distribution of the Dayton school population as presently constituted, when that distribution is compared to what it would have been in the absence of such constitutional violations. The remedy must be designed to redress that difference, and only if there has been a system-wide impact may there be a system-wide remedy."[30] Although the Court cited *Keyes* for this proposition and acknowledged no deviation from its principles, *Dayton I* was widely interpreted as having shifted to plaintiffs the heavy, often impossible, burden of proving causation, thus severely restricting the availability of the desegregation remedy.

That supposition, however, was to be short-lived. In companion Ohio cases decided in 1979—*Columbus Board of Education* v. *Penick*[31] and a second round of *Dayton Board of Education* v. *Brinkman*[32] *(Dayton II)* —the Court reaffirmed the presumption rule of *Keyes* and narrowly limited the applicability of *Dayton I*. In both cases it affirmed decisions of the court of appeals requiring system-wide desegregation on the basis of miscellaneous de jure violations both before and after *Brown I*. Its principal opinion, written for the *Columbus* case, endorsed the conclusion "that there was system-wide segregation in the Columbus schools that was the result of recent and remote intentionally segregative actions of the Columbus Board."[33] *Dayton I* was distinguished on the ground that it involved only a few seemingly isolated violations; in these circumstances, apparently, the *Keyes* presumption does not arise and the desegregation remedy must be tailored to those "incremental segregative effects" that are affirmatively shown. By contrast, where purposefully discriminatory actions affecting a significant portion of the school district are found, as in *Columbus* and *Dayton II*, the trial court is entitled, and in the absence of contrary proof even required, to conclude that the radiating effects of these actions are of system-wide scope.

The burden of proof on causation might not matter greatly if the evi-

dence bearing on this issue were judged by normal standards of adequacy. Causation is not a question on which the record is likely to be
silent or the evidence finely balanced. School authorities, once aware of
their burden, can often marshal circumstances that tend to minimize the
impact that their unlawful conduct has had on the current racial makeup
of the system. *Columbus* and *Dayton II*—though they do not hark back
to the *Keyes* notion of geographic separateness—nevertheless make clear
that the presumption of system-wide segregative effects will not be overcome by any ordinary showing, and that the burden of proof with which
defendants are now firmly saddled will be almost impossible to meet.

The *Columbus* case is illustrative. The district court found that, prior
to 1954, the school board had deliberately created an enclave of five all-
black schools on the near east side of Columbus, assigning them all-black
faculties and gerrymandering their attendance areas so as to fence blacks
in and whites out. The only specific instance of gerrymandering noted by
the court was a boundary change that converted racially mixed Pilgrim
School into an all-black school by shifting some of its white students to
the all-white Fair Avenue School.[34]

The board maintained that these violations could not have had any influence on the racial composition of the school system at the time of trial,
since the faculties of the surviving schools (two had closed) were fully
desegregated by the time of the trial, and with the expansion of the black
community, the schools were now located so far from any white neighborhoods that they would inevitably be all-black no matter how the
boundaries had been drawn. In this connection the record showed that
Fair Avenue, the formerly white school to which Pilgrim's white students
were shifted, had by 1964 become like Pilgrim, nearly all-black,[35] so that
the gerrymandered boundary made absolutely no difference to the current racial composition of the two schools.

The board made equally detailed arguments with respect to the handful of miscellaneous post-1954 acts and omissions found by the district
court to have been intentionally segregative. Yet the district court, without commenting specifically on any of these factual contentions, dis-
posed of the causation issue in a single sentence blanketing both the pre-
1954 and the post-1954 violations: "Defendants have not proved that the
present admitted racial imbalance in the Columbus Public Schools would
have occurred even in the absence of their segregative acts and omissions."[36] The Supreme Court, in affirming, was almost equally suc-
cinct.[37] So casual a dismissal of the board's detailed showing of non-

causation is understandable only on the premise that the level of proof required to overcome the *Keyes* presumption is far higher than the usual preponderance-of-evidence standard.

That conclusion emerges even more clearly in *Dayton II*, in which the court of appeals, later seconded by the Supreme Court, went so far as to reverse district court findings in favor of the defendant on the question of causation and to substitute its own contrary findings of system-wide segregative impact without serious discussion of the detailed evidence that had persuaded the district court the other way. To be sure, the district court had mistakenly assigned the burden of proof to the plaintiffs; this and other legal errors were the main grounds of reversal. But it was clear that the district court, after careful consideration of each of the found and alleged violations, was convinced that none of them had significantly affected the current racial composition of the system; and the ease with which the appellate court rejected the defendant's proof—without explanation and without addressing the considerations on which the district court had relied—was defensible only on the premise that the required burden of proof was exceptionally heavy. Indeed, if the evidence of noncausation in these two cases was not enough to defeat the *Keyes* presumption and foreclose a system-wide desegregation order, it is hard to imagine what evidence would be.

The stringency of the defendant's burden of proof on the question of causation is in contrast to the leniency of the plaintiff's burden on the question of segregative intent. The courts, we have seen, readily infer the latter fact from circumstantial evidence, often minimal; plaintiffs are not expected to produce a "smoking gun." Yet that is precisely what *Columbus* and *Dayton II* seem to require of defendants when it comes to causation. In one sense the difference is incongruous: the causation question —whether Y would have happened, but for X—by its very nature can be answered only speculatively and circumstantially, whereas, with respect to intent, one can at least imagine what a smoking gun would look like (an express declaration by school board members, for example). At a deeper level, however, the contrasting standards of proof, both favoring the plaintiff, are reconciled in the notion that factual uncertainties, whether of intent or causation, should be resolved in favor of the asserted constitutional rights.

The causal hypothesis underlying both the *Swann* and *Keyes* presumptions and the desegregation remedy itself—that yesterday's de jure violations have shaped the racial composition of today's schools through their

ripple effects on neighborhood racial patterns, school locations, or both
—is, as we shall see, highly dubious. Before examining it, however, there
is an important point to be made. The bare fact that a school originally
made black (or white) by intentionally segregative state action continues
to be black (or white) at the time of trial does not alone establish a causal
relationship between that unconstitutional action and the current racial
composition of the school. The current composition may be entirely
the result of factors independent of the original constitutional violation.

Assume for a moment that, contrary to the Court's thesis, school segregation statutes and practices have not in fact influenced residential patterns or school locations. All would agree that a pre-*Brown* segregation
statute, as long as it remained in force, was the sole cause of the segregation it mandated, even assuming that precisely the same racial separation
would otherwise have resulted from the use of a colorblind geography-
based assignment policy in a community where neighborhoods were
highly segregated. The notion of causa sine qua non does not exhaust
what we ordinarily mean by the term *cause*. Whenever two or more factors or sets of factors, each independently sufficient to bring about a certain result, combine to produce that result, neither is a causa sine qua
non, but both are nevertheless causes—call them operative or generative
causes—in a sense that is intuitively obvious, however difficult to expli-
cate (Hart and Honore, 1959, pp. 216-229). Even more clearly, such a
factor does not cease to be a cause, indeed the sole cause, merely because
there is another factor that, in its absence, *would* have operated to produce the same result.

Once the segregation statute, however, had been replaced by a neutral
neighborhood-assignment policy, any subsequent racial imbalance in the
system would no longer have been a consequence of the former statute
(in either of the senses distinguished above) but a consequence solely of
the new rule operating in conjunction with residential segregation. This
seemingly obvious point is sometimes obscured by a tendency to think of
the student body of a school as a single entity (like the building in which
the school is housed)—and of its racial composition as a single continuing condition that (like the color of the building) remains at all times the
product of the "paint job" that originally generated it. Such thinking
easily leads to the conclusion that the school board that initially painted
the school black (or white) now has an affirmative duty to repaint it in
two-tone, regardless of any intervening causal considerations. The paint
analogy, however, is false. The student body of a school is not a single
continuous entity but an annually revolving class of individuals, the

membership of which is determined anew each year by the pupil-place-ment rules *currently* in effect, not by the superseded rules of the past. Past official action can be said to have "current segregative impact" only if it is causally linked to the most recent installment of the series, not merely to earlier installments.

In the northern situation the problem is more complicated because the assignment rules generated by the original intentionally segregative state action—the gerrymandered boundaries, optional attendance zones, feeder patterns, and the like—are usually still in force at the time of trial. Nevertheless, these rules, though still operative, may no longer be a con-tributing cause of segregation even in the very schools to which they apply: A boundary change originally intended to segregate may, as resi-dential patterns change, cease to have that effect, and indeed may have the opposite effect.[38] Furthermore, a racial-balance-busing remedy would seem unwarranted even in cases where the tainted assignment rule does continue to have segregative impact; for that impact would be ended, along with the rule itself, simply by reversing the original uncon-stitutional action (for instance, by restoring the pregerrymander bound-ary). Such a change, whether or not it significantly altered the racial composition of the schools in question, would assure that any subsequent racial imbalance was no longer attributable to purposeful discrimination by the state.[39] In sum, as long as the underlying constitutional violations are "reversible" pupil-placement rules, rather than "irreversible" school siting and construction decisions, and as long as these placement rules do not in turn influence private housing decisions and therefore racial resi-dence patterns, busing or other racial balancing would never be necessary to eliminate the vestiges of unconstitutional state action. To the extent the offending placement rule still contributed to current racial imbalance, that contribution could be terminated simply by reversing or canceling the rule itself.

It is now time to assess the supposed causal linkage between de jure school practices and residential segregation. This linkage is immediately suspect—if only because of the universality of residential segregation, both in the South and in the North, in school districts both guilty and guiltless of de jure violations. In the pre-*Brown* southern context the theory, presumably, was that the existence of segregation statutes caused families, both black and white, who would otherwise have fanned out into racially mixed neighborhoods, to cluster instead around the schools reserved for members of their race. This theory, whatever its validity for whites, is plainly fanciful when applied to blacks. It assumes a degree of black mobility, and of white receptiveness, that all experience belies; poverty and housing discrimination, the twin obstacles to residential de-segregation even today, were surely not less formidable in the days when restrictive covenants were in flower and fair-housing legislation was not yet on the books. If anything, school segregation statutes may have had exactly the opposite of the postulated effect: they may have tended to lessen residential segregation by reassuring white families that it was unnecessary to maintain the whiteness of their neighborhoods in order to preserve the whiteness of their schools. This may explain why, according to some demographic evidence, residential segregation in the pre-*Brown* South was less severe than it has subsequently become, and less severe than it was in the North, a relationship that has now been reversed (Taeuber and Taeuber, 1969).

In the northern situation, where de jure violations are of the gerry-mandering variety, the hypothesis that school segregation brings residen-tial segregation is more complicated. The main idea is that residentially mobile white families are drawn to neighborhoods served by schools they perceive to have been earmarked for whites. (Whether residentially mo-bile black families are apt to be influenced by earmarking and, if so, the relative attractiveness to them of alternative school racial compositions are thornier questions.) Moreover, the official earmarking of schools may trigger discrimination in the housing market designed to fulfill the expectations of the white community that their favored schools and at-tendance areas will remain white. Finally, earmarking aside, official ac-tions that reduce the white presence in racially mixed schools below some critical tipping point may cause the remaining whites in those schools to desert them. For example, if an act of gerrymandering shifts a white neighborhood from school A (50 percent white) to school B (80 percent white), many of the remaining whites in A, finding themselves a minority or fearing that the authorities have written off their school, may head for whiter pastures elsewhere in the city, in the suburbs, or in private or parochial schools. And the ripple effects need not be confined to the immediately affected schools: whites in racially mixed neighborhoods in other parts of the district may perceive B as a haven school and be drawn to it; and their departure may in turn tip the balance in their former schools, triggering further white defections.

Even on its face, this scenario must be taken with a grain of salt. Ger-rymandering in the North typically occurs in formerly white areas under-going racial transition. It is hard to see how such violations can signifi-cantly have influenced the racial composition of schools in the older ghetto areas that were all black, or nearly so, decades earlier. Nor is it clear why official action aimed at preserving the whiteness of schools already white should make those schools more attractive than they previously have been. Finally, the very fact that gerrymandering so often occurs in schools where the transition from white to black (in a school such as A) is already well under way and reflects a judgment by school authorities that this process is certain to continue (that the school is destined to become all-black anyway and that its whites, unless reassigned, will flee the system) suggests that the gerrymander may have no significant effect other than to hasten the inevitable. And when, as often happens, the surrounding schools (such as B in our example) likewise become black—despite the efforts of school authorities to keep them white—the long-term segregative impact of the gerrymandering becomes all the more suspect.

Most empirical evidence seems to be against the hypothesis that school racial composition has corresponding effects on neighborhood racial composition. If that were true, one would expect to find that in a district where schools are racially mixed, the neighborhoods served by those schools are likewise racially mixed; yet this is rarely the case. As Wolf (1977) has observed: "Small towns with small black populations typically have but one secondary school, but its biracial character has not created racial dispersion. A study of a number of Philadelphia suburbs with busing programs that include even the elementary schools found residential segregation to be unchanged as a consequence. Nor is there any evidence —or even claims—that the system-wide school dispersion programs in Berkeley, Pasadena, Princeton, Evanston, and elsewhere have had a corresponding effect on housing patterns, although these programs have been in existence for several years."[40]

The Supreme Court's approach to causation, however, has not been grounded on the simple premise that school racial mix determines neighborhood racial mix. Rather, the Court has stressed the role of school-siting decisions; these, it has said, reciprocally interacting with private decisions on housing, simultaneously produce both segregated schools and segregated neighborhoods.[41] To what extent is this hypothesis valid?

Even if racially motivated school-siting decisions had no influence whatever on private residential decisions and therefore on the racial composition of neighborhoods, they could nevertheless have significant long-term effects on the racial composition of schools—effects that cannot, like those generated by pupil-placement rules, be erased simply by reversing the original decision. In the pre-*Brown* situation, the existence of segregation statutes undoubtedly made it necessary to select school sites with an eye to the racial character of the population to be served. In communities with racially segregated neighborhoods, it was more efficient to locate schools near the center of the racial enclaves than on their fringes (though the latter locations might have been equally or more efficient under a colorblind assignment system). Once established, this configuration assured that even after statutory segregation gave way to neighborhood schools, attendance areas designed by colorblind school boards for efficiency alone would continue to correspond with the racial enclaves for whose convenience the school sites were initially selected.[42] The original de jure "fit" between school locations and neighborhood racial concentrations must in many cases have been perpetuated as a de facto fit.

The importance of this school-location factor as a cause of southern segregation after *Brown* is difficult to estimate. In districts where blacks and whites were thoroughly dispersed, the location of schools could have made little difference to their racial composition; similarly, in districts where blacks were heavily concentrated in large ghetto areas, almost any pattern of school locations would have produced racially homogeneous schools. It is only in those districts where racial enclaves existed but were relatively small, so that a high proportion of schoolchildren lived in fairly close proximity to members of the other race, that the choice between alternative, equally efficient school locations could have made a major difference to the racial composition of schools.

Within that limited category the long-term segregative impact of school-siting decisions would be hard to determine even on a careful case-by-case basis. Such an inquiry would require a comparison between the existing configuration of school locations and attendance areas and the one that would have evolved under a racially neutral assignment system. To describe that alternative site-zone set would have been no easy matter. The existing patterns developed through countless individual siting and zoning decisions over the course of decades; for each decision there were doubtless one or more alternatives; in each instance the choice may have depended on a multiplicity of factors (present and projected population, traffic, safety, land acquisition costs, competing land uses, and others) and upon information no longer available at the time of trial. No better argument exists for the Court's unwillingness to make causation a subject for case-by-case proof in southern desegregation cases than the impossibility of reconstructing school location patterns that would have occurred in the absence of segregation laws.

In the northern situation school-location effects have probably been less significant and in any case are far more amenable to proof. Here the relevant de jure violations are the racially motivated siting decisions themselves, not, as in the South, the segregation statutes that engendered them. And whereas in the South nearly all school-location decisions must have been made with an eye to race, purposefully segregative siting decisions in the North, one suspects, have been fewer and more recent; the alternatives more easily identified and more narrowly circumscribed by preexisting, innocently generated patterns of school locations; and the evidence recent enough to be retrievable for purposes of litigation. For all these reasons, it would be far more difficult to justify a conclusive presumption of school-location effects in the North than in the South.

Case-by-case inquiry, moreover, is apt to disclose that the initial segregative effects of school-siting decisions are often almost immediately swamped by rapid demographic change. The *Denver* case is an illustration. The most notable of the de jure violations in *Keyes* was the establishment of the Barrett School, just west of Colorado Boulevard, as an all-black school. The purpose and effect of this action were to confine black children to Barrett as their families moved east toward and across Colorado Boulevard, and thus to preserve the whiteness of Stedman Elementary School, eight blocks to the east. Within three years, however, Stedman itself had become overwhelmingly black and it was clear in retrospect that no redistribution of students between the two schools, and no alternative location for Barrett, could have produced a lasting biracial mix in either school; such measures could only have hastened the transformation of Stedman from a white school to a black one.

It is fair to conclude that in northern cases such as *Keyes, Columbus,* and *Dayton II*, and even in southern cases such as *Swann*, most of the racial imbalance eliminated by system-wide desegregation decrees bears no actual causal relationship to the underlying constitutional violations. This lack of fit between wrong and remedy was obscured throughout much of the last decade by uncertainty about the constitutional status of de facto segregation. Many observers believed that the real constitutional vice was racial imbalance per se, that the Court would eventually so hold, and that the remedial decisions would in retrospect be seen as milestones on the road to that holding. When *Dayton I* finally made clear that intentional segregation alone is unconstitutional, in thus limiting the scope of the wrong it simultaneously appeared to limit the scope of the remedy by requiring affirmative proof of causation. Only with *Columbus* and *Dayton II* has the problem of misfit between wrong and remedy become acutely evident.

This problem is more than a doctrinal quibble. To the extent that the supposed causal relationship between unconstitutional state action and current school racial imbalance is mythical, the de facto-de jure distinction, and the sweeping racial-balance remedy prescribed in the de jure cases, can lead to massive disparity in the treatment of similarly situated communities. Some school districts remain free to maintain systems of single-race neighborhood schools while others, in which de jure violations are found, become subject to burdensome and intensely unpopular busing requirements on the false premise that those violations caused or contributed to the existing racial makeup of the schools. The Court introduced a further anomaly through its holding that an offending school board is not responsible for correcting racial imbalance that develops after a court-approved desegregation plan becomes operational.[43] Thus predecree and postdecree racial imbalance receive different treatment even though both stand in the same real relationship (or lack of it) to the underlying constitutional violation.

In principle, at least, the proof-of-causation requirement in *Dayton I* would have eliminated the misfit between wrong and remedy, and along with it the practical anomalies just described. It would, however, have created new difficulties and anomalies of its own. Had the Court strictly enforced the causation requirement in the manner seemingly contemplated by *Dayton I*, district court judges would have found themselves ordering busing, not on the basis of relevant educational or logistical considerations, but on the basis of inevitably speculative historical judgments about whether the racial composition of a particular school was traceable to prior constitutional violations. Busing orders thus might have been issued to some, but not all, schools within the same district. This visible and concrete disparity of treatment of children in the same district might have been worse than the more abstract disparity between de facto and de jure districts, which in any case may become less and less significant as the courts routinely classify districts de jure for the reasons earlier discussed. Moreover, any weakening or abandonment of the *Keyes* presumption would run the risk of creating a new and more sensitive kind of interdistrict disparity cutting across regional lines. Prior to *Keyes* the thoroughgoing desegregation imposed by the Court on the South stood in sharp and embarrassing contrast to the northern situation, where it was not clear that any affirmative desegregation remedies at all would be imposed. *Keyes* put that fear to rest, saddling northern de jure districts with remedial duties comparable to those previously laid on the South pursuant to *Swann*. A broad application of *Dayton I* might have led to notable relaxation of busing requirements in many northern communities, based on a found absence of causation, leaving southern communities, once again, with a legitimate basis for complaint.

Even in purely conceptual terms, the frailty of its factual underpinnings does not automatically discredit the strong presumption of continuing system-wide causation on which the racial-balancing decisions declaredly rest. To be sure, the strongest justification for any such burden-shifting presumption is the expectation that it will produce more accurate results than the alternative rule, which places the burden of proof on the plaintiffs. Such an expectation would be warranted if there were sound basis for an empirical generalization that intentionally segregative acts and omissions by school authorities, though distant in time and limited in scope, do typically have current system-wide impact, albeit difficult to prove in the individual case. We have seen that this generalization is unfounded. Still, even if it were conceded that the *Keyes* presumption yields accurate results no more often, and probably much less often, than the alternative *Dayton I* rule, shifting the burden might still be justified by a value judgment that an erroneous finding of causation is better than an erroneous finding of noncausation. Just as the strong presumption of innocence in criminal cases finds justification in society's judgment that an erroneous conviction is more to be avoided than an erroneous acquittal, so the *Keyes* presumption of causation might be defended on the ground that it is preferable to err on the side of the possible victims of wrongdoing than on the side of the wrongdoer, and in favor of the constitutional right to nonsegregated education than the competing governmental interest in neighborhood schools, which, while important, is of less than constitutional stature.

The *Keyes* presumption, so weak in its empirical basis, depends critically on this normative preference. Yet the moral and policy considerations that underlie the preference, and that ultimately account for the willingness of the courts to find causation despite its manifest improbability, are the very ones (deterrence, punishment, frustration of the wrongdoers' unlawful objective) that might be advanced to justify comprehensive racial balancing quite apart from causation. This suggests that the Court's lip service to the notion of vestiges or "continuing segregative effects" may be largely rhetorical; that its more basic insistence on an appropriate fit between wrong and remedy is properly understood as a requirement of moral proportionality rather than causal connectedness; and that this proportionality requirement is satisfied once it is determined that the underlying violations are more substantial and reprehensible than the handful of isolated instances thought to be involved in *Dayton I*. Indeed, as will be discussed below, there is language in *Columbus* and *Dayton II* that can be construed as authorizing system-wide racial balancing even in the absence of findings of current system-wide causation.

Before examining that alternative rationale, however, it may be worth pointing out some further possible variations on the vestiges theme. Even if current school and neighborhood racial concentration were conceded to be in no way a consequence of earlier constitutional violations, other theories can be advanced to justify court-ordered busing as a means of undoing the harmful effects of those violations. First, it might be argued that black children educated in purposefully segregated schools have suffered psychological and educational disadvantage for which the state is obligated to compensate them; one of the first purposes of any remedial scheme is to make the victim whole. Whatever other compensation may be due, the state owes them, at the very least, termination of the condition that produced the disadvantage. It is on this basis that the Supreme Court has upheld a desegregation decree providing compensatory education for children in the formerly segregated schools.[44] If school authorities have a duty to provide more-than-equal educational opportunities for the victims of segregated education, a fortiori they must provide at least equality.

This otherwise powerful argument has certain limitations. In the northern situation it would seem applicable only to children who attended the particular schools in which de jure segregation was practiced. And even in the southern case it applies only to students enrolled in the system during the period of purposeful segregation; children who entered after the violations ceased have no straightforward claim of injury. Thus, after a sufficient period of time has passed so that none of the children currently in the system were the victims of purposeful segregation, the duty would seem to lapse. One wonders, incidentally, whether desegregation is an altogether appropriate "compensatory" remedy. Ironically, those children who have spent the most time and therefore suffered the greatest disadvantage from purposefully segregated schools may be the least likely to benefit from desegregation; and, conversely, those most likely to benefit are the children—first- or second-graders, for example— who have suffered little or not at all.

Children who started school after purposeful segregation had ceased can argue further that they are disadvantaged as a result of the inferior segregated education received by their parents a generation earlier. But even if one grants its factual premise, this argument is unpersuasive. The parents are likely to have been educated in a school system, and in a state, other than the one in which the child is now enrolled. To demand that one state remedy the constitutional violations of another would, to say the least, be novel doctrine. If valid, however, the case for vicarious responsibility would seem applicable to de facto no less than to de jure districts, since the violations to be remedied are not in either case those of the defendant school district itself.

A more plausible theory would focus on attitudinal effects of the underlying wrongs. According to this view, purposeful school segregation—particularly the systematic, long-sustained segregation of the South—caused black schools to be perceived (by parents, teachers, children, the community at large) as inferior places in which children cannot learn. This attitude still survives and has become a self-fulfilling prophecy: Children are not expected to learn, do not expect to learn, therefore are not taught and do not learn. Only by eliminating identifiably black schools can these harmful attitudes, the legacy of past constitutional wrongs, be destroyed. The weakness of the argument is the highly conjectural nature of its accumulated factual premises. That the supposed attitudes exist, that they are attributable to past de jure school violations, that they have the feared educational effects—each of these speculations is at least as open to question as the much-criticized findings of psychological harm in *Brown*.

As has already been pointed out above, the *Columbus* decision did not hinge exclusively on the findings of "current segregative impact." Another strand of reasoning—if anything, more prominently featured —was that the Columbus board was operating a dual system at the time of *Brown*, was at all times thereafter under an affirmative constitutional duty to dismantle that system, and failed to discharge that duty. "Whatever the Board's current purpose with respect to racially separate education might be, it knowingly continued its failure to eliminate the consequences of its past intentionally segregative policies."[45] On its face this language would seem to mean that current segregative impact—the existence of a causal relationship between intentionally segregative official actions and the racial composition of the system at the time of trial— is not, after all, a prerequisite to a system-wide desegregation decree. It implies that such a decree would have been justified in *Columbus* even had the district court found that the pre-1954 violations were without current effect, and that none of the board's post-1954 acts or omissions were intended to segregate.

The retrospective judgment that the system was dual as of 1954 did presuppose a causal relationship, as of that time, between prior constitutional violations and the *then* current racial imbalance in the system. But any nexus there may once have been between pre-1954 violations and system-wide segregation in the Columbus schools was eroded if not totally eliminated long before the time of trial by two developments: First, the system had more than doubled in size in the interim, and most of the schools in the district in 1976 had been built or annexed subsequent to 1954.[46] Second, intervening demographic change—notably, the expansion of the black community—soon swamped the initial segregative impact of the pre-1954 gerrymandering even in the very schools originally affected. In effect, the Supreme Court held that once an affirmative duty of system-wide desegregation attaches, the duty becomes indefeasible, frozen; it does not dwindle or disappear (though it may expand with the district) merely because the causal relationship on which it was originally predicated no longer exists at the time of trial.

The reasoning, though not explicitly stated by the Court, may be that ever since *Brown II*, school authorities operating dual systems have been on notice that they were under a constitutional duty to rid those systems of racial imbalance; they should not be permitted to escape or limit that duty by claiming the benefit of superseding demographic events and should, on the contrary, be forced to bear the risk that the scope of their duty may expand as the system itself expands. The contrary position would enable noncomplying boards to profit from their own dilatoriness and provide incentives for foot dragging. It is precisely for this reason that, if a decree requiring system-wide desegregation had actually been issued in 1954 to a school board, such as the one in Columbus, operating a dual system, that decree, until obeyed, would have continued to encompass all schools in the district, whether constructed before or after 1954, and without regard to whether the school's racial composition was any longer attributable, or ever had been attributable, to the underlying substantive violations. To be sure, prompt compliance with such an order would have relieved the board of responsibility for resegregation resulting from post-1954 demographic changes;[47] but, failing to comply, it could hardly expect such relief. In effect, the Court's affirmative-duty theory treated the Columbus board as though it had actually received a system-wide desegregation order in 1954 and simply disregarded it for a quarter century. The decree that did eventually issue in 1976 did not impose a new remedial obligation, but merely confirmed the obligation that had existed all along.[48]

There are two major difficulties with this approach, at least in its application to the *Columbus* case. First, its underlying factual premise—that the Columbus board was operating a dual school system, a system in which segregation existed on a district-wide basis as a matter of official policy—rested on the slenderest of evidence. The fact that four elementary schools and one high school, all located in a traditionally black area, had overwhelmingly black student bodies proved no more than de facto desegregation. There was no indication in the record, and no finding by the trial court, that the school locations had been selected with race in mind. The fact that the board had assigned all-black faculties to each of these five schools was insufficient in itself, as the Supreme Court acknowledged,[49] to support an inference of racial purpose in the assignment of students. Yet, faculty segregation apart, the only other instance of racially motivated official action cited by the district court was the gerrymandering of a single attendance area, that of Pilgrim School, in 1938. Even if this were enough to justify the district court's finding that the five enclave schools had been deliberately segregated—a debatable proposition—it was scant basis for any sweeping inference of segregative impact or intent on a system-wide scale, since the enclave schools accounted for less than 5 percent of the total school population and, it would seem, substantially less than half of the black children,[50] and since the district court acknowledged that substantial racial mixing had occurred in other schools.[51]

The Supreme Court bridged this evidentiary void by a heroic application of the *Keyes* rule, that proof of segregation in a substantial part of a district is prima facie evidence that the whole system is "dual."[52] But the *Columbus* case put far greater strain on this bridge than the *Denver* case had. Whereas in *Denver* proof of de jure violations in the Park Hill section had served as the basis for an inference that proven wide-scale segregation elsewhere in the district was intentional or causally connected, in *Columbus* the fact of racial imbalance elsewhere in the system was itself unproven. One wonders whether the Court would have been prepared to find a system-wide constitutional violation in *Keyes* had the record been silent on the number, size, and racial composition of any school outside Park Hill.

Finally, even assuming that intentionally segregative action with respect to the five named schools may have had some sort of ripple effects throughout the district, it is clear that racial imbalance in the system, particularly in the enclave schools themselves, would have been severe even in the absence of those violations. Expert testimony showed that residential patterns in Columbus were extremely and uniformly segregated throughout the period between 1940 and 1970.[53] The level of segregation was every bit as high at the beginning of the period, before all but the earliest of the de jure violations cited by the district court, as at the end, after three decades of the "dual school system." In such a setting any configuration of attendance areas based, as in Columbus, on the principle that all children should be able to walk to school, was certain to produce a high level of racial imbalance.

Granting, however, that a system-wide desegregation order would have been justified in 1954, we come to the second difficulty with the affirmative-duty theory—the unfairness of treating the Columbus board as though such an order had in fact been issued. As we have seen, it was not until *Green* in 1968 that the Court first indicated that school boards have an affirmative duty to eliminate the continuing effects of past segregative action, and not until *Keyes* in 1973 that it disclosed that acts of gerrymandering in part of a district could trigger a duty to desegregate the whole. One could argue, therefore, that any remedial duty of a punitive or disciplinary nature, going beyond what is necessary to undo the current consequences of past violations, should date, not from 1954, but only from 1973. So limited, the duty might well have been satisfied in the *Columbus* case, since the record showed that the board had taken various desegregative actions in recent years.[54]

Even if the law had been clear, the facts assuredly were not: in the absence of an authoritative determination, the board arguably could not be charged with knowledge that its pre-1954 violations were of system-wide impact; that question, ultimately resolved by the district court in 1976 on the basis of a presumption rule established only in 1973 and in the absence of rebuttal evidence that might have been available at an earlier date, was at the very least a matter of considerable uncertainty prior to trial. This uncertainty admittedly did not relieve the board of its responsibility to eliminate 1976 racial imbalance traceable to its prior substantive violations, but it did weigh against the imposition of any wider duty based on what the board "should have known" or "should have done" earlier. Admittedly, a case can be made the other way: that the board should have realized as early as *Brown I* that is was acting unconstitutionally and was required to adopt at least minimal corrective measures (such as modifications of the gerrymandered boundaries), and that failure to take even those steps deprived it of any legitimate defense based on lack of notice.

The Question of Balancing

Even if the causal connection between past de jure practices and current racial imbalance were far more apparent than it is, the post-*Brown* desegregation decisions would still be open to serious criticism. Traditionally, equity courts grant injunctions only after balancing the competing interests to determine whether such relief is cost justified. Yet neither the Supreme Court nor any lower court has seriously attempted to weigh the benefits and costs of school desegregation. In the original 1954 cases the Court found that state-imposed segregation damaged the hearts and minds of black children[55] without serving any legitimate governmental purpose;[56] no balancing was necessary because one of the scales was empty. There are no empty scales in the busing issue. Busing for racial balance ordinarily means the end of neighborhood schools, a not insignificant social cost; the question is whether the benefits of desegregation outweigh those costs.

These benefits, however, are highly uncertain. The Court's original suggestion in *Brown*, that an all-black school environment generates feelings of inferiority in black children, seems not to have been borne out by subsequent research (Epps, 1975)[57], and the more recent hypothesis that black children will do better academically when exposed to a white peer group and their teachers is a matter of controversy. Few investigators seem prepared to say that the academic benefits to black children are very great and there is evidence that such benefits may be realized only in majority-white situations often impossible to achieve in any sizable number of schools. All in all, the benefits and costs of court-decreed desegregation remain a question upon which reasonable and fair-minded people of both races—educators, behavioral scientists, school officials, and ordinary citizens—can and do disagree.

It may be objected at this point that important constitutional rights do not yield to any ordinary state interest, any straightforward utilitarian judgment. Purposeful racial discrimination, the argument goes, can be justified, if at all, only by a state interest that is truly "compelling"; by the same token, nothing less than an extraordinary public interest—a very large preponderance of remedial costs over remedial benefits—should suffice to justify the failure to provide a fully restorative remedy for such discrimination. The best answer to that objection is that a person's right to be free from state-imposed discrimination based on race is entitled to far greater constitutional protection than his interest in not being disadvantaged as a remote consequence of prior state-imposed discrimination against other members of his race—or, put differently, his interest in attending a school from which all vestiges of prior racial discrimination have been eradicated. Under this view a decree ordering the state to stop discriminating would be warranted at almost any cost; but a decree requiring the restoration of the status quo ante, the erasure of all traces of past discrimination, is appropriate only if the expected benefits exceed the expected costs or, at the very least, only if the benefits are clear and substantial.

A further question is the degree of deference to be given the balance already struck by school authorities. If one assumes that maximum feasible desegregation is required in the absence of an extraordinary state interest, the Court should perhaps make an independent decision because school authorities presumably have not addressed that question. If one assumes instead that the desegregation remedy is demanded only if its expected benefits to black children exceed its expected cost to the entire community, a strong case can be made that the reviewing court should defer to the reasonable judgment of those whom the community has chosen to make such social value judgments. This proposition is supported by familiar considerations of democratic theory that need no rehearsal here.

Fiss (1975) has written with customary insight on this set of issues but has reached, in my view, a questionable conclusion. He acknowledges that "the more uncertain the underlying proposition, the less appropriate it is to impose obligations through the least representative branch" and that "decisions of those institutions more directly responsive to the citizenry—such as the legislature or the school board—seem more self-imposed, less intrusive, less coercive, and thus are more compatible with a high degree of uncertainty" (p. 194). Fiss maintains, however, that this argument loses force where "the benefits of the obligation are to be primarily conferred on a racial minority and the costs imposed on all," since the resultant decision runs a high risk of being merely "a manifestation of majority self-interest." Recognizing that this argument may call into question the superiority of the democratic process in general, he limits it to cases in which the interests of the black minority are at stake—a minority whose "special historical position" in this country "gave it a discrete set of interests and diminished its power in a way that cannot be corrected simply by the extension of the franchise" (pp. 210-211).

The notion that the federal judiciary is the preferred decision maker whenever the interests of the black minority and white majority come into conflict has mind-boggling implications for democratic theory and practice. Even if it were valid in other contexts, this view would have little application in the school desegregation area, for here the preferences and self-perceived interests of the two racial communities are not in sharp conflict. Busing is not an issue that divides the community neatly along racial lines; overwhelmingly unpopular among whites, court-decreed racial balancing is also strongly opposed by many blacks, especially among those most immediately affected. If the issue were put to a plebiscite in which blacks and whites were represented equally (rather than in proportion to their numbers), I dare say it would be soundly defeated. Thus, the case for a judicial guardianship must rest on the premise not only that whites do not know or care what is good for blacks, but that black parents do not know what is good for their own children. Such an aspersion would be insulting and patronizing in any context but is doubly out of place in an area where no one can be sure of the answers and where the variability of children's responses to desegregation would seem to make the parent's individualizing judgment particularly valuable.

The Multidistrict Problem

The exodus of white families from the public-school systems of the larger cities has made meaningful desegregation increasingly difficult. The school population of many cities is now heavily black, so that even if the remaining whites were spread evenly throughout the system, thereby achieving racial balance in the narrow sense, the hoped-for benefits of integration would still not be realized. A crucial question, therefore, is the power and duty of a federal judge to issue a desegregation decree transcending the boundaries of the city system itself in order to bring urban blacks and suburban whites together in school. Such multidistrict remedies could come in various shapes and sizes, from a plan that treats an entire metropolitan area as a single unit for purposes of racial balance to modest arrangements for busing black volunteers to suburban schools.

The issue came to the Supreme Court in 1974, in *Milliken* v. *Bradley* (*Milliken II*).[58] The district court, having found a variety of de jure violations within the heavily black Detroit school system, concluded that a city-only decree would produce no effective desegregation. It therefore designated Detroit and fifty-three surrounding suburban systems, all predominantly white, as a "desegregation area" and ordered the preparation of a plan aimed at making all schools racially representative of that entire area. The court of appeals affirmed the decision, but the Supreme

Court reversed it, holding in essence that de jure violations committed within a single school district, and affecting only schools in that district, did not justify a decree embracing neighboring districts as well. The Court stressed the importance of local control over public education ("No single tradition in public education is more deeply rooted than local control over the operation of schools; local autonomy has long been thought essential both to the maintenance of community concern and support for public schools and to quality of the educational process"[59]), but that was not the basis for its decision.

The Court did not dispute that a state (Michigan) is responsible for constitutional violations committed by the local (Detroit) school authorities to whom it delegates certain aspects of its educational function, and it acknowledged that, local autonomy notwithstanding, an interdistrict remedy might be warranted when necessary to undo the effects of constitutional violations. The real basis for the holding was the absence of any such effects. "Before the boundaries of separate and autonomous school districts may be set aside by consolidating the separate units for remedial purposes or by imposing a cross-district remedy, it must first be shown that there has been a constitutional violation within one district that produces a significant segregative effect in another district. Specifically, it must be shown that racially discriminatory acts of the state or local school districts, or of a single school district, have been a substantial cause of interdistrict segregation."[60] The decision thus applied to the multidistrict situation the principle repeatedly declared, though not faithfully applied, in single-district cases: The purpose of the desegregation remedy is to eliminate the consequences of purposeful segregation, that and no more.

There was this difference: In the single-district case, the burden of proof on the question of causal relationship lay with the school authorities; in the multidistrict case, it lay with the petitioners. Justification for that burden shifting could be found, as we have seen, in the state's local-autonomy interest—an interest insufficient to relieve the state of its duty to eliminate the proven consequences of unconstitutional acts, but weighty enough (as neighborhood school values alone were not) to condition that duty upon affirmative proof of those consequences.

Just as *Dayton I* has not proved a significant obstacle to systematic desegregation in the single-district case, there are signs that *Milliken I* may not be an impossible roadblock to metropolitan desegregation. The lower federal courts have continued to order interdistrict remedies and in at least three important cases—involving Louisville, Wilmington, and

Indianapolis—have done so even without finding a causal nexus between acts of purposeful segregation by school officials and interdistrict racial imbalance. A full discussion is necessary in order to convey the current status of the interdistrict remedy.

In *Newburg Area Council* v. *Board of Education of Jefferson County, Kentucky,*[61] the Sixth Circuit, on remand from the Supreme Court after *Milliken I,*[62] reaffirmed an earlier decision ordering that the school districts of Louisville and neighboring Jefferson County be desegregated without regard to their district boundaries. The court of appeals drew a number of distinctions between the Detroit and Louisville situations. In the former, the outlying districts were innocent of de jure violations, whereas in the latter, both districts had maintained dual systems. Two districts in a single county could be combined more easily than fifty-four districts in three counties. Louisville's school district boundaries were more artificial: They were not coterminous with the boundaries of the city itself; they had repeatedly been disregarded by the authorities, who had bused students across them in both directions; and under Kentucky law counties, not school districts, were the basic educational units. These considerations amply supported a conclusion that interdistrict desegregation would be less costly, less disruptive, less difficult to administer, less burdensome for the district courts, less damaging to local-autonomy interests in Louisville than in Detroit.

While the balance of equities was thus more favorable to a metropolitan solution, the essential prerequisites for an interdistrict remedy under *Milliken* were nevertheless missing. The Court made no finding either that the boundaries of the city and county systems were racially inspired or that the underlying constitutional violations had produced interdistrict segregative effects that could not be cured simply by discontinuing those violations (for example, refraining from further busing of white students from Louisville to county schools or of black students the other way). In the absence of such findings, interdistrict racial balancing in Louisville would seem to go beyond its appointed function of cleaning up the consequences of prior constitutional wrongs.

In *Evans* v. *Buchanan*[63] a three-judge district court, after finding de jure violations within the predominantly black Wilmington school system, concluded that the appropriate remedy would embrace both that system and the adjoining predominantly white suburban systems of Newcastle County. One of two independent grounds for this action was the fact that Wilmington had been uniquely exempted from a statute authorizing the consolidation of school districts by state-level administrative action rather than through the cumbersome popular referendum process previously required. The effect, said the court, was to perpetuate the existing racial imbalance between Wilmington and its suburbs. The court acknowledged that the exception for Wilmington was not racially motivated[64] but held that "effective, as well as intentional racial classifications . . . require special scrutiny under the Equal Protection Clause."[65] This assertion, not altogether unsupported by previous precedent, seems squarely at odds with the principle, later explicitly announced in *Davis*[66] and *Dayton I*, that only purposeful racial classifications are constitutionally suspect.

The second basis for the interdistrict remedy was that governmental officials, both state and federal, had condoned and encouraged racially discriminatory practices in the public and private housing markets and thus prevented black families from gaining entrance to suburbs and their schools. This rationale for busing, adopted by several lower courts in single-district cases,[67] has not yet been approved by the Supreme Court.[68]

The district court's decision was affirmed by the Supreme Court without opinion.[69] This action is difficult to interpret. Unlike a denial of certiorari, a summary affirmance is technically a decision on the merits; moreover, had the Court merely wished to sidestep the issues, there were highly plausible jurisdictional grounds on which it could—and according to three justices[70] should—have vacated the decision below without reaching the merits even in that technical sense. But while the *Buchanan* affirmance must therefore be deemed an authoritative approval of the district court's judgment, the precise grounds of approval and the legal proposition for which the case stands remain obscure.

Reasoning remarkably similar to that in *Evans* provided one of the two bases for an interdistrict remedy in a desegregation case involving the Indianapolis metropolitan area.[71] There the district court found, in addition to de jure violations within the Indianapolis school system, that the school authorities in Marion County had for years rejected proposals to combine the schools with those of Indianapolis into a single consolidated county school system; and it found that the state legislature, in merging the municipal governments of Marion County, including that of Indianapolis, into a county-wide government (Uni-Gov), had expressly exempted the public schools. The court made no finding that the de jure violations in Indianapolis had contributed to the racial imbalance between the city and suburban systems or that the refusal to create a county-wide school district was racially motivated. Yet the district court decree ordered an interdistrict remedy calling for the busing of Indianapolis blacks to white suburban schools, and its order was upheld by the Seventh Circuit. This time, however, the Supreme Court vacated the judgment and remanded the case to the court of appeals for reconsideration in the light of *Davis.*[72]

Without special circumstances such as the state statutes in the Wilmington and Indianapolis cases, proving that de jure violations within a city system have contributed to racial imbalance between city and suburban systems will ordinarily be a difficult, if not impossible, task. More often than not, one suspects, the effect of such violations—indeed their very purpose—is to do just the opposite, to discourage the leakage of white families to suburban, private, or parochial schools by assuring the continued availability of white public schools in the city. This need not always be the case. There may be instances in which placement practices designed to preserve the predominant whiteness of certain schools—by channeling in white families, or channeling out black families—have the unintended effect of reducing the ratio of whites in the transferor schools below a critical tipping point, thereby causing the remaining whites in those schools, who might otherwise have stayed put, to take flight to the suburbs.

Interdistrict segregation will be easier to show in cases, like Louisville and unlike Detroit, where the suburban districts themselves have operated dual systems. When a suburban district attempts to maintain racially separate schools, the effect may well be to attract urban whites seeking homogeneous white schools, to retain suburban whites who might otherwise have opted for private schools, and to repel urban blacks who want integrated schools; all three effects would accentuate the existing racial polarity between the city and suburban public-school populations. It should be stressed, however, that the existence of de jure violations in both city and suburban systems does not automatically warrant interdistrict relief. Unless those violations have had the effect of heightening the racial differential between or among the districts, the appropriate remedy under *Milliken I* would seem to be separate decrees for each district providing, at most, for racial balance within that district. The interdistrict disparity would remain, but not as the product of any unconstitutional state action.

Indeed, even in cases where suburban violations were found to have contributed in modest degree to white flight, it is doubtful that *Milliken I* would sanction a decree calling for all-out racial balancing between the districts. Few would deny that the racial polarity between cities and their suburbs is primarily a consequence of economic disparities and housing discrimination, and that the contribution of school-assignment policies has been marginal at most. Both the reasoning and the express language of the Court's opinion indicate that it is only the increment of segregation attributable to constitutional violations that district judges have the duty or power to eliminate. Such fine tuning is, of course, impossible in practice. But the limits the Court has sought to impose upon interdistrict desegregation would be thoroughly undermined if a finding (typically based on an unrebutted presumption) of de jure violations in suburban districts, together with a finding (almost inevitably based on speculative inference) that these violations have added marginally to white flight, were enough to justify a Detroit-like decree mandating racial balance on a metropolitan scale and the merger of all offending school districts.

Nevertheless, the Court's sweeping stricture against any and all interdistrict remedies lacking interdistrict effects may go further than the underlying logic of *Milliken I*. Let it be granted that the absence of interdistrict effects rules out Homeric remedies that treat an entire metropolitan area as though it were a single district in order to create a uniform ratio of whites to blacks in all schools throughout the area. One can still argue that, even without interdistrict effects, the state should be required, if necessary, to use interdistrict means to eliminate vestiges of purposeful discrimination within the offending district (usually the city system) itself. Where racial concentration within a city school system is pervasively the product of de jure violations but cannot be relieved by a reshuffling of students within the system itself, the state must bring in a sufficient number of suburban whites to achieve, in as many city schools as possible, the black-white ratio that would have prevailed in the absence of the violations.

This duty might arise, for example, in situations where certain black city schools lie beyond reasonable busing distance from white neighborhoods in the city but within range of white neighborhoods in the adjoining suburbs, so that a racial mix representative of the city system can be created in those schools only by busing in suburban whites, perhaps in exchange for blacks bused to suburban schools. It might also arise in situations where whites in the city system, though uniformly distributed among the several schools, are too few in number to provide a meaningful interracial environment—though this, of course, is much more doubtful and would depend on whether desegregation requires not only a "representative" but also a "beneficial" racial composition.

This argument does not assume that the racial disparity between city and suburban school systems is a consequence of official discrimination, nor does it demand that the interdistrict disparity, as such, be eliminated. The objective would not be to reform the racial composition of the suburban schools but merely to use available suburban whites as resources to improve the racial mix of the black city schools. The rationale is simply that the state must use all feasible means to desegregate the city system, and the busing in of suburban whites is one such means.

Notes

1. Dayton Bd. of Educ. v. Brinkman (Dayton I), 433 U.S. 406 (1977).

2. The decision was strongly foreshadowed a year earlier in Washington v. Davis, 426 U.S. 229 (1976), an employment discrimination case, in which the Court held that official action having a disproportionate impact upon members of a minority group does not violate the equal protection clause in the absence of any discriminatory intent.

3. " 'Segregation of white and colored children in public schools has a detrimental effect upon the colored children. The impact is greater when it has the sanction of the law; for the policy of separating the races is usually interpreted as denoting the inferiority of the negro group.' " Brown v. Board of Educ., 347 U.S. 483, 494 (1954) (quoting "a finding in the Kansas case").

4. Deal v. Cincinnati Bd. of Educ., 369 F.2d 55 (6th Cir. 1966); Downs v. Board of Educ., 336 F.2d 988 (10th Cir. 1964); Bell v. School City, 324 F.2d 209 (7th Cir. 1963).

5. Spencer v. Kugler, 404 U.S. 1027 (1972).

6. Keyes v. School Dist. No. 1, Denver, 413 U.S. 189, 212 (1973).

7. Id. at 208.

8. United States v. School Dist. of Omaha, 521 F.2d 530, 535-536 (8th Cir. 1975); Hart v. Community School Bd. of Educ., New York School Dist., 512 F.2d 37, 50-51 (2d Cir. 1975); Oliver v. Michigan State Bd. of Educ., 508 F.2d 178, 182 (6th Cir. 1974).

9. Dayton Bd. of Educ. v. Brinkman (Dayton II), 443 U.S. 526, 536 n.9 (1979).

10. 413 U.S. at 208.

11. Id. at 210-211.

12. Id. at 210.

13. Mt. Healthy City School Dist. Bd. of Educ. v. Doyle, 429 U.S. 274 (1977); Arlington Heights v. Metropolitan Housing Development Corp., 429 U.S. 252, 270-271 (1977).

14. Green v. County School Bd., 391 U.S. 430 (1968).

15. Swann v. Charlotte-Mecklenburg Bd. of Educ., 402 U.S. 1 (1971).

16. 413 U.S. 189 (1973).

17. 391 U.S. at 438 n.4.

18. 402 U.S. at 15.

19. Id. at 28.

20. Id. at 20-21.

21. Id. at 21.
22. Id. at 25-26.
23. 413 U.S. at 202.
24. Id. at 203.
25. Id. at 205.
26. Id. at 203.
27. Any such equation would be unwarranted. Proof that part of a district (such as Denver's Park Hill section) is geographically isolated from the rest seems neither necessary nor sufficient to negate the possibility that de jure violations in that area have an effect on the racial composition of neighborhoods and schools elsewhere in the district. The hypothesis that the racial earmarking of schools in Park Hill may have attracted whites to that area from other parts of the city would have been no less (and no more) plausible had Colorado Boulevard been a river spanned by a single bridge or a ridge of hills crossed by an occasional canyon road.
28. Milliken v. Bradley (Milliken I), 418 U.S. 717 (1974).
29. 433 U.S. 406 (1977).
30. Id. at 420.
31. Columbus Bd. of Educ. v. Penick, 443 U.S. 449 (1979).
32. 443 U.S. 526 (1979).
33. 443 U.S. at 463-464.
34. Penick v. Columbus Bd. of Educ., 429 F. Supp. 229, 235-236 (S.D. Ohio 1977).
35. Plaintiff's Exhibit No. 383, 21 February 1979 at 777, 443 U.S. 449 (1979).
36. 429 F. Supp. at 260.
37. The Court noted the board's argument that "because many of the involved schools were in areas that had become predominantly black residential areas by the time of trial the racial separation in the schools would have occurred even without the unlawful conduct of petitioners." It concluded, however, that "petitioners' evidence in this respect was insufficient to counter respondents' proof" and that "the phenomenon described by petitioners seems only to confirm, not disprove, the evidence accepted by the District Court that school segregation is a contributing cause of housing segregation." 443 U.S. at 465 n.13.

This last point is puzzling. The "reciprocal-effects" theory—that school segregation contributes to housing segregation, as well as vice versa—maintains that when certain schools are earmarked for blacks or whites, private residential decisions cause the attendance areas served by those schools to take on the same racial character as the schools themselves, with black families being drawn to identifiably black schools and white families to "haven" schools identifiably white. The demographic phenomenon described by the Columbus board was exactly the opposite—not, primarily at least, the movement of more blacks into the already overwhelmingly black attendance areas served by the enclave schools, but the expansion of the black population into the surrounding residential and school attendance areas formerly occupied by whites and served by schools (such as Fair Avenue Elementary) earmarked for whites. This phenomenon, contrary to the Court's assertion, tends to disprove, rather than confirm, the reciprocal-effects hypothesis.

38. A concrete illustration may help to clarify. In a school district half white and half black, elementary schools A and B, serving contiguous attendance areas, are respectively 75 percent black and 75 percent white. All the whites who attend A live in neighborhood x, while all the blacks who attend B live in neighborhood y. Bent on segregation, the school board modifies attendance-area boundaries so as to transfer neighborhood x to B and neighborhood y to A, thereby making both schools uniracial. If no demographic changes occur by the time of trial, the offending boundary change will be responsible for part of the current racial imbalance of the two schools, but that contribution can be eliminated simply by reinstating the original boundaries. A and B will still be racially imbalanced, as they were from the beginning, but none of that imbalance will result from the unconstitutional gerrymander, and there will be no occasion for racial balancing by the court either through adjustments in the A-B boundary or the busing in of students from elsewhere in the district.

Now let us assume that, by the time of trial, x has changed from an all-white to an all-black neighborhood. No longer can it be said that its inclusion within zone B rather than zone A, pursuant to the original gerrymander, currently makes for segregation; on the contrary, it is a factor that mitigates segregation, at least if the rest of zone B remains all or mostly white. If the rest of zone B has become, like zone A, homogeneously black, the rule assigning neighborhood x to B rather than A will have no current effect one way or the other on the racial composition of either school: Both would be all-black with or without the gerrymander, indeed no matter how the boundary was drawn.

The matter is a bit more complicated if x remains all-white while the rest of B becomes, like A, all-black; the assignment of x to B would then have two equal and opposite effects—segregative with respect to A, desegregative with respect to B. One can argue that the two influences cancel one another out or, contrariwise, that the continuing unfavorable effect on A cannot be netted against or redeemed by the favorable effect on B. Even on the latter view, the segregative effect can be eliminated merely by revoking the boundary change and restoring the original boundaries: no further court-ordered racial balancing would be called for.

39. It might be objected that if a condition of racial imbalance in certain schools were found, at the time of trial, to be a consequence of unconstitutional gerrymandering, a court order commanding the elimination of all such consequences would necessarily require that the condition itself be eliminated, not merely supplied with a new and sanitary pedigree. This view would create an anomaly: that the existence of a racial-balancing duty would depend on whether the restorative boundary change occurred before or after trial, though in either case the postrestoration racial compositions of the affected schools, and their relationship to the underlying substantive violations, were exactly the same. Furthermore, the argument that "the condition itself," not merely its tainted pedigree, must be eliminated, runs counter to the propositions that racial imbalance per se is not unconstitutional and that the purpose of the desegregation remedy is achieved if there is no racial imbalance in the system that is attributable to unconstitutional state action. Without "residential" or "school-location" effects, racial balancing would be justified only on the assumption that the desegregation remedy has some prophylactic, deterrent, or punitive purpose above and beyond the restoration of the status quo ante, in which case the whole question of causa-

tion would become largely irrelevant.

40. E. Wolf, Northern school desegregation and residential choice, in 1977 *Supreme Court Review* (Kurland, ed.) at 63, 68.

41. Swann v. Charlotte-Mecklenburg Bd. of Educ., 402 U.S. at 20-21.

42. Imagine, for example, a square-shaped district with eight-mile boundaries. The northern half of the district is all-black, the southern half all-white. Given a segregation statute, it is efficient to locate the "black" and "white" high schools at the geographic centers of the two racial enclaves—that is, halfway between the eastern and western boundaries of the district and two miles from the northern and southern boundaries respectively. In that way no child would have to travel more than four miles in an easterly or westerly direction or more than two miles in a northerly or southerly direction. When the statutory regime is replaced by a colorblind zoning policy, it is more efficient, given the location of the schools, to define the two attendance areas by means of a line bisecting the district from east to west and creating two racially homogeneous school zones than by means of a line bisecting the district from north to south and creating two biracial zones. For under the former, the maximum north-south home-to-school distance would continue to be two miles, whereas under the latter it would be six miles. Had the two schools been differently located in the first instance—at the centers of the western and eastern halves of the district, for example, or at the centers of the southwestern and northeastern quadrants—the north-south bisector would have produced attendance areas at once efficient and biracial.

43. *See* Pasadena City Bd. of Educ. v. Spangler, 427 U.S. 424 (1976); Swann v. Charlotte-Mecklenburg Bd. of Educ., 402 U.S. at 32.

44. Milliken v. Bradley (Milliken II), 433 U.S. 267 (1977).

45. 443 U.S. at 461.

46. 429 F. Supp. at 237; Appendix, Plaintiff's Exhibit No. 383, 21 February 1979 at 775-787, 443 U.S. 449 (1979).

47. Pasadena City Bd. of Educ. v. Spangler, 427 U.S. 424 (1976); Swann v. Charlotte-Mecklenburg Bd. of Educ., 404 U.S. at 32.

48. This version of the affirmative-duty theory is admittedly hard to square with the Court's statement in *Columbus* that a finding "that the Board's purposefully discriminatory conduct and policies had current systemwide impact" continues to be "an essential predicate" for a system-wide remedy. 443 U.S. at 466 n.14. The distance between the current-impact and affirmative-duty theories can be narrowed somewhat by an alternative formulation of the latter. This second formulation would preserve the requirement of a causal relationship between unconstitutional state action and current racial imbalance, but would broaden the notion of "unconstitutional state action" to include a host of post-1954 nonracially motivated acts and omissions (including perhaps the failure to bus) that effectively perpetuated the condition of racial imbalance. In this view the ongoing remedial default, though not intended to segregate, would count as a fresh and continuing constitutional violation, and its current system-wide impact would be plain.

This version of the affirmative-duty theory, like the one outlined in the text, depends on the premises (a) that the pre-1954 substantive violations or their radiating effects were of system-wide scope, giving rise to a system-wide remedial duty (if they were narrower—confined, for example, to a single school or pocket of schools—the remedial duty would be correspondingly narrow, and the breach of that duty would not have system-wide segregative impact at the time of trial), and (b) that the Columbus board was or should have been aware of the full scope of its remedial duty from 1954 on (otherwise the continuing breach of that remedial duty could not fairly be treated as a new and independent constitutional violation).

It may not be immediately evident why this version of the affirmative-duty theory should yield any different results than the straightforward approach requiring a causal nexus between purposefully segregative acts and current racial imbalance. Why should the breach of a remedial duty make any greater contribution to current racial imbalance in a system than the underlying substantive violation that gave rise to that duty? If, for example, a school board gerrymandered certain boundaries prior to 1954 as the Columbus board did, and then preserved those boundaries after 1954 without racial motive, whatever segregative effects might flow from this remedial default—whether those effects be broad or narrow, and whether or not they include residential changes—would also be attributable to the original gerrymandering. For that reason it would be utterly absurd, even without the remedial default theory, for a court to absolve school authorities from responsibility for current racial imbalance on the ground that it was a consequence of the colorblind retention rather than the color-conscious establishment of the existing pupil-assignment arrangements; and conversely, a finding that the latter had no current segregative impact would apply to the former as well.

There may be cases, however, in which the continuing remedial default does add an increment of its own to current racial imbalance. The school gerrymander may have bred residential segregation, and that, in turn, further school segregation remediable only by an extensive busing program that, had it been adopted, would have had a stabilizing influence on neighborhoods and schools above and beyond those affected by the original gerrymander.

The same sequence can be imagined, even without postulating demographic changes, where the underlying violation involves irreversible action such as a school-siting decision: The choice of one location over another may produce a black school rather than a mixed school; the school being immovable, extensive busing may be the only adequate remedy; failure to do so may, as in the earlier example, have a lasting segregative effect even though the substantive violation no longer does. The later expansion of the black community into the area served by the rejected alternative site may erase the segregative effects of the siting decision, but the remedial default, the failure to bus, again may have a continuing segregative effect of its own. In this fashion the affirmative remedial duty may, over time, expand by accretion, as the accumulating effects of the breach of that duty are added to the effects of the substantive violation itself.

49. Dayton Bd. of Educ. v. Brinkman (Dayton II), 443 U.S. at 536 n.9.

50. These estimates are based on extrapolations from incomplete data in the record. The total public-school population of Columbus in 1954 must have been about 60,000, since the record indicated that it was 46,352 in 1950 and increased by an average of 3,700 per year in the following decade. 429 F. Supp. at 237. The

82 *Frank Goodman*

black student population in 1954 must have been at least 15 percent of this total, or 9,000, since the percentage of blacks among all Columbus residents increased from 11.7 percent to 18.5 percent from 1940 to 1970, id., yet was at all times much smaller than the percentage of black children in the school system. And the total enrollment of the five enclave schools, judging by the average enrollment in 1975 of the three schools then still operating, must have been well short of 2,000. Appendix, Plaintiff's Exhibit, 21 February 1979 at 745, 443 U.S. 449 (1979).

51. 429 F. Supp. at 236.
52. 443 U.S. at 458, 467-468.
53. 429 F. Supp. at 258.
54. Id. at 239-240, 259.
55. Brown v. Board of Educ., 347 U.S. at 494 (1954).
56. Bolling v. Sharpe, 347 U.S. 497, 500 (1954).
57. After reviewing the research, Epps concluded that "there is little evidence that desegregation seriously impairs black self-esteem; nor can it be said that desegregation, in itself, enhances self-esteem." Epps, Impact of school desegregation on aspirations, self-concepts and other aspects of personality, *Law and Contemporary Problems* 39 (1975): 312.
58. 418 U.S. 717 (1974).
59. Id. at 741-742.
60. Id. at 744-745.
61. Newburg Area Council v. Board of Educ., 510 F.2d 1358 (6th Cir. 1974).
62. Board of Educ. v. Newburg Area Council, 418 U.S. 918 (1974).
63. Evans v. Buchanan, 393 F. Supp. 428 (D. Del. 1975).
64. Id. at 439.
65. Id. at 439.
66. Washington v. Davis, 426 U.S. 229 (1976).
67. *See* Brewer v. School Bd., 397 F.2d 37, 41-42 (4th Cir. 1968).
68. *See* Milliken v. Bradley (Milliken I), 418 U.S. 717, 728 n.7 (1974).
69. Buchanan v. Evans, 423 U.S. 963 (1975).
70. Id. at 967-968 (Rehnquist, J., dissenting).
71. United States v. Board of School Commissioners, 541 F.2d 1211 (7th Cir. 1976), *vacated and remanded*, 429 U.S. 1068 (1977).
72. 429 U.S. 1068 (1977). The court of appeals in turn remanded the case to the district court for findings on whether the action of the state legislature in separating the boundaries of the Indianapolis school system from the newly expanded boundaries of the city itself, now merged with the county, was racially motivated. 573 F.2d 400 (7th Cir. 1978). On remand, the district court held, among other things, that the state legislature had, after all, acted with racial motivation. 456 F. Supp. 183 (S.D. Ind. 1978).

References

Epps, Edgar S. 1975. Impact of school desegregation on aspirations, self-concepts and other aspects of personality. *Law and Contemporary Problems* 39:300-313.

Fiss, Owen M. 1975. The jurisprudence of busing. *Law and Contemporary Problems* 39:194-216.

Graglia, Lino. 1976. *Disaster by Decree*. Ithaca, New York: Cornell University Press.

Hart, H. L. A., and A. M. Honore. 1959. *Causation in the Law*. Oxford: Oxford University Press.

Taeuber, Karl E., and Alma F. Taeuber. 1969. *Negroes in Cities*. New York: Atheneum.

Wolf, Eleanor. 1977. Northern school desegregation and residential choice. In 1977 *Supreme Court Review*, ed. Philip B. Kurland, vol. 6, pp. 63-85. Chicago: University of Chicago Press.

4   The Effects of School Desegregation on Children: A New Look at the Research Evidence

NANCY H. ST. JOHN

Chief Justice Earl Warren voiced the expectations for desegregation in his famous opinion in *Brown I*. Separation in schools solely because of race, he stated, denies minority children equal educational opportunity and thus equal protection of the law. This is so "even though the physical facilities and other tangible factors may be equal." The Chief Justice then noted the opinion of social scientists about the psychological damage to black children: segregation "generates a feeling of inferiority as to their status in the community that may affect their hearts and minds in a way unlikely ever to be undone." Thus the 1954 judicial mandate for desegregation stressed: (a) equality of educational opportunity; (b) nontangible characteristics of schools, including racial isolation, and their psychological effects; and (c) protection of minority children, rather than benefits to all children.

Although the Court suggested broad expectations for benefits from desegregation, liberals who welcomed the Court's decision have broadened them still further to include the following propositions: (a) by eliminating the dual school system of the South, desegregation would undermine the caste social structure there and assure equal occupational opportunity for black adults; (b) a unified school system would ensure schools that were indeed equal in facilities, personnel, and curriculum; (c) desegregation would not only improve the self-esteem of black children, but would encourage their educational motivation and vocational aspirations; (d) white children as well as black children would benefit, because contact with blacks would make them less racially prejudiced.

This chapter does not treat the first of these expectations—that desegregation would result in gains in the political and economic development of the black community and in the racial attitudes of white adults, and thereby would arrest the movement identified by the National Advisory Commission on Civil Disorders (1968) toward two separate Americas.

Nor does it analyze the second, that desegregation would result in schools that are equal in facilities, personnel, and curriculum. However, there is considerable evidence that even before 1954 the imminence of the *Brown* decision provoked a push to make separate schools equal, and that equalization proceeded apace during the next decade as implementation of *Brown* was fought through the courts. Certainly *Equality of Educational Opportunity* (Coleman et al., 1966) found that differences between schools attended by black and white students were on the whole rather minor and that variations in test scores were not related to these differences. Nevertheless, there are undoubtedly still enormous discrepancies in hard-to-measure characteristics of the schools attended by poor blacks and those attended by middle-class whites, and thus there is support for the conviction of many blacks that a majority-white school is inevitably better equipped and better staffed than a majority-black school.

The task of this chapter is perhaps simpler—to assess the outcomes of school desegregation in regard to the academic achievement, psychological health, and racial attitudes of children, black and white. In 1974 I reviewed twenty years of published and unpublished research on this topic, over a hundred separate studies. The book that resulted (*School Desegregation: Outcomes for Children*) is a major source for this chapter, as are a number of reports of research findings and several reviews that have appeared since January 1975. Research findings published after September 1977 are not covered here.

All reviewers stress two problems that beset the literature. First, there is an absence of well-developed and commonly accepted theory to guide the questions researchers ask or the way they interpret their findings. Most researchers make a polite bow to some strand of social theory in the introduction to their final report, but rarely do they ground their concepts, methodologies, or variables in a common body of theory. This hinders the comparability of findings and the cumulation of knowledge. Second, much of the research on school desegregation has so many methodological limitations that the validity of the findings is in serious doubt. For instance, more studies are cross-sectional than longitudinal—that is, they compare children who are in segregated and desegregated schools at one point in time rather than matching children by background factors, randomly assigning them to segregated and desegregated schools, and then comparing the results. We cannot be sure, therefore, that the desegregated children were not originally more academically oriented, or more self-confident, or less racially biased than the segregated children before the two groups were exposed to different types of schools. Many studies also lack a proper control group: for instance, if a whole district desegregates, there are no segregated children with whom to compare the desegregated. Comparisons with past records may prove little, since changed conditions outside the school rather than the percentage of whites in the school may be affecting the children.

Control of contaminating factors is not the only problem of desegregation research. Size and randomness of sample, definition of desegregation and length of exposure to it, measurement of key outcome variables, tests of statistical significance—these and other aspects of the research may be flawed. Such problems are so common (often because of characteristics of the field situation rather than blindness of the investigator) that a purist might conclude that there is no research worth reviewing. In any case, each reviewer must decide where to draw the line between studies that are satisfactorily executed and those that are not, and must decide which findings to treat as real and which as nonfindings.

In the face of such methodological problems, the prejudices of either the researcher or the reviewer can make a serious difference in the conclusions they reach. Policy makers must be aware of this danger but should not exaggerate it, provided the research is directed by those trained as social scientists. The ethic of honesty is very strong in the discipline, and conflicting findings can in fact result from myriad factors other than bias.

With these cautions in mind, let us consider the extent to which expectations for the positive outcome of racial mixing in schools have been realized in terms of three major goals for desegregated schools: closing the black/white gap in academic achievement; improving the self-concept and motivation of black children; and encouraging more favorable racial attitudes and behavior among children of both races.

Academic Achievement

The most important source of nationwide cross-sectional data for the comparison of the academic achievement of segregated and nonsegregated schoolchildren is *Equality of Educational Opportunity* (Coleman et al., 1966). The proportion white in a school was found to be positively related to verbal achievement, but this finding disappeared when background characteristics of students were held constant. However, reanalysis by the U.S. Commission on Civil Rights (1967) of some of the same data for the high-school level indicated that the racial composition of the classroom did have an independent relation to achievement. Black children in majority-white classrooms tended to have higher scores than black children in majority-black classrooms. A partial reason for this correlation is probably that students are assigned to classrooms on the basis of test scores. Nevertheless, the commission also found that the earlier the grade in which blacks reported having white classmates, the higher their achievement.

In my previous review of the literature on desegregation and school achievement (St. John, 1975) I summarized the findings of 64 smaller studies, of which 13 were cross-sectional, 14 longitudinal but without a control group, and 37 quasi-experimental in that measurements were taken at two points in time for two samples that differed in the racial mixture of their schools. These studies were of children of varying ages, kindergarten through high school, but most often at the elementary level. They were conducted in all regions of the country, in cities of varying size. Desegregation came about in at least four ways—through residential change; through school-board rezoning, or closing of a segregated school and transfer of pupils with or without busing; through voluntary transfer of selected pupils to distant schools; and through total district desegregation in which all children were assigned to schools of the same racial mix. There was no evidence that region, city size, method of desegregation, or length of exposure to mixed schooling affected the relation of racial mix and academic outcome.

I concluded that these studies did not provide strong, clear evidence that desegregation will rapidly close the black/white gap in achievement, "although it has rarely lowered and sometimes raised the scores of black children. Improvement has been more often reported in the early grades, in arithmetic, and in schools over 50% white, but even here the gains have usually been mixed, intermittent or non-significant. White achievement has been unaffected in schools that remained majority white but significantly lower in majority black schools" (p. 119).

Crain (1976) challenged my conclusion that only 11 of the 64 studies I reviewed had an adequate research design (pretests and posttests for experimental and control groups, matching on family background, application of tests of significance to the results). I reported that the findings of those 11 studies were wholly positive in one case, mixed in 6 cases, and no difference in 4 cases. Crain applied a different criterion of methodological rigor to the 64 studies and counted 19 that met his standard. "The most common results for all grades were positive and significant; and in three, significant positive results occurred simultaneously with significant negative results. None of the 19 studies showed results that were more often negative than positive" (p. 374). Since Crain did not clarify his criteria or name the studies he selected, it is impossible to judge his conclusion.

I have located four more recent studies of desegregation and achievement. In Harrisburg, findings were mixed (Beers and Reardon, 1974); in Pasadena, city-wide test scores of both blacks and whites declined in the four years following desegregation (Kurtz, 1975); in Grand Rapids, no significant difference appeared between the segregated and desegregated (Schellenberg and Halteman, 1976); and in Indianapolis, the trend was positive but not significantly so (Patchen et al., 1977).

Over the past dozen years Weinberg has compiled successive bibliographies of the school desegregation literature. In his review appearing in the spring of 1975 he covered most of the same studies I did, but included also four or five investigations I had missed, the findings of which he judged to be more positive than negative. The most important of these is Crain's (1973) evaluation of the Emergency School Assistance Program, which reported academic gains for desegregated black male high-school students (apparently not for female students). In spite of such evidence, Weinberg's conclusion seems somewhat overdrawn: "Overall, desegregation does indeed have a positive effect on minority achievement levels" (p. 268). The impression of overall positive effect results from the fact that when findings are mixed, Weinberg regularly reports only the positive results and ignores the grade levels or subject areas in which children made no gains or lost ground. (See also Weinberg, 1977.)

Miller's close examination (1977) of the studies Weinberg categorized as having a positive outcome revealed that: (a) in a number of instances the positive outcome cannot with any certainty be attributed to desegregation; and (b) in certain other cases the outcomes are not particularly positive. According to Miller, Crain's categorization of the studies I had examined yielded only a slightly more favorable outcome than my own regarding the effect of desegregation on minority academic achievement. He concluded that a dispassionate review of the desegregation literature makes it quite apparent that "simply distributing students in each school of a district as a whole, without simultaneous initiation of numerous other programs, is very unlikely to provide a desirable kind of integrated learning experience, or to improve academic achievement of minority children" (p. 2).

Another review of the literature, by Clement, Eisenhart, and Wood (1976), reached the same conclusion as St. John and Miller.

The studies referred to above used three different measures of the educational outcomes of desegregation: grades, IQ scores, and achievement-test scores. Each has its drawbacks. Since teacher-assigned marks tend to be normalized in relation to the classroom mean, disadvantaged children entering mixed classrooms can be expected to experience a decline in their marks. To the extent to which tests of IQ measure stable characteristics in pupils, they are insensitive to changes in the school environment. Both IQ and achievement tests suffer from the fact that they are more or less culturally biased. Not standardized or validated on a population similar to that being tested, they tend to have low predictive validity for under-privileged minority-group children and differentiate poorly among them.

There is another measure of educational outcome that has been little used in desegregation research, as it entails long-term or follow-up studies, but in a couple of studies it has been utilized to good effect. This is educational attainment—the degree to which those who attend desegregated schools (a) graduate from high school, and (b) pursue higher education.

In recent decades nationwide school retention rates have climbed dramatically for all youth, especially for blacks. Despite this trend, a number of commentators have noted an alarming increase in high-school withdrawals, suspensions, and expulsions of black youth in some desegregating systems, especially in the South (Bryant, 1968; Clement et al., 1976; Felice and Richardson, 1977). In Boston the first year of desegregation saw innumerable white withdrawals as well. How many of these young people are "dropping out" of their own volition or in protest over conditions in mixed schools and how many are being "pushed out" by prejudiced school personnel is not clear. In either case an unexpected and serious problem has been flagged.

At the other end of the spectrum is the finding that voluntary participation in busing programs that bring ghetto children to middle-class suburban schools results in increased college attendance among graduates. Thus Armor (1972) found bused students much more likely to enter college than their siblings who remained in city schools, although the college dropout rate was higher for the bused students, so that by the end of the sophomore year 59 percent of the bused and 56 percent of their siblings were enrolled full-time in college. Similarly, Perry (1973) reported that 94 percent of ghetto youth placed by the ABC (A Better Chance) program in independent schools entered college, compared with 62 percent of matched non-ABC students, and the colleges entered by the ABC students were more selective. Crain and Mahard (1978), analyzing data from the National Longitudinal Study of the senior class of 1972, reported that in the South black graduates of predominantly white high schools are less likely to attend and survive in college than those from predominantly black schools. In the North, however, the opposite is true: black college attendance and survival in college are higher for the graduates of predominantly white schools. Further analysis of the data led the authors to conclude that "self-selection" is probably partly responsible for the apparent negative impact of desegregation in the South, but cannot account for the positive impact in the North.

That the benefits of desegregation do not end with college attendance is indicated by Crain's earlier (1971) survey of black adults in the urban North. He found that those who had attended integrated public schools had better jobs and higher incomes throughout at least three decades of their lives, although the differences in income were not accounted for by higher educational attainment or more favorable social background. A retrospective survey of this type cannot demonstrate that integrated schooling was the cause of later success; nevertheless the results suggest that desegregation has long-term economic benefits.

Self-Concept and Motivation

Three reviews of research on the psychological effects of school desegregation appeared in the years 1975 and 1976: Epps, 1975; St. John, 1975; and Clement at al., 1976. An important book by Gerard and Miller (1975) also appeared, which summarized their ten-year study of school desegregation in Riverside, California, and reported on their analysis of psychological outcomes. I shall look now at the collective evidence in several different areas.

Anxiety
St. John (1975) summarized 7 studies of anxiety in desegregated black children as indicating that although, in general, black children show more signs of anxiety than white children, there is no marked increase following desegregation. However, Gerard and Miller (1975) reported that over time the younger black children display a much larger increase in general anxiety than do the younger Anglo or Mexican-American chil-

dren. Epps (1975) cited a study by Mercer, Coleman, and Harloe (1974) as evidence that the impact of desegregation upon anxiety depends on the educational environment of the school.

Aspiration

I reported in 1975 that a significant positive relationship is rarely found between percent white within a school and either educational aspiration (16 studies) or occupational aspiration (13 studies) of the students. Epps (1975) referred to only a few of these studies (and to no new ones), but drew a somewhat different lesson from the evidence: "No study of black aspirations has shown that they are substantially lowered by introducing these students into a desegregating system" (p. 302). This is true: only a proper experimental design could demonstrate such an effect. Most studies of aspirations are cross-sectional and cannot show change over time.

Veroff and Peele (1969) and Gerard and Miller (1975) interpret a reduction in aspiration on a laboratory task on the part of desegregated children as evidence of increased realism and hence positive gain. (See also Travis and Anthony, 1975.) If we adopt this line of reasoning, we need not consider that lower aspiration on the part of desegregated children (as measured by a pen-and-paper test) lends support to school segregation, but rather that desegregated youth may have more realistic ambitions than those in segregated schools.

Self-Concept

Many researchers have found that black children tend to indicate a higher degree of self-esteem than white children, but that desegregation often has a discouraging effect. Twenty-five studies of the relation of black self-concept and school percentage white were summarized in St. John (1975). Of these, 9 found that desegregation had a negative effect (3 significantly so), 7 no effect, 5 mixed effects, and 4 a significantly positive effect. But the most careful study among these (Rosenberg and Simmons, 1971) was one of those that found self-esteem significantly lower in desegregated schools. Academic self-concept of blacks is much more negatively related to school percent white than is self-concept in general. Gerard and Miller (1975) say they found in Riverside no support for the assumption that desegregation will increase the minority (in this case primarily Chicano) child's self-esteem. Instead, his academic adjustment is disturbed, while that of the Anglo child is not. It appears to me, therefore, that desegregation tends to threaten the self-esteem of minority children.

Again, Epps (1975) interprets the evidence somewhat differently. Reviewing many of the same studies, but adding one that suggests a positive effect (Shaw, 1974) and one that suggests a negative effect (Weber, Cook, and Campbell, 1971), he concludes that desegregation has no effect on black self-esteem—or lowers it only slightly. In partial support of this conclusion, I found in my study of Boston sixth-graders that although academic self-concept was related negatively to present school percent white, it was related positively to past school percent white, suggesting that the long-run benefits of a more challenging academic environment may be greater than the short-run discouragement involved (St. John, 1971a).

Sense of Environmental Control
For black children, the sense of control over environment is regularly found to be more positively related to school percent white than are any of the other psychological outcomes, a correlation first noted by Coleman (1966). Reanalyses of the same data by the Commission on Civil Rights (1967) and by McPartland (1968) substantiated this finding. So did my study of Boston sixth-graders (1971a) and Bachman's (1970) study of tenth-grade boys in eighty-seven high schools. However, Gerard and Miller (1975) report that desegregation had no effect on this variable for the grade-school children they studied in Riverside.

Racial Attitudes and Behavior

With regard to the educational and psychological effects of desegregation, the expectation has been that *minority youth* would be the beneficiaries. Racial prejudice, on the other hand, has been seen as a *white* problem. Therefore, change in the attitudes and behavior of white youth has been a major goal of interracial schooling. This goal has clearer theoretical support than those previously discussed. Allport (1954) and other social psychologists (Amir, 1969) have used theory and experimental evidence to support the proposition that contact between ethnic groups leads to reduced prejudice, but only if such contact is prolonged, intimate, noncompetitive, between equals in pursuit of common goals, and sanctioned by those in authority. As we shall see, researchers have been too quick to assume that the interracial classroom satisfies these conditions.

Three types of studies are available: (a) comparison of racial beliefs or attitudes in segregated and desegregated schools; (b) studies of interracial

friendship choice or behavior in desegregated settings that attempt to relate such behavior to previous interracial contact, to racial percentages in
the classroom, or to time spent in the desegregated setting; and (c) case
studies of racially mixed schools or classrooms. St. John (1975) summarized 41 studies of the first two types, spanning the years 1937 to 1973,
many of them in northern high schools. For blacks and whites both, positive findings are less common than negative findings, but in many cases
there is no effect or the effects are mixed. The direction of findings by
type of study design or sophistication of methodology, by manner in
which desegregation came about (neighborhood, mandatory or voluntary busing), and by characteristics of subjects (age, sex, social class,
achievement level) are generally inconclusive. Positive findings are somewhat more likely for younger children, for black males or white females,
for situations in which the races are not too diverse in social-class background, and where the community and school climate is not markedly
hostile.

Case studies confirm the inconclusive results of comparative studies
and suggest the great range in interracial climate from school to school.
In some there is considerable friendly interaction, in others peaceful but
separate coexistence, and in still others tension or violent conflict. More
recent investigations do not change the picture. Gerard and Miller (1975),
for instance, found that following desegregation ethnic separation increased over time for both friendship and work partner choices, while
Schofield and Sagar (1976, 1977) found that in a well-integrated setting,
racial desegregation decreased over time for sixth- and seventh-graders,
while it increased for eighth-graders enrolled in either a predominantly
white accelerated academic track or a predominantly black regular track.
(See also Silverman and Shaw, 1973; Wolf and Simon, 1975; Jacobson,
1976; Schafft, 1976; and Bullock, 1978.)

A review of the literature by Cohen (1975) corroborates my conclusion. She refers to several additional articles (Williams and Venditti,
1969; Wade and Wilson, 1971; Patterson and Smits, 1972; Coats, 1972;
and Bullock and Braxton, 1973), but writes that the studies analyzed
for her article appear to yield "the same mixed results as the studies reviewed by St. John." While she deplores the methodological inadequacies of investigations in this area, she stresses that they are especially defi-
cient on theoretical grounds.

Cohen's own experimental work that attempts to produce equal-status
behavior in interracial groups of students working together on tasks is an
example of the type of research we need—research grounded in well-

developed theory. In this case the theory derives in part from Allport's hypothesis regarding the importance of equality of status for prejudice-reducing contact. Cohen goes beyond this, identifying the intrinsic difficulty in overcoming general expectations for greater competence of higher-status group members (whites), and successfully uses expectation training to counteract this "disability."

This very promising effort in testing a theoretically derived proposition leads into the last major topic we shall consider: what are the key variables in the desegregated school that affect achievement of the desired goals?

Conditions of Effective School Desegregation

In 1975 I suggested two basic reasons for the mixed and inconclusive findings on outcomes of desegregation for children. First, desegregation is a multifaceted phenomenon that can be simultaneously beneficial and detrimental. Second, whether the benefits outweigh the disadvantages depends both on a child's individual needs, and (more important) on how desegregation is implemented by school staff. Resorting to various strands of social psychological theory, I predicted the necessary and sufficient conditions for successful implementation, but there were relatively few studies that tested my predictions.

Since that time several summaries of research evidence on this topic have appeared: an essay by Orfield (1975); an Educational Testing Service survey and interview study of effective school desegregation in ninety-six elementary schools and seventy-two high schools (Forehand, Ragosta, and Rock, 1976); and a set of principles relevant to successful school desegregation, drafted by Miller (1977) for the guidance of the Los Angeles school board as it moves to comply with court-ordered desegregation and signed by a number of social scientists with long experience in the field. In addition, reviews of the literature (Weinberg, 1975; Epps, 1975; and Cohen, 1975) indicate key variables found to affect outcomes. Unfortunately, no matter how convincing their sets of principles appear to be, all these authors have been handicapped by the paucity of hard empirical evidence. There are some common major themes, however, and where possible I shall refer to research findings that support the suggested policy.

Role of the Principal

All observers stress the role of the principal in planning for and implementing desegregation. Orfield (1975) writes that it is the principal who must provide the educational leadership and see that the social climate supports integration. Willie's (1973) case study of the desegregation process in a middle-sized northern city also underscores this point. Forehand, Ragosta, and Rock (1976) found that principals' racial attitudes seem to have direct influence on the attitudes of teachers in elementary schools and on teaching practices in high schools; these variables in turn directly affect the racial attitudes of white students. The principal's role in communication with parents and involvement of the community in the desegregation process is stressed by Collins and Nobbitt (1976) and by Miller (1977).

The power erosion of the black principal following desegregation is found by Buxton and Prichard (1977) to be endemic in one southern state, and to have potentially serious consequences for black pupils because it deprives them of a role model and leads to a decline in school discipline. Discipline and outbreaks of violence are major issues in many desegregating secondary schools. The principal must lead the staff in crisis prevention, in perception of community needs, and in restructuring the school environment. Forehand, Ragosta, and Rock (1976) found that the racial attitudes of black high-school students reflected their perception of the fairness of the school to them, the absence of conflict over discipline, and the equality of influence of black and white teachers, students, and parents.

Teacher Selection and Training

The experts agree on the importance of developing an interracial staff at all levels and of assuring minority and majority group faculty equal status in the life of the school. A number of studies suggest that faculty and counselors are more effective in raising the expectations of students of their own racial background (Entwisle and Webster, 1974; Darkenwald, 1975; Erickson, 1975). The importance of teachers (black or white) who communicate to students high expectations for their performance is demonstrated by the Gerard and Miller (1975) finding that minority children whose teachers exaggerated their intellectual inadequacies at the beginning of the year showed much greater decline in verbal achievement than peers in classes of less biased teachers. Brookover and colleagues (1976) found that students' sense of academic futility contributes more than any other climate variable to low achievement, especially in schools with black students. High- and low-achieving predominantly black schools were distinguished from each other by the fact that teachers in the high-achieving schools did not "write off" their slow students but arranged more instruction time and gave a great deal of positive reinforcement.

Cohen's (1975) laboratory experiments also demonstrate the need for black and white instructors who are models for high expectations.

The racial attitudes of teachers are flagged by all our experts as the key variable. The Forehand group (1976) reported that at the tenth-grade level, as at the fifth-grade level, the single variable that seems to have the largest impact on students' racial attitudes is teachers' racial attitudes as reported by teachers and students. A related and important condition, according to Forehand, is obvious support for integration by teachers, administration, and students. In integrated sixth-grade classrooms in Boston, I found that black pupils of teachers rated "nurturant" by outside observers showed improved reading, conduct, and attendance. They believed their teachers approved of them in spite of low grades and, if the class was majority-white, named whites as best friends. Black and white students under teachers rated "fair" were significantly friendlier to the other race than those in classrooms under teachers not so rated (St. John, 1971b). For integration to benefit students, the principal must give strong leadership and must develop a faculty that supports integration and is unprejudiced and fair—no easy task. Careful screening of candidates for teaching positions and innovative and flexible techniques of in-service training are called for (Orfield, 1975; Forehand, Ragosta, and Rock, 1976).

Curriculum and Instruction
Orfield (1975) insists that successful desegregation requires basic modifications of teaching methods, a process that teachers often find very difficult. The major problem is how to handle a wide range of achievement levels in a single classroom, as schools must do if they are to avoid resegregation at the classroom level. The Emergency School Assistance Program found that tracking had a consistently negative effect on students' attitudes toward integration at the elementary level (Crain, 1973). As an aside, Koslin and associates (1972) found that interracial attitudes were more favorable when classrooms had approximately equal numbers of black and white students. In order to minimize the adverse effects of the achievement gap, investigators advise individualization of instruction (Orfield, 1975), use of competency-based testing (Miller, 1977), extra instruction time for slower students, and team competition rather than individual competition in academic subjects (Brookover et al., 1976).

A number of researchers have identified a very promising technique that challenges all students and does not discourage the slow learner, the use of cooperative learning teams. For instance, as developed by Slavin at Johns Hopkins University, this technique involved the study of academic material in biracial teams of four or five students of different ability levels. All then compete in a game or tournament to demonstrate their knowledge, each individual's contribution to his team's score being based on how well he does relative to others of similar ability. Slavin (1977, 1978) has found repeatedly that seventh-graders in these classrooms make greater academic gains and more cross-racial friends than similar seventh-graders in traditional classrooms. Other researchers also have achieved positive results from some variation of the cooperative-learning team approach.

The importance of the use of integrated texts and multicultural curricula is stressed by all experts (see especially Forehand, Ragosta, and Rock, 1976). But Orfield (1976) warns that minority as well as majority teachers require more than superficial training in the development of new materials and teaching units. In an integrated high school using all the above programs, Lachat (1972) found significantly more friendly interaction between races than in a high school that was merely desegregated.

Equal-Status Contact

In Miller's (1977) words, "desegregation plans should explicitly implement the conditions for favorable contact"—that is, the contact should be on an equal-status basis, long-term, intimate, in pursuit of common goals, and sanctioned by those in authority. Many of the principles discussed in the two preceding sections would contribute to these conditions. In addition, Forehand, Ragosta, and Rock (1976) found that race relations were more favorable in schools where the staff deliberately structured class assignments and extracurricular activities to maximize equal-status contact. Cohen's (1975) success in expectation training built upon the same principle.

A major hurdle to achieving equal-status majority/minority contact in schools is difference in social class. Porter (1971), on the basis of field observations with preschool children, concluded that differences in race and social class should not be allowed to reinforce each other (see also Bain and Anderson, 1974). Forehand and associates (1976) report that positive racial attitudes are strongly reinforced by socioeconomic similarity of black and white students. In a study of Boston sixth-graders St. John and Lewis (1974) found that the smaller the white/black gap in social class and achievement, the greater was the relative friendliness of each race to the other as measured by sociometric choice. As Rosenberg and Simmons (1971) demonstrated through their interviews with Baltimore elementary and secondary students, racial isolation protects the lower-class black child from realizing his or her low social status, low academic status, and low racial status. Social-class desegregation strips the first two defenses from the student, while racial desegregation exposes him to awareness of prejudice against his race. Depressed self-concept in the desegregated school is often the result.

Since it is impossible in our present-day society to equalize social background in desegregated classrooms everywhere, school staffs must look for innovative ways of neutralizing the differences that children bring to school and of creating "equal status, dignity, and access to resources within the contact situation itself" (Pettigrew et al., 1973).

Conclusion

Has social science contributed to an understanding of the outcomes of desegregation? Crain (1976) answers "In no way." He criticizes researchers as having been too little concerned with determining *how* desegregation should be achieved, too little concerned with long-term as opposed to short-run effects, and too quick to conclude that desegregation has not been beneficial. His explanation of why desegregation research has been beset with these problems is, first, that the expense of research in time and money, the strings attached to federal funding, and the structure of the university reward system combine to encourage short-term studies of easily gathered achievement-test scores. Second, he feels that the ideology of researchers leads them to conclude that desegregation has not been beneficial.

Long-term studies are badly needed, as are more studies that pinpoint the conditions for successful integration. It is true that shortage of time and money has been a major handicap. But I do not agree that the ideology of the researcher typically leads to a decision that desegregation has not been beneficial. It is my impression that the influence of ideology is in quite the other direction. I believe with Metzger (1971) and Wolf (1972) that the values of social scientists are so often prointegration that many tend to underreport negative findings or to report them in a way that they believe will have less of an anti-integration effect on policy. I also question whether all the research on outcomes, rather than on conditions, has been wasted effort. It has taken us a long time to realize what probably should have been obvious in the first place—that moving children around like checkers will not in itself improve matters. But now that twenty years of research have made this abundantly clear, we are ready for the next stage—long-term studies to identify conditions within schools and classrooms that will improve educational achievement.

Cohen and Weiss (1976) have written gloomily about social research on education and race, arguing that though research has steadily improved, it has only produced "new arguments and complications." Whereas in physical science the result of improvement is convergence, in social science the result is a "richer, more diverse picture of things." This is so, they suggest, because research reveals how complicated social reality is; the use of different methodologies multiplies mystification; and other social-science disciplines, each with its own angle of vision, are drawn in. Naturally policy makers and courts become exasperated with the resultant complexities and contradictions of research findings. While their essay is insightful and its separate points are persuasive, I take issue with their central argument, that research on school and race results in divergence rather than convergence of knowledge and therefore can give no clear guidance to policy makers.

In fact, on the specific topic of this review—the outcomes of school desegregation for children—one can find a high degree of consensus among social scientists by keeping one's eyes on the woods rather than the trees. As implemented to date, racial mixing in schools has rarely harmed majority-group children. Minority-group children have gained in some respects, but may have suffered in others. Whether for children of either race the benefits outweigh possible harm seems to depend on how desegregation is accomplished in schools—on the leadership given by the principal, on a teaching staff that is unbiased and trained in ways of handling diversity in the classroom, on the cultural pluralism of the curriculum, and—above all—on equality of status for each racial group within the school. A school with these assets might be called truly integrated. To date, because social scientists have studied the effect on children of "mere desegregation," their findings appear inconclusive. If, as, and when school settings become more thoroughly integrated, I firmly believe that all children will benefit, measurably and immeasurably.

References

Allport, Gordon W. 1954. *The Nature of Prejudice.* Reading, Massachusetts: Addison-Wesley.

Amir, Yehuda. 1969. Contact hypothesis in ethnic relations. *Psychological Bulletin* 71:319-342.

Armor, David J. 1972. The evidence on busing. *Public Interest* 28:90-126.

100   *Nancy H. St. John*

Bachman, Jerald G. 1970. *Youth in Transition*, vol. 2. Ann Arbor: Institute for Social Research, University of Michigan.

Bain, Robert K., and James G. Anderson. 1974. School context and peer influences on educational plans of adolescents. *Review of Educational Research* 44:429-445.

Beers, Joan S., and Francis J. Reardon. 1974. Racial balancing in Harrisburg: achievements and attitudinal changes. *Integrated Education* 12:35-38.

Brookover, Wilbur B., John H. Schweitzer, Jeffrey Schneider, Charles H. Beady, Patricia K. Flood, and Joseph M. Wisenbaker. 1976. Elementary school social climate and achievement. Paper presented at American Sociological Association meeting, New York, August 30-September 3.

Bryant, James C. 1968. Some effects of racial integration of high school students on standardized achievement test scores, teacher grades and drop-out rates in Angleton, Texas. Doctoral dissertation, University of Houston.

Bullock, Charles S. 1978. Contact theory and racial tolerance among high school students. *School Review* 86:187-216.

——— and Mary Victoria Braxton. 1973. The coming of school desegregation: a before and after study of black and white student perceptions. *Social Science Quarterly* 54:132-138.

Buxton, Thomas H., and Keith W. Prichard. 1977. The power erosion syndrome of the black principal. *Integrated Education* 15:9-14.

Clement, Dorothy C., Margaret Eisenhart, and John W. Wood. 1976. School desegregation and educational inequality: trends in the literature, 1960-1975. In *The Desegregation Literature: A Critical Appraisal*, ed. Ray Rist. Washington, D.C.: National Institute of Education.

Coats, W. 1972. A longitudinal survey of desegregation in Kalamazoo, Michigan. Paper presented at American Psychological Association annual convention, Honolulu, September 7.

Cohen, David, and Janet Weiss. 1976. Social science and social policy: schools and race. In *Education, Social Science and the Judicial Process: An International Symposium*. Washington, D.C.: National Institute of Education.

Cohen, Elizabeth G. 1975. The effects of desegregation on race relations. *Law and Contemporary Problems* 39:271-299.

Coleman, James S., Ernest G. Campbell, Carol J. Hobson, James McPartland, Alexander M. Mood, Frederic D. Weinfeld, and Robert L. York. 1966. *Equality of Educational Opportunity*. Washington, D.C.: U.S. Department of Health, Education and Welfare, Office of Education.

Collins, Thomas W., and George W. Nobbitt. 1976. The process of interracial schooling: an assessment of conceptual frameworks and methodological orientations. In *The Desegregation Literature: A Critical Appraisal*, ed. Ray Rist. Washington, D.C.: National Institute of Education.

Crain, Robert L. 1971. School integration and the academic achievement of Negroes. *Sociology of Education* 44:1-26.

———. 1973. *Southern Schools: An Evaluation of the Effects of the Emergency School Assistance Program and of School Desegregation*. Chicago: National Opinion Research Center, University of Chicago.

————. 1976. Why academic research fails to be useful. *School Review* 84:337-351.

———— and Rita Mahard. 1978. School racial composition and black college attendance and achievement test performance. *Sociology of Education* 51:81-101.

Darkenwald, Gordon G. 1975. Some effects of the "obvious variable": teacher's race and holding power with black adult students. *Sociology of Education* 48:420-431.

Entwisle, Doris R., and Murray Webster, Jr. 1974. Expectations in mixed racial groups. *Sociology of Education* 47:301-318.

Epps, Edgar G. 1975. The impact of school desegregation on aspirations, self-concepts, and other aspects of personality. *Law and Contemporary Problems* 39:300-313.

Erickson, Frederick. 1975. Gate-keeping and the melting pot. *Harvard Educational Review* 45:44-70.

Felice, Lawrence G., and Ronald I. Richardson. 1977. Effects of desegregation on minority student dropout rates. *Integrated Education* 15:47-50.

Forehand, Garlie A., Majorie Ragosta, and Donald A. Rock. 1976. *Conditions and Processes of Effective School Desegregation: Final Report*. Princeton, New Jersey: Educational Testing Service.

Gerard, Harold B., and Norman Miller. 1975. *School Desegregation*. New York: Plenum Publishing Corp.

Jacobson, Cardell. 1976. Racial-ethnic composition and student attitudes: a longitudinal study. Paper presented at American Sociological Association meeting, New York, August 30-September 3.

Koslin, Sandra, Bertram Koslin, Richard Pargament, and Harvey Waxman. 1972. Classroom racial balance and students' interracial attitudes. *Sociology of Education* 45:386-407.

Kurtz, Harold. 1975. The educational and demographic consequences of four years of school desegregation in the Pasadena Unified School District. Unpublished report to the Board of Education, Pasadena (California) Unified School District.

Lachat, Mary Ann. 1972. A description and comparison of the attitudes of white high school seniors toward black Americans in three suburban high schools: an all-white, a desegregated, and an integrated high school. Doctoral dissertation, Columbia University.

McPartland, James. 1968. The segregated student in desegregated schools: sources of influence on Negro secondary students. Report no. 21, Center for Social Organization of Schools, Johns Hopkins University.

Mercer, Jane, Marietta Coleman, and Jack Harloe. 1974. Racial/ethnic segregation and desegregation in American public education. In *The Uses of the Sociology of Education*, ed. Calvin W. Gordon. Chicago: National Society of the Study of Education.

Metzger, L. Paul. 1971. American sociology and black assimilation: conflicting perspectives. *American Journal of Sociology* 76:627-647.

Miller, Norman. 1977. Principles relevant to successful school desegregation: a social science statement. Los Angeles: Social Science Research Institute, University of Southern California. Unpublished.

National Advisory Commission on Civil Disorders (Otto Kerner, chairman). 1968. *Report of the Commission.* Washington, D.C.: Government Printing Office.

Orfield, Gary. 1975. How to make desegregation work: the adaptation of schools to their newly integrated student bodies. *Law and Contemporary Problems* 39:314-340.

Patchen, Martin, James D. Davidson, Gerhard Hofmann, and William R. Brown. 1977. Determinants of students' interracial behavior and opinion change. *Sociology of Education* 50:55-75.

Patterson, David L., and Stanley J. Smits. 1972. Reactions of inner-city and sub-urban adolescents to three minority groups. *Journal of Psychology* 80:127-134.

Perry, George A. 1973. *A Better Chance: Evaluation of Student Attitudes and Academic Performance, 1964-1972.* Boston: A Better Chance.

Pettigrew, Thomas F., Marshall Smith, Elizabeth L. Useem, and Clarence Nor-mund. 1973. Busing: a review of the evidence. *Public Interest* 30:88-118.

Porter, Judith D. R. 1971. *Black Child, White Child: The Development of Racial Attitudes.* Cambridge, Massachusetts: Harvard University Press.

Rosenberg, Morris, and Roberta G. Simmons. 1971. *Black and White Self-Esteem: The Urban School Child.* Washington, D.C.: American Sociological Association.

St. John, Nancy H. 1971a. The elementary classroom as a frog pond: self-con-cept, sense of control and social context. *Social Forces* 49:581-595.

————. 1971b. Thirty-six teachers: their characteristics and outcomes for black and white pupils. *American Educational Research Journal* 8:635-648.

————. 1975. *School Desegregation: Outcomes for Children.* New York: Wiley Interscience.

———— and Ralph H. Lewis. 1974. Children's interracial friendships: an explora-tion of the contact hypothesis. Unpublished.

Schafft, Gretchen E. 1976. White children in a majority black school: together yet separate. *Integrated Education* 14:3-7.

Schellenberg, James, and John Halteman. 1976. Busing and academic achieve-ment: a two-year follow-up. *Urban Education* 10:357-365.

Schofield, Janet W., and Andrew Sagar. 1976. Interracial interaction in a new magnet desegregated school. Paper presented at 84th convention of Ameri-can Psychological Association, Washington, D.C.

———— and Andrew Sagar. 1977. Social relationships in an integrated school. *Integrated Education* 15:117-119.

Shaw, Marvin E. 1974. The self-image of black and white pupils in an integrated school. *Journal of Personality* 42:12-22.

Silverman, Irwin, and Marvin E. Shaw. 1973. Effects of sudden mass school de-segregation on interracial interaction and attitudes in one southern city. *Journal of Social Issues* 29:133-142.

Slavin, Robert E. 1977. Effects of bi-racial learning teams on cross-racial friend-ship and interaction. Report no. 240, Center for Social Organization of

Schools, Johns Hopkins University.

———. 1978. Effects of student teams and peer tutoring on academic achievement and time on task. Report no. 253, Center for Social Organization of Schools, Johns Hopkins University.

Travis, Cheryl B., and Sharon F. Anthony. 1975. Ethnic composition of schools and achievement motivation. *Journal of Psychology* 89:271-279.

U.S. Commission on Civil Rights. 1967. *Racial Isolation in the Public Schools*. Washington, D.C.: Government Printing Office.

Veroff, Joseph, and Stanton Peele. 1969. Initial effects of desegregation on the achievement motivation of Negro elementary school children. *Journal of Social Issues* 25:71-91.

Wade, Kenneth, and Warner Wilson. 1971. Relatively low prejudice in a racially isolated group. *Psychological Reports* 28:871-877.

Weber, S., T. Cook, and D. Campbell. 1971. The effect of school integration on the academic self-concept of public school students. Paper presented at Midwestern Psychological Association meeting, Detroit.

Weinberg, Meyer. 1975. The relationship between school desegregation and academic achievement: a review of the research. *Law and Contemporary Problems* 39:240-270.

———. 1977. *Minority Students: A Research Appraisal*. Washington, D.C.: National Institute of Education.

Williams, Robert L., and Fred Venditti. 1969. Effect of academic integration on southern Negro students' expressed satisfaction with school. *Journal of Social Psychology* 79:203-209.

Willie, Charles V., with Jerome Beker. 1973. *Race Mixing in Public Schools*. New York: Praeger.

Wolf, Eleanor. 1972. Civil rights and social science data. *Race* 14:155-182.

Wolf, Robert L., and Rita J. Simon. 1975. Does busing improve the racial interactions of children? *Educational Researcher* 4:5-10.

PART TWO

Individuals, Groups, and Attitudes

5   The One and the Many

HAROLD R. ISAACS

School desegregation is part of the struggle for change in America in which classroom teachers have had to become frontline soldiers. The "enemy" they face is confusion, uncertainty, and all the legacies of a past they did not make, only inherited. They are like troops that have been thrown into action in a critical salient with orders to hold on come what may, to save the day while the generals try to figure out what to do to win the battle, not to say the war. And as usually happens in wars, the fog gets thickest when it comes to trying to understand what the war is all about, what the "war aims" are and what they are not. One way or another, this is what the teacher is dealing with every day in every classroom in coping with the tensions and problems of "race," in trying to meet the new demands and new definitions of "ethnic heritage" and the relationship involving not only "blacks" and "whites" but all the many kinds of people whose children populate American classrooms.

The purpose of these notes is to deal with those "war aims," with some aspects of the evolving American group identity and the so-called new ethnicity as they underlie both the large problems of school desegregation and the "small" ones that every teacher has to face somehow every working day in the classroom.

There is, to begin with, the larger context. School desegregation is part of the great wrenching rearrangement of racial and ethnic pecking orders, perceptions, behaviors that has been going on in American society since the end of World War II. This in turn has been part of a larger history: the American white supremacy system could not survive the collapse of the system of Western white dominance everywhere in the world except, so far, in southern Africa. As the long-established power systems

This chapter appeared previously in *American Educator* 2(1978):4-14 and is reprinted here by permission of the American Federation of Teachers.

came down, so did the accompanying styles of perception and self-perception and relative status of peoples grouped in their many tribes, races, and nationalities. This has forced everyone to stumble around amid the rubble and ruins looking for new ways of existing and coexisting on new and largely unfixed terms. It has meant trying to cope with all the social, economic, psychological, and political carry-overs and consequences of how it was while trying to shape how it is to be hereafter.

The new shape of things could not be created simply by transferring sovereignties in the ex-colonies from old to new masters nor in the American society simply by judicial, legislative, or administrative decisions. But it did take change of quake-like force to pull the legal and institutional foundations out from under those old orders of things: it took history's greatest and bloodiest global war to bring all those old flags down and run up all those new flags in more than a hundred new states. It took the pressures and outcomes of that global war to give effect to a generation of civil rights struggle in the American society. It took A. Philip Randolph's March-on-Washington strategy to produce Roosevelt's fair employment order in 1941, a nascent civil disobedience movement to bring on Truman's desegregating the armed forces in 1948, and a deeper recognition of the changes required by the war to produce the Supreme Court's *Brown* decision in 1954. Ten years later, following upon the massive freedom movement initiated by Martin Luther King in Alabama, came the civil and voting rights acts of 1964 and 1965 which gave the new era the full force of law. With all this, the American society finally began to become what it had claimed to be all along in the matter of assuring equal protection of the law and equality of opportunity to *all* its members.

In the ex-colonial world, the removal of the mantle of white rule brought back into view and into action all the many tribal-racial-ethnic-religious-national divisions in all these societies. These became the crux of the new national politics almost everywhere and brought on new lunges for pelf, power, and turf, leading to bloody collisions that have taken somewhere between 10 and 20 million lives during the last thirty years in dozens of countries around the world.

In the American society, these events ushered in a time of great change not comparably lethal but comparably quake-like and incomparably more positive and fruitful in scope and consequences despite all its formidable incompleteness and continuing turmoil and confusion. This turmoil and confusion, moreover, comes not only out of the breakdown of old patterns of racial-ethnic-religious status and behavior, but out of a far more inclusive erosion during these same decades of moral, social, and cultural norms of every kind. In the wake of Vietnam and Watergate, the new normlessness spread like the floodwaters of a great river into all domains of life. It has made disaster areas out of what had been the more or less fixed, the more or less ramshackle, at least the more or less recognizable domains of our governing notions about political institutions, family, education, sex, marriage, high and low politics, high and low religion, high, low, and lowest arts. This came along with a profoundly shaking loss of belief in the idea of the unending progress of science and technology that would lead more and more people toward greater and greater well-being and felicity. This flood has inundated much of the old bottomland that used to renew these old crops for us year after year. It has carried away many of the old structures in which we lived and worked and it damaged most of what remains, blocking entrances and exits, cutting off much of the power that used to keep these places lit, warm, and habitable, and many of the communication lines that used to keep them in some kind of touch with each other.

It is no doubt easy to exaggerate this: from the roof of a flooded house, the whole world looks pretty grim. But even after making extensive corrections—for distortion via our amplified media or via the prism of personal fatigue or despair—the scene still surely resembles a confused shambles more than a functioning order, a landscape painted by a Dali, not a Wyeth. It is not an exaggeration to apply the metaphors of earthquake and flood to the context of our present discussion. In the span of time that most of us have known—taking in the time that includes our parents, ourselves, and our children—we have experienced two world wars and countless others, multiple great revolutions, all the transforming effects of swift technological change, and the redoubling of the world's population, all of it with no happy endings, or hardly any.

Nor does it help much when we narrow the subject down to our own racial or ethnic behavior and the time down to the last thirty years; no happy endings either, or hardly any, or so, at least, everyone seems to feel. Much has changed—a lot more than the despairing among us acknowledge—yet very little comes out "right." And so, the question has to be, what else is new? And the answer is Victor Serge's—when France fell—"The world is always new, if your nerves are strong enough." If they are not strong enough, it has to be a comfort to know that anyone can make a good case for projecting personal frustration, failure, impotence in these matters onto the larger screen of the human condition. If, by whistling a lively tune, jogging, or just by being young enough, you do keep those nerves strong enough, you have to keep on facing the choice of *what* values, *what* norms to have and to hold and defend as best for the greatest common good, and what action, if levers can be found, to promote and maintain them.

This, I take it, is the purpose of our present exercise, trying to confront the new problems created by efforts at school desegregation. This is part of trying to find new and better ways of dealing with our diversity, to make our society over in its own better image, to begin shaping the "one" we want to come, finally, from the "many." What *one?* What *many?* Organized by what ethos, creating what kind of social and political system, giving what substance to the shared group identity called *American?* What is to be the relation between whatever continues to mark us apart, by race, religion, heritage, and what we all hold in common? These are large questions, easier to answer in general than in particular. Yet particular answers are being provided every day that are in some measure already shaping the new actualities, in court decisions, administrative actions, and, perhaps most influentially of all, by what goes on in every schoolroom where this generation of children is being treated to the full effects of our present confusion and disarray.

Again, what *one?* What *many?* And what is to lie between them? We have been getting mostly bad news about the one for some years now, and mostly good news about the many. Indeed, in our great distress over the state of the one (Vietnam, Watergate), quite a few people have been indulging in a romance with the many (the "new ethnicity," "Roots"). It is time, past time, perhaps, to redress the balance between how we see our "one" and our "many" without being too romantic about either one.

"Americans" are a great array of mixed and diverse peoples of many kinds and origins. Figures on this diversity are not easy to come by. From census and related studies, it would appear that there are roughly 35 million "nonwhites"—including about 25 million blacks, 2 million "Orientals," and some uncertain proportion of those called "Spanish" or "Mexicans" or "Latin." There are about 95 million Americans who identify themselves as having this or that particular European origin (that is, 31 million English-Scots-Welsh, 25 million German, 16 million Irish, 10 million Italian, 8 million Slav and so on; the 6 million Jews often disappear in the census under "Russian"). This total included 33 million (in

1971) called "foreign stock," meaning foreign-born or having at least one foreign-born parent.

"An appreciable segment of the population," says a 1973 census publication, "remains uncommitted to any specific origin group." That "appreciable segment" turns out to be roughly of the order of 90 million people. This figure needs to be pondered most thoughtfully by enthusiasts for the "new ethnicity." There are some 90 million people so mixed or so distant from their origins that they can only describe themselves as "Americans." Of the 95 million who *do* identify a European origin, the overwhelming majority (including all but marginal elements in the European immigrant stock of the last two or three generations) sees itself essentially and primarily—often aggressively—as "American" and, only in some secondary way, by origin and attachment and continuing association, something else at the same time, a distinctive background preserved in the church, home, and family, in styles of food, preserved homeland customs, in the names they bear. Only at the margins of these groups, always being reinforced numerically and emotionally by oncoming waves of new immigrants, do we find those who still identify themselves primarily with their homelands and only in some secondary way as "American." Similarly among American blacks, with all their prolonged experience of oppression, exclusion, and rejection, only small, mostly tiny nationalist-separatist currents have over time carried the idea that blacks in this society are not "Americans" but must establish their own nation somehow somewhere else. Some of the most remarkable figures in black history, like Martin Delany, lived out their lives coping with the ambivalences of what DuBois called the inescapable "twoness" of being black *and* American.

This extraordinary diversity and continuing mobility explains why the American group identity, more perhaps than any other, has always been and still is coming into being. New people, new forces, new circumstances have worked constantly to shape it, sometimes—although not always—trying to make it fit more closely the vision with which it was originally created. This vision was eighteenth-century Enlightenment vision at its loftiest: popular sovereignty, inalienable rights guaranteed to all individual citizens in their pursuit of life, liberty, and happiness in whatever form they might seek and find it. The actuality was deeply flawed: it carried within it from the beginning the cancer of slavery. It is far from certain now, after all the crises and remissions and recurrences of all the years, that the body politic is not still mortally sick with this malignancy, that its failures as an open society might not yet overtake its successes and strike it, finally, in some vital part.

In their many kinds, Americans came together in a society whose ethos was nominally to make "one" out of these "many." In practice until quite recently it made "one" only out of some (essentially white Americans of northern European Protestant origin) while partly excluding others (mainly whites of other origins, Catholics, Jews) and more or less totally excluding still others (its nonwhites, blacks, browns, yellows, reds). This was still for all practical purposes the structure of American society as recently as 1945. In the decades since, we have been going through great changes occurring in all their uneven ways with all their uneven results. During these turbulent years, we have touched highs and lows of expectations and outcomes in this ongoing process. In the civil rights revolution that finally brought down legal racial segregation and opened the assault on its entrenched customary forms, it seemed possible to see the beginning of the closing of the gap between what the society had claimed to be and what it actually was. Then in the America of the burning ghettos, Vietnam, and Watergate, what had begun to put itself together after 1945 seemed to be falling apart. New illusions about the coming of racial justice and old ones about the nature of the society, its political system, its role in the world, were laid punctured on all sides. The battle of Little Rock in 1957 had led only to the battle of Boston, twenty years later, and other battles still unfinished elsewhere. Whatever real gains lay in between remained largely obscured in the fog of the continuing war.

The changes that have affected blacks have been the most uneven of all but that does not mean they are as minimal, even negligible, as so many would now make them out to be. The entrenched and persisting legacies of the past drag at the process of change, hemming in every new "solution" with new problems of the most formidable kind. But the terms of the struggle and the grounds on which it is fought are enormously different now compared to what they were. A black Rip van Winkle who went to sleep in 1945 and woke up this year and looked around him would find much of his world gone and much of the new world quite unrecognizable. This would be truer if he were a middle-class black Rip van Winkle than if he were a member of the ghetto poor, but it would still be a discovery of great transformation at almost every level, much of it for the better—for example, the effects of restored voting rights on the political

landscape of the country—and a great deal of it so far for the worse—
the problems of employment and employability in the urban ghetto populations and especially the urban black youth caught in the grinding mill
of inherited deprivation and inadequate new opportunity. Dealing with
the pathologies created by this situation is one of the heaviest burdens
thrust upon the schools, called upon to cope somehow with problems
that the society has so far been unable to solve.

Blacks are, and rightly, so much at the center of this swirling change
process that much that has affected others goes somehow hardly noticed
anymore. What has not yet opened enough to blacks in this society in
these turbulent decades, has in fact opened wide to other groups in the
population previously subject to their own different measures of exclusion. It seems hardly remembered now even as notable that it was only
during these same years that the deeply embedded anti-Catholic biases of
Protestant America, with its accompanying systems of denigration, exclusion, and discrimination, lost effect and all but disappeared from the
public domains of the society. This change was symbolically heralded by
the election of the country's first Catholic president in 1960, an event
that also marked the ultimate inclusion at all levels of the common society of the Irish, barely two generations away from being the niggers of
Yankee Boston.

It now goes largely unremarked too that in this same thirty-year period, high barriers against Jews and Japanese-Americans and Chinese-
Americans came crumbling down, enabling them for the first time to
enter freely many spheres of life from which they had been excluded in
the past, in academia, the professions, politics, business, and industry.
Except for a few totally surrounded outposts of surviving old-fashioned
racial/religious bigotry, members of these groups now move unhindered
virtually everywhere in the society except to its political summits. Election of a Jewish or Japanese-American or Chinese-American president is
presumably still some way off, partly because of their small numbers,
partly because the change in their status and in the perceptions held of
them by the rest of the population remains fragile and insecure.

In this regard, at least, the speed of change has probably been swifter
for members of other still-hyphenated European-origin immigrant
groups of the last three generations, the largely Catholic Italian-Ameri-
can, Polish- and other Slav-American populations whose place in the
social scheme of the country has also radically changed in these years.
They often still carry with them the burdens of the past, but their mobility to all levels and in all directions in the society is no longer hampered,

as it was, by restriction and exclusion based on prejudice against their Catholicism or their other-European origins.

Indeed, if it did not stand bracketed and hemmed in by so much else that remains unresolved, the end of the more egregiously active forms of religious bigotry and discrimination in the American society, so largely achieved in these same decades, would surely stand out more notably than it does. This does not mean that all the old-style prejudices do not continue to exist—nothing ever quite disappears, everything coexists, only the measures change. It *does* mean that for almost all, if not quite all, practical purposes, these particular anti-Catholic and anti-Semitic prejudices can no longer dominate and determine the lives of the people at whom they are directed. They cannot be openly applied in the public domain as they once were. They have been driven back into the private domain of individuals. The old familiar American-as-apple-pie-Know Nothing-KKK variety of bigotry survives, but under severe legal constraints and broad public—if not equally broad private—disapproval. It will remain with us in its old forms, but under the impact of the changes of these decades, intra- and inter-group hostilities have for the most part moved into new arenas.

One most striking, and possibly the most important, effect of these events on American blacks in this time has been the progressive shedding of long-encrusted patterns of self-rejection imposed by generations of enforced inferiority. Again, these deeply embedded holdings have obviously not just dissolved and disappeared; again, it is the measure of them that changes. They have been powerfully countered in these years by a new and strong self-acceptance and self-assertion. A new generation of black Americans is growing up discovering and measuring themselves in new ways not yet at all clearly visible or sharply defined but vastly different from the self-images acquired by generations past. Much of this has to work itself out in the resolution of inherited circumstances and new problems, many of them forbiddingly formidable. Yet the change is there as an immensely positive force. Not a little of its essence is expressed in the new usage of the term *black* as a name to go by, a matter I have dealt with at some length elsewhere and too much of a subject to deal with briefly here beyond indicating it.

This strong black self-reassertion, rising sharply in the 1950s and 1960s, touched off what has sometimes been called an "ethnic revival." What may have begun in some places as "backlash" became a far more complex reawakening of ethnic consciousness among some members of many other groups in the American population. This remains a complicated happening that is still poorly reported and hazily seen. No one has yet adequately traced its extent or distinguished its sounds, sometimes loud, from its substance, sometimes meager, sometimes considerable. Its message, abbreviated here as simplified and amplified by the media is this: if it is beautiful to be black, Chicano, Puerto Rican, or Indian, then it is no less beautiful, nay, more beautiful to be Irish, Italian, Jewish, Polish, Ukrainian, Slovak, Greek, Armenian, or whatever your origins indicate that you can now be proud to be. Here again, a subject much too large for this small space.

There is so much about so much of it, moreover, that seems to me limited, questionable, and unpromising, that I want to be sure to put as strongly as I can what I see to be its most positive meaning. It suggests a new measure of healthy self-acceptance, more people of almost every kind coming to accept themselves for what they are. It suggests that they are shedding the feelings of relative inferiority generated by the old American pecking order with its placement of who is up and who is down, who high and who low, not by class or the money measure but by the ascribed status assigned to people by their race, color, religion, national origin.

If I am right about this—and it is a hunch supported by what has emerged for me from scores of interviews with many different people during the last three years—then it could be just possibly the most important single thing that has happened in our society in this time. If decently self-respectful self-acceptance is the beginning of good mental health, it could be another beginning of the making of a brave new American world. If this be wishful optimism, I want to make as much of it as I can. For its meaning depends on how "American" this new self-image comes to be, on how our sense of the "one" is coupled with our rediscovery of merit in the "many."

For ethnic group consciousness is not exactly the stuff of brotherly love, not even among the brothers themselves. It is not the stuff of humane coexistence with others who are different in the critical respects of physical characteristics, history and origins, language, religion, and nationality. Every basic group identity, as I undertook to show in some detail in *Idols of the Tribe* (Isaacs, 1977), has its built-in we-they syndrome. This has not often in history yielded to any doctrine or practice of tolerance, mutual respect, and friendly acceptance of such differences. Quite the contrary. It has had more to do with more people fearing, demeaning, rejecting, dominating, hating, killing more people than any other single cause since time began. The great American social experiment has not enjoyed any exemption; all the varieties of people who came to make up the American design brought to it all their matching varieties of virulent and violent mutual prejudices, their patterns of fear, rejection, antipathy, hatred. The resulting virulence and violence of bigotry in American life yields to none in depth and scope. But the uniqueness of the American happening lies in the fact that all these different people who came together in America also at the same time shared the experience of becoming something new, that is, *American.*

Just what being "American" means is a matter still being worked out in the process and it will probably continue that way indefinitely. But one thing seems possible to say about it: if being "American" finally gets to mean accepting the ethos of mutual respect and acceptance of differences among people, then the outcome will depend not on how we maintain our differences but on how "American" we become. Mutual respect and acceptance between and among different kinds of people can be achieved only when what they hold in common outweighs what holds them apart. This does *not* mean, as some tribunes of the "new ethnicity" idiotically keep insisting it means, that we all become *all* alike.

It is a cliché among ethnic revivalists that all those ethnic differences among Americans did not melt after all in that melting pot. This is summoned up as a Crushing Fact which they call upon all of us to face, accept, recognize. It compels us to revise whatever notions we might have had about what it means to be or become "American" and dispels illusions about the possibility of creating a more integrated American society.

For the purposes of this argument, the "melting pot" has to be visualized as a great vat into which all varieties of the American population were poured as they arrived, all intended to come out the other end like a string of frankfurters, each one stamped with a label bearing the likeness, say, of Elliot Richardson. Indeed, in some versions, this "melting pot" was used by the wicked Wasps of the Old Northeast precisely to boil away all the rich pure stuff of non-Waspness and cook up a great thin mess of pasty gruel-like second-class Waspness which became the substance of that hot dog, common American culture. This all took place in the American/dream/nightmare from which some of these rediscoverers of ethnicity see themselves as happily waking at last, looking with newly rubbed and cleared eyes on the beauties of their own non-Wasp heritages. Anyone who thinks this is parody should reexamine some of the literature of unmeltable ethnicity, white, black, brown, red.

The reality is that *all* group identities, especially all the American varieties, are made in melting pots and always have been ever since peoples and cultures began meeting and clashing and blending with one another. What is being produced in the American society by this process is not a second-class "Wasp" (a term, incidentally, added by its users in this context to the characteristic ethnic vocabulary that includes nigger, wop, kike, mick, spic, chink, honky). Nor is he a frankfurter-like or clone-like creature summoned up for this purpose out of interpretations of the Crevecoeur-Turner-Zangwill versions of melting pot "theory." He is, for better or worse, a one-class American who is made up of his various melded parts. These include the melded/changed survivals of his biological and cultural heritage in immensely varying measures depending on how much time and how many elements have gone into the melding. These elements include all that come from the experience of American life itself, all the effects of coming up, generation after generation, in a new and ever-changing culture.

This happened in one degree or another to all the varieties of northern European Protestant stock which made up the earlier "majority" of the new nation. It happened swiftly, in one to three generations, to the great masses who came a century or so later from eastern, central, and southern Europe and whose children in all their intermingled varieties may very well be by now the new "majority" of the population. It also happened in their degree to the blacks held in thrall throughout this time at the bottom of the society. They became biologically as well as culturally removed from their African origins and became "American" to an extent which many only discovered, some to their dismay, when they came back into contact in recent years with descendants of their African forebears. They had become Afro-*Americans*, something very different from Africans despite all that they still held in common. Similarly, Italian Americans have discovered that they are just that, Italian-*Americans*, not Italians, Japanese-*Americans*, not Japanese, and so on. American Jews in Israel have had the same experience. The distinctivenesses are there, the feelings about heritages are there, and, if I am right and not merely wishful about what is happening in our society now, it is the quality of these feelings that has been changing, feelings of low status, inferiority and shame about antecedents giving way to some new measure of prideful and more realistic acceptance. I take this as the beginning of a new shaping, a new maturing of the group identity called *American*.

The question becomes one of the balance and weight of our melded parts. Some prophets and tribunes of the "new ethnicity" argue that the "American" identity fails to meet the deepest needs of people, that these are met by the ancestral or inherited identities which must be restored as the organizing core of existence, the key to the making of the better life. There is nothing at all to keep this proposition from being put to the test that is itself peculiarly "American." For by the ethos that we want to prevail, any person or any group that wants to organize the inner core of life around any such identification, racial, religious, even national, is utterly free to do so and to carry it as far as its own vitality and capacity can take it *within its own private domain*. It is that individual's business, that group's business, not the public's business. Such private domains exist in many forms. Such are the churches and other religious institutions, whose tax-exempt status *is* an encroachment on the public purse which has enjoyed the common consent, or at least the absence of serious objection. Such also—and without any such encroachment—is the very large network of "nationality" groups established by many immigrant groups, including social clubs and associations, mutual aid societies, a foreign language press—there were still 350 foreign language publications by fairly recent count—along with distinctive nationality churches of various persuasions and languages.

But we come in this matter to a wide range of scales and levels of apartness, some of them spilling over from the limits of private choice and association into the public sphere, especially the political sphere. In the working of the American political system, especially at the local and state levels, nationality groups became interest groups and pressure groups, using the local political process as leverage to achieve greater power and mobility. The "balanced ticket" with all its pulls and pushes and pluses and minuses has long been a fixture of the American political scene, serving both as a strongly divisive force in community and political life and as a way for both groups and individuals to move up and out into the larger common arena where competition for place gets to be based on broader identifications and capacities. The rise of the Kennedys out of Irish Boston is of course the classic case. The Muskies, Inouyes, Brookes, Marshalls, Pastores, Rodinos, Siricas, Brademases, Javitzes, and Ribicoffs, and their similars all mark the many places where the ethnic is giving way to national concern and identification in what could still be, one doggedly hopes, the new world still a'coming. In cities across the country, on the other hand, the new racial ethnic assertion is reflected now in tensions and confrontations sharper perhaps than they have ever been. It is a condition from which there will be no discharge as long as the accumulating crises of urban life go unresolved. Ethnic apartness and political separation, indeed apartheid, is what the white segregationists were still practicing and defending only yesterday. In new forms created by the new circumstances, the same or similar kinds of separateness could appear. This too could be the shape of some things to come.

In quite other ways, ethnic apartness in the form of political separation has been and still is part of the scene. The bitter experience of exclusion and rejection led to the various Back-to-Africa and other migration or separatist movements among blacks across the many years. It is still the program of small black nationalist groups who do not believe there is any tolerable future for blacks in the American society. It is the option of some radical Chicanos who want a separate Chicano state of their own, the Puerto Rican independistas, and in their unique historical context, some Indian groups. All such movements have been most characteristically marginal, tiny, or small minorities within their own constituencies. Groups of quite other kinds, like the Amish, have also, out of their own strong sense of separateness and distinctiveness, sought to remain in their own enclaves, however small.

More generally and more pragmatically, however, most of our current ethnic revivalists who want to maintain their ancestral identities want to do so in some continuing form within the American system. As I have already remarked, there is wide latitude inherent in the system for doing so. Unlike the older immigrant-nationality groups who always considered this strictly their own business, however, many of the current revivalists explicitly or implicitly seek to reshape and reorganize the system itself. They want not only to pursue their own thing in a permissive and tolerant setting. They want recognition and public support of their separatenesses. In effect, they want their separatenesses to be incorporated into the legal and political structure, to have them become part of the public domain. The vision of the society that goes with this view is often pictured as a "mosaic" whose multihued pieces lie sharply separate but snugly together to form a beauteous—and a bounteous—American whole.

This is astigmatic ethnic vision. Surviving racial/ethnic ghettos and enclaves notwithstanding, the American reality does *not* resemble a mosaic. It looks much more like a Jackson Pollock painting, its great swirls and blurs of lines and colors totally entwined, mixed, and mutually absorbed, each bit in its own way distinct but inseparable from the whole. This is the kind of image that far more truly reflects all those millions of Americans who can no longer single out any specific national origin for themselves. It also describes, for that matter, most of those millions who do name some one ancestral background but who do not even remotely yield up thereby their primary sense of identity as "Americans." The same holds true, by all the evidence, of the great majority of the second- and third-generation descendants of our most recent European immigrant stocks, who all together now make up nearly another half of the total population. Because he knows this so well, Andrew Greeley, one of the most prolific and expressive among the new ethnic tribunes who speak of an American mosaic, usually likes to say that he means a mosaic "with permeable borders." It is only at the darkest end of the color spectrum where despite all the mixing, sizable pieces of the design still stand more apart than folded into it. As between all extremes in human culture, this bridging is the most difficult to achieve. It is in this that the past American failure has been greatest and the new challenge to its future the most demanding.

The ethnic-group-centered vision of society—as opposed to the individual-centered ethos of the American system—has its antecedents in the nationality-based societies of the old Hapsburg and Romanov empires, essentially preserved as such now in the Communist power system which succeeded them. It also has a not-too-distant cousin in the millet system of the old Ottoman empire. Under these systems the many different segments of the various populations, usually but not always living in their own territory or enclaves, were sorted out by their racial, ethnic, and religious origins, assigned some limited autonomy in their own local affairs, mainly enforcement of their own religious codes. They remained in all other matters subject to the overarching absolute power of the emperor, sultan, or now more absolute than any, the Communist politbureau at the center. In these societies each person acquires the advantages or disadvantages attached to the identity stamped on his face or in his passport. The pecking order range was wide in the old empires; it is certainly not less wide in the Communist states. As we move farther along the spectrum we come to systems where the gulf is widest of all, for example, the Southern African apartheid system with its rigid racial classifications and distributions of power and powerlessness, and finally the Nüremberg law system, with *its* variety of grandfather/grandmother clauses to determine not only who gets what but who lives and who dies.

The nationality-system models have their own possible relevance for postcolonial states with multiethnic populations rent by deep and ancient divisions. They are reappearing in Western Europe, where Britain is feeling new stresses in its old parts, as in Spain. It is the explosive breakup of two such nationality/religious systems of government that we have been witnessing in Ulster and Lebanon. Every country in the Communist world suffers some of its worst internal political strains because of nationality divisions. The collision between Communist Vietnamese and Communist Cambodians simply illustrates again, like the Sino-Soviet conflict, how little the cement of the Communist ideology can do to pull together ethnic/national cleavages of such depth and strength.

In the American society the chance of a different outcome exists uniquely because instead of remaining "Vietnamese" and "Cambodian", "Hausa" or "Ibo," "Basque" or "Scots," "Serb" or "Croat," we have all been becoming "American." I suppose one way of putting the matter would be to say we are engaged in a test to see whether the "American" melding that took place in that famous pot of ours has turned out something more durable than anything produced by any other formula for holding different kinds of people together in a common order in which they all can live. The reason it is stronger is that all political systems based on race/tribe/nationality are in total contradiction with the fundamental concept on which the American society is trying to base itself, namely, popular sovereignty resting not on "groups" but on the franchise of individual citizens, accountable and replaceable government, and the effective guarantee of the same political, legal, and human rights to *all* citizens regardless of race, creed, national origin, and now also, sex. This is the ethos which generations of people of many kinds have struggled to make practice instead of preachment. This struggle has begun in our own years to give greater promise of coming into its own. The question is how we keep moving in the direction we want to go. This is not only a means question, it is an ends question too: do we get to where we want to go by traveling in the opposite direction?

Ironically enough, the main push to give new ethnic shapes to our system is coming not from any generalized ethnic "movement"—the "new ethnicity" is much too diffuse, confused, and unfocused for that. It is coming rather from acts of the government itself, laws, court decisions, and administrative fiats of the bureaucracy. These are having the effect of reclassifying people in arbitrary racial and national-origin categories for purposes of receiving or not receiving assorted sets of benefits, admissions, selections, funding, employment. And this is taking place, with the most "benign" intentions, as part of the effort to enforce the new civil rights dispensation which was aimed to remove these distinctions from all parts of the public domain.

These actions all have to do with complex, difficult, and often intractable problems to which none of us can pretend to have very good answers at this time, all the more especially since this is a time not of adequate economic growth but of contraction in the society, a time of new limits, not expanding opportunities.

Still, some questions need asking. Some examples:

• Are arbitrarily fixed categories by race and national origin currently restored as a basis for legal and official action more acceptable—indeed any more *legal* now—because they are used now for "benign" purposes and not malevolently, as in the past?

• Does effective affirmative action to correct past inequities depend, as so many now would have it depend, on the application of racial quota systems throughout the society? If so, where does this lead, legally and in everyday life, as group after group rushes to assert its particular "groupiness" and demand its place in the process?

• Who chooses the categories, and on what basis? Who decides, and on what basis, who belongs to what "race"?

• What definition of "race" governs HEW enforcement action? For purposes of the laws and civil rights enforcement, what does "Hispanic" mean? (Previous uses of "Spanish," "Spanish-speaking," "Spanish-surnamed," all ended in remarkably compounded confusion.) What does "Oriental" mean? Does "Native American" mean *only* the person descended or claiming to descend from earlier Asian immigrants to North America, and if so, what is everyone else? How is anyone's membership in any of these categories to be determined when disputes arise? (We have already had the scene of teachers filing up to "black" boxes and "white" boxes to get their school assignments. We have already seen school officials, in a disputed transfer case, set up *"visual inspection"* boards to decide who is black and who not. Where will *this* lead us?)

• HEW's selection of five deserving categories includes women (who seem to me to be quite something else again, the problem of women and their deprivations and their rights cutting across all other groups). But then how about others who can make *their* case for being deserving too? In 1979, for example, effective lobbying by ethnic professionals produced passage of an amendment to the Civil Rights Commission authorization act to include in its coverage "Americans who are members of eastern- and southern-European ethnic groups." Members of a group of Chassidic Jews in New York tried, less successfully, to get themselves included among the victims of discrimination especially favored by the Small Business Administration. The matter of vocabulary in this process is not trivial. Just what, for example, does "minority" now mean? It is coming to be used as a singular noun to describe individuals who belong, or claim to belong, to this or that "minority." But just what single, not to say singular, person is not a "minority" and what narrowly defined "group" is not a "minority" in American society?

• What can raise ethnic consciousness higher and faster than handing out either advantages or disadvantages by race and origin? How is it proposed to deal with the new collisions, confrontations, and general hostility that this brings about? Consider the black-Jewish and black-Puerto Rican tensions in New York, the black-Chicano tensions in Los Angeles, the Irish-black-Italian-Polish-Puerto Rican-you-name-it tensions in Chicago, the Chicano-Puerto Rican-Cuban-Dominican-all-other-Latin tensions *wherever* these "Hispanics" meet? Consider the tensions and angers aroused among all who see themselves as having been down there with everyone else at the bottom of the pecking order and suddenly, as *they* see it, have *their* chances for mobility snatched away. ("We Italians were just reaching the point where we could pass the principal's exams and get those jobs," said a bitterly angry Italian politician in New Jersey, "we played by the rules and just when we can win at last, they change the game and appoint by color." Etc., etc., etc.)

• In the matter of ethnic heritage studies, what is the responsibility of schools maintained by everyone's taxes? What is the balance to be struck between what is common to all and what is particular to some? In dealing with the many particulars, who decides, and on what basis, *whose* version of any particular heritage is to be studied? How far can any such program be carried beyond inclusive and reasonably objective treatments provided to all for the benefit and knowledge of all? What justification is there for spending public funds on the active promotion of any single brand of any particular ethnic identification among its own presumed communicants? What is the difference between such consciousness raising and religious instruction? (A small but rich experience in the doling out of public funds for ethnic heritage studies was accumulated in 1975-76 by the HEW bureau allocating the federal money, fortunately a small sum, appropriated to this end. The harried and astounded bureaucrats, every one of them "benign" to his fingertips, discovered just how non-uniform and nonhomogeneous, and how internally torn and divided virtually every so-called ethnic group actually is. They tried to establish a "multiethnic" norm—as opposed to "monoethnic"—for their grants. Instead they found themselves caught in crossfire between "old" nationality groups and "new" ones, for instance, between secular Jewish scholars and religious scholarly Jews.)

• What are the implications in this context of bilingual teaching programs as they have developed with heavy federal funding since 1968? How have they fared in serving the nominal "transitional" purpose for which they were created and to what extent have they become subject to the quite different notion of "culture maintenance"?

There are more such questions and their substance could be almost indefinitely expanded upon. How far, they all ask, how far are we prepared to go in using racialist means (the difference between "racialist" and "racist" is something like the difference between "stubborn" and "persevering") to achieve what we hope will be "benign" ends? Racism and tyranny have always claimed benign, even divine, sanctions for themselves and their purposes. Can we get only a "little" pregnant now with more of same, trusting that circumstances—to say nothing of our indubitable virtue—will enable us to have a "safe" abortion before it is too late?

The argument here is not that we have been putting too much emphasis on the "many" but too little on the "one." The balance needs redressing. The agreed purpose is, presumably, the creation of a more open society. What do we mean by it? It may sound now like questing after the Holy Grail or building the City of God, or maybe just waiting still for Godot, but it has to continue to be remembered that the goal of the civil rights struggle across more than a century was something called *integration*. No one was ever sure, or still can be, just what it meant. But it clearly meant more than desegregation. *Brown*, remember, had something of the quality of a second coming: the victors really believed for an exhilarating moment that this was the beginning of the end of the systematic exclusions of the postslavery century and the beginning of a new color-blind inclusion of blacks, and by extension of *everyone*, in the exercise of rights and opportunities that had always in theory in America been commonly available to all. It was the coming of a second chance to begin building the kind of society the founding fathers said they were creating when it all began. It has become fashionable to say—wearily or with scorn—that this was all too dreamy, too American dreamy, too Martin

Luther King dreamy. But this was where it was and where—with whatever better-educated more realistic expectations—it still has to be. If *integration* remains the goal, then all our best effort has to bear most heavily on defining and strengthening what we have in common, not on all that keeps us apart.

I keep remembering what William Morris once wrote: "Men fight and lose the battle, and the thing they fought for comes about in spite of their defeat and when it comes it turns out to be not what they meant, and other men have to fight for what they meant, under another name." Generations of Americans have been fighting for a society offering rights to all *regardless of* race, creed, or national origin. If what we get instead is a society that offers rights *according to* race, creed, or national origin, it will not be what we meant at all, not what we meant at all, and others will have to fight for what we meant, perhaps in some other place, under some other name.

Reference

Isaacs, Harold. 1977. *Idols of the Tribe: Group Identity and Political Change.* New York: Harper & Row.

6   The Demographic Basis
of Urban Educational Reform

CHARLES V. WILLIE

Two theoretical positions are generally accepted as predictive of the future of urban educational reform in the United States. One theory holds that urban school desegregation will be severely limited, especially in large cities, because not enough whites will be left to desegregate their public-school systems. The other states that urban schools are likely to experience an "exceedingly rapid rise in the proportion of 'high cost' disadvantaged students and a corresponding drop in overall educational performance," since "the central cities are increasingly becoming the domain of the poor and the stable working class" (Wilson, 1978, pp. 114, 115).

It is probably a coincidence that these theories have been set forth by two sociologists both affiliated with the University of Chicago. James Coleman, in a deposition submitted to the Dallas division of the U.S. district court, said, "Based on my research, it is my opinion that extensive desegregation of schools within larger central cities has two effects: first, by reassignment of children within the district, it has a direct and immediate effect in eliminating predominantly black schools. Second, it increases the loss of white children from the district, and as a consequence, it has the long-term effect of re-establishing predominantly black schools in the central city" (quoted in Willie, 1978, p. 28). William Wilson said, "The racial struggle for power and privilege in the central city is essentially a struggle between the have-nots." He characterized "the relatively poorly trained blacks of the inner city" as being "locked in the low-wage sector" with "inferior ghetto schools" (Wilson, 1978, pp. 116, 121).

It is my contention that there are enough whites in central cities now, and there will be in the future, to achieve meaningful desegregation of their public-school systems. I believe, furthermore, that city populations are diversified, do not today consist overwhelmingly of poor people, and are unlikely to be so constituted in the future. These contentions are supported by the analysis that follows.

Definition of Desegregation

A definition of school desegregation is an appropriate beginning; it has a great deal to do with how population data are interpreted. In the 1960s the Syracuse, New York, school district transferred approximately sixty black children from an inner-city elementary school with a predominantly black student body to a predominantly white elementary school in a middle-class neighborhood. The president of the school board, who was white, Protestant, and a captain of industry, said the desegregation program was successful. However, the same individual labeled as a failure a program launched the following year to desegregate a predominantly black inner-city school, because only sixty-eight white children volunteered to transfer to the thousand-pupil school. The board had hoped seven hundred white children would voluntarily transfer; if this had occurred, the school board officer stated, the program would have been classified as a successful desegregation experience. Because of the small number of whites who volunteered, this desegregation program was canceled.

Elsewhere, I have summarized the meaning of this experience: "The numbers involved in the two programs were about the same, but the perspective of the board president varied according to the situation . . . A black student who was a minority in a white setting was acceptable; but a white student who would be a minority in a black setting was not acceptable" (Willie, 1978, pp. 8-9). The customary definition of desegregation is bringing a black minority into the presence of a white majority. Actually, desegregation is possible with whites or any other racial population as the minority.

Desegregated education brings together people from different populations for the purpose of exchanging knowledge and understanding. The nature of the exchange depends in part upon the social location of both parties. Majority status and minority status are significant locations in American society. This Syracuse experience denied whites the opportunity of obtaining the knowledge and understanding associated with a minority status when the desegregation program was canceled because blacks would outnumber whites. Most discussions of school desegregation assume that majority-white student bodies are the most appropriate arrangements, as they are the customary arrangements. That is *not* the assumption of this chapter. Effective urban school desegregation programs are possible with black, brown, or white students as the majority.

Size of Population and Desegregation

The claim that the white population in central cities is too small to desegregate public schools is summarized by Harry Gottlieb, a specialist in housing and finance: "in growing numbers of cities, there are not only too few whites to achieve meaningful racial desegregation; often there are also not enough economically advantaged people to achieve meaningful economic desegregation" (Gottlieb, 1976, p. 158). While this opinion has been repeated often enough to become conventional wisdom, it is entirely at odds with the facts. Let me emphasize this point. Claims that the central cities in the United States have become black ghettos, devoid of whites, are incorrect. Of the 184.8 million whites in the United States 24 percent, or 44.5 million, lived in central cities in 1978. While the proportion of blacks in central cities (55 percent) was twice as large as the proportion of white city dwellers, the black proportion represented only 13.7 million people. Thus whites outnumbered blacks 3 to 1 in central cities. There are plenty of whites to go around for school desegregation or any other purpose.

It is true that whites are not an overwhelming majority in all central cities as they once were and as they now are in the suburbs. In most central cities, however, they still are a majority. Even though city whites have dwindled to a relatively small majority and must adapt to their new numerical situation, no real change has occurred in their status as the majority in most American cities.

Even in the few cities where blacks are a majority, enough whites remain to desegregate the public-school systems. When I testified in the Dallas school desegregation case in the mid-1970s, the attorney for the majority-white school board (the defendant) asked me if there was not a danger that Dallas would become like Atlanta if court-ordered school desegregation was implemented. Before answering, I asked the attorney to define Atlanta's problem and was informed that the student body of that public-school system was more than 80 percent black. I replied that this was of no consequence so far as education was concerned, that I had known of several good public-school systems that were 80 percent or more white. The point is that good public-educational systems may be majority black, brown, or white if they are unitary systems in which resources are equitably distributed among all schools.

A desegregated school is one in which a majority is educated in the presence of a minority or minorities of different backgrounds and experiences. A unitary school system is one in which there is equal access to educational opportunities for both majority and minority, and equitable distribution of educational resources. A public-school system that is predominantly black, brown, or white can be a unitary and desegregated system. This is what the Constitution requires; it does not require whites to be a majority; it does not prohibit whites from experiencing minority status. Enough whites are present to desegregate the urban school systems of this nation, if it is not necessary for whites always to be the majority. Actually, in most cities there are enough whites to permit desegregated school systems in which whites are and will continue to be the majority. It may be easier to design desegregation plans that encompass total metropolitan areas, but it is also possible to limit desegregation plans to central cities.

Socioeconomic Status of City Residents

The claims that central cities have become settings of the poor and that the affluent, by and large, have escaped to the suburbs also are in error. Wilson has observed the increasing black population in cities and assumes that the blacks are poor. He quotes from *Urban Education* by Hummel and Nagle, who state that cities have lost "valuable human capital to the suburbs"—meaning middle-class whites; then Wilson asserts that "the mounting financial problems of urban schools seem to go hand in hand with their rapidly changing racial composition" (Wilson, 1978, pp. 114-115). Again, the facts do not support these assertions.

In 1978, approximately six out of every ten white families in the suburbs had annual incomes above the national median; in the central cities the figure was approximately five out of ten. Thus, a high proportion of city and suburban whites were affluent. While blacks in central cities and elsewhere continued to experience racial discrimination and consequently were disadvantaged economically, they still were not poverty-stricken. In fact, nearly three out of every ten urban black families in 1978 had an annual income that was above the national median; seven out of every ten nationwide were above the official poverty line. Central cities are far from being ghettos of the black poor.

It is true that the proportion of poor people in central cities is larger than the proportion of poor people in the suburbs. But since the number of white poor in the city is one-third larger than the number of black poor, it is inappropriate to characterize the central cities of America as ghettos of poor black people. Most people in cities are *not* poor. While whites constitute the largest number of poor people in central cities, only one out of every ten whites families has an income that is below the official poverty line. The proportion of blacks at this low-income level, although nearly three times greater, still represents less than three out of ten black families.

To recapitulate, there are several facts it is important to remember when discussing the future of urban education and school desegregation: (1) whites outnumber blacks 3 to 1 in central-city populations; (2) most people in city populations, blacks as well as whites, are not poor; (3) among the poor in cities, whites outnumber blacks 3 to 1. Enough whites, then, are available in central cities to achieve meaningful school desegregation and most cities, in terms of the socioeconomic status of their residents, are capable of financing desegregated, unitary school systems (although additional help may be needed from nonlocal sources).

Regional Location of Future Educational Reform Movements

The future is likely to bring increased efforts in all parts of the nation to achieve unitary school systems that provide equal access for minority and majority populations and equitable distribution of educational resources. This movement, initiated in the South, has and will continue to spread to the North and West because of the changing characteristics of the black population in cities of those regions. The demographic phenomenon, incidentally, that will enable blacks to marshal the power to press for reform in urban educational systems would not exist if minorities were randomly distributed throughout the nation.

Black people are no longer concentrated in a single region (about half now live in the South and half reside elsewhere in the nation). However, the black population is concentrated in cities. About three-fifths of all blacks live in central cities of metropolitan areas. The suburbs contain slightly less than one-fifth of all blacks. But, according to Harold Rose, "the most active suburban growth communities [for blacks] are spatial extensions of central city ghettoes" (Rose, 1976, p. 263).

In 1968 the *Report of the National Advisory Commission on Civil Disorders* (Kerner Report) stated that "thousands of Negro families have attained incomes, living standards and cultural levels matching or surpassing those of whites . . . yet most Negro families have remained primarily within predominantly Negro neighborhoods, primarily because they have been effectively excluded from white residential areas'' (National Advisory Commission, 1968, p. 44). The residential segregation of blacks is more prevalent than that of any other minority group. Elaborating on the theme that the segregation of blacks is not caused solely by income, the commission analyzed fifteen representative cities and found that ''white upper- and middle-income households are far more segregated from Negro upper- and middle-income households than from white lower-income households'' (p. 247). Dealing with the same theme, Karl and Alma Taeuber came to this conclusion: ''The net effect of economic factors in explaining residential segregation is slight . . . Economic differentials diminished, but residential segregation persists'' (Taeuber and Taeuber, 1969, p. 94).

If blacks were dispersed throughout the nation without discrimination, they would constitute not more than 11 percent of the total population in any locality. Under these conditions their relative strength in numbers would be below the critical mass of approximately one-fifth that is necessary to mount effective campaigns for educational reform against community institutions practicing racial segregation and discrimination. By limiting blacks largely to central cities and thereby concentrating their numbers, whites have given this racial-minority group more power than it would otherwise have. Indeed, by controlling a few cities, urban blacks have obtained a disproportionate amount of power in this country. With that power they are now shaking the foundations of the nation, demanding reform in public education and other human services.

I have a theory about the circumstances and conditions associated with the increasing power of subdominant populations to press for institutional reform: a subdominant population is likely to intensify its press for affirmative action with reference to equal access and equitable distribution of community resources when it grows in numbers from a small minority to a large minority, and when it changes socioeconomically from a homogeneous to a heterogeneous population. Essentially, the size of a subdominant population and its socioeconomic differentiation are interrelated phenomena that determine the pattern of its press for social action.

An assertion by William Robert Miller gives an appropriate perspective. He feels that the most remarkable achievement of Martin Luther King, Jr., was his success in making middle-class blacks the backbone of a crusade for human dignity (Miller, 1968, p. 308). The group most likely to press for social change in education and in other institutional systems is a large minority that comprises people of differentiated status positions. During the 1950s blacks were sufficiently differentiated into middle-class and other status groups to do this.

The history of social action by blacks in this nation has proceeded in accordance with this theory. A century and a half ago the relative size of the black population was larger than it is today; in 1820 nearly one of every five people (18.4 percent) was black. Yet no social movement toward desegregation and reform was initiated by blacks because this relatively large minority was more or less undifferentiated; most blacks were slaves. Effective social action is possible only when a group has some members who are free to plan and to deal with matters that go beyond the immediate requirements for personal survival. The undifferentiated, relatively large minority of blacks during the age of slavery was unable to mount a movement for reform.

When King began his work in the South, one-fifth of the population in that region was black and at least one of every three southern blacks was above the poverty line. This proportion, beyond the clutches of daily worry about minimum physical survival, apparently was sufficiently great to spark and sustain a revolutionary movement for reform—to become its backbone. This demographic fact is the reason the civil rights movement started in the South when it did.

The northern population of blacks has always been more differentiated in terms of socioeconomic status. As early as 1960 two-thirds of the blacks in the North were above the poverty line, a proportion that would appear to be sufficient to sustain a reform movement. However, the relative size of the black population in the North was small, only 7 percent of the total number of northerners. The socioeconomic resources may have been sufficient, but the critical mass was not. With the containment of blacks in central cities of the North because of racial discrimination, their proportion of the urban population in several cities has increased to one-fifth and higher, providing them with the critical mass and the socioeconomic differentiation to initiate effective movements for educational and other institutional changes. As reform efforts in education, particularly those involving school desegregation, have developed in the North, they have originated in those cities with relatively large black populations of diversified socioeconomic status. Because residential containment of racial minorities in central cities in the North and West does not appear to be leveling off and because these areas have a sufficient number of middle-class minority people who tend to serve as the backbone of reform movements, I predict that the social movement among blacks and Hispanics with reference to educational reform and other human services will intensify. Reform efforts will continue as long as residential discrimination results in the containment and concentration of racial minorities.

Minority and Majority Responsibility for Social Action

Ultimately every group must accept responsibility for the circumstances and conditions under which it lives. The probability is high that a minority group (or any population that is subdominant in terms of power) will continue to suffer the oppression of inequity and blocked opportunities as long as it continues to cooperate in its own oppression. In colloquial terminology: they'll do it to you as long as you let them.

In most instances resistance and reform movements are initiated by the oppressed and not by the oppressors, by those with less power and not by those with more. For this reason we should study the mood of the minorities and the subdominant peoples for some indication of future reform of urban education. Among most scholars in this field, investigation and analysis tend to be limited to the interests and activities of the majority or those in power. For example, Daniel Patrick Moynihan's policy study of community action in the war on poverty, *Maximum Feasible Misunderstanding*, contains not a single reference to Martin Luther King, Jr. It is as if the demonstrations during the 1950s and 1960s had had no effect, which, of course, is patently untrue. Moynihan discusses the Johnson administration's war on poverty as if it had been concocted out of the minds of university professors and as if the main issue were a contest between Columbia and Harvard professors about the appropriate way to fight the war (Willie, 1978, p. 35). In like manner, too, many studies of urban education concentrate on the actions and reactions of whites when it is the blacks who initiated the shaking of the foundations of this nation over segregated education.

Despite all I have said about minorities, the majority also plays a crucial role in social movements; by its actions, minorities are driven to reactions. If the racial oppression in the South had not been as brutal as it was (and had not eradicated opportunities to earn a decent living), blacks would not have fled in droves to the North, raising their numbers there to the critical mass sufficient to sustain a reform movement. If racial discrimination by residential area had not been practiced in the North, blacks and other racial minorities would have randomly distributed themselves throughout the region and would not have concentrated in cities, thereby obtaining a disproportionate amount of power to initiate change in urban institutions. That the reform movement in urban educa-

tion has expanded from the South to the North, and will surface elsewhere in this nation in the future, is the result of two demographic factors, concentration and differentiation among minorities. Since, of
course, the concentration of minorities in the central cities of metropolitan areas derives largely from the actions of the majority, the majority
has only itself to blame for the revolution in urban education, initiated
by minorities, that has come upon us.

Goals of Educational Reform

I predict that desegregated public education in the future will emphasize
the integration of people of different social classes as well as races. Along
with the new pluralistic populations in schools will come new educational
goals that emphasize *truth* and *honesty*, as well as proficiency in communication and calculation. These changes will occur as the minorities of
this nation, whoever they may be, continue to practice the grand tradition of serving as creative dissenters by insisting that the nation live up to
its basic constitutional doctrine of freedom and justice for all. A merito-
cratic educational system, such as we have now, considers calculating
and communicating skills to be very important outcomes of an education. In fact, two of America's foremost educators, David Riesman and
Christopher Jencks, declared in 1968 that "the best single measure overall" of academic competence is the "verbal aptitude test" (Riesman and
Jencks, 1968). Most racial minorities would disagree.

   The liberation and reform of public education by the school desegregation court cases initiated by minorities is reminiscent of the way that
societies have been renewed and regenerated in the past. Commenting on
this role of minorities, Richard Korn has reminded us of the wisdom of
Polybius. Centuries ago (in *The Histories, Book 57*) Polybius said,
"When a new generation arises and the democracy falls into the hands of
the grandchildren of its founders, they have become so accustomed to
freedom and equality that they no longer value them and begin to aim at
preeminence . . ." Korn's interpretation of this statement is that "the in-
heritors of greatness waste the heritage . . . The passive beneficiaries of
liberty become oppressive." Then Korn asks, "Who . . . is left to keep
the flame alive—whence comes the regeneration?" His answer, which
also is my answer, is this: regeneration of the system tends to come from
the oppressed. Said Korn, "Where is the light more cherished than in the
darkness? And this, perhaps, is the complacent bigot's most bitter purga-
tive: in the end he can be saved only by those who survived the worst he
could do to them—his victims" (Korn, 1968, pp. 195-196).

In the future, the educational goals of urban desegregated schools will be changed radically to accommodate the goals of the parents of racial-minority children who rank honesty and truthfulness as important skills to learn. Desegregated schools with black and brown as well as white students will have to adapt to the needs of their new clients. And the education of all will prosper.

References

Gottlieb, Harry. 1976. The ultimate solution: desegregated housing. In *School Desegregation*, ed. Florence Hamlish Levinsohn and Benjamin Drake Wright. Chicago: University of Chicago Press.

Korn, Richard R. 1968. *Juvenile Delinquency*. New York: Thomas Y. Crowell.

Miller, William Robert. 1968. *Martin Luther King, Jr.* New York: Avon Books.

Moynihan, Daniel P. 1969. *Maximum Feasible Misunderstanding*. New York: Free Press.

National Advisory Commission on Civil Disorders. 1968. *Report*. New York: Bantam Books.

Riesman, David, and Christopher Jencks. 1968. *The Academic Revolution*. Chicago: University of Chicago Press.

Rose, Harold M. 1976. *Black Suburbanization*. Cambridge, Massachusetts: Ballinger.

Taeuber, Karl E., and Alma F. Taeuber. 1969. *Negroes in Cities*. New York: Atheneum.

Willie, Charles V. 1978. *The Sociology of Urban Education: Desegregation and Integration*. Lexington, Massachusetts: Lexington Books of D. C. Heath.

Wilson, William J. 1978. *The Declining Significance of Race*. Chicago: University of Chicago Press.

7   Race and the Suburbs

NATHAN GLAZER

One of the solutions prescribed freely for attaining school desegregation is "Integrate housing." If blacks and whites lived in the same neighborhood, the argument runs, the neighborhood school would be an integrated school, one that would not require busing and would not therefore arouse antagonism by breaking up what is seen to be the normal pattern of public-school assignment in the United States. So the question arises, why isn't housing more integrated in the United States, and what can we do to make it more integrated?

There is no question that one of the most striking embarrassments and failures of American society is the distribution of blacks and whites within metropolitan areas. The overall picture is familiar: the suburbs are overwhelmingly white; the central cities have far more than the national proportion of black. And if our common aim is an integrated society—integrated in its schools, its work, its residence, its armed forces, its international representation, its culture—clearly the failure of integration in residence, and consequently in residentially based public schools, is the great exception to what I think is an overall success. While the Kerner Commission report in 1968 spoke of the danger of two societies—one white, one black—in most fields we have put that specter behind us. Workplaces are more and more integrated, up to the highest levels. Government is more and more integrated, up to the highest levels. But residence remains separated, most strikingly between suburb and central city, but strikingly also *within* suburbs and central cities.

Sociologists have been charting the degree of segregation for some time, generally by use of a measure known as the segregation index, which tells us what proportion of one race or the other would have to move to give us an even distribution of the races within cities and metropolitan areas. There are good reasons to have expected a reduction in segregation in recent years. In 1968 discrimination by race, religion, and national origin was barred in both ownership and rental of housing. Government-subsidized housing—which has had a checkered career in the last decade or so—not only bans discrimination but requires some "affirmative" effort, in location and in rental and sales efforts, to get a social mix. Attitudes have improved greatly: in 1956, 46 percent of whites said they would object if a Negro with the same income and education moved into their block; by the late 1960s, the figure was down to 21 percent.

There have also been improvements in the economic position of blacks. There are increasing numbers of blacks of higher education and stable family patterns. Indeed, young black families that comprise both a husband and a wife now have incomes quite close to the national average. Certainly there are enough blacks of respectable income to permit a much higher level of integration than we actually find. Only about 5 percent of blacks live in suburbs, a figure that has not changed in decades, even though the *number* of blacks living in suburbs has increased. If we look into the matter in detail, we find that much of the black suburban population is concentrated in predominantly black residential enclaves. Even that 5 percent of blacks in suburbs, which is one-half the proportion of blacks in the country as a whole, suggests a much higher degree of integration than actually exists.

A recent study by Ann B. Schnare (1978) of the Urban Institute provides some rather sad illumination of this question. She has analyzed the distribution of blacks and whites in metropolitan areas by census tracts (a tract holds on the average 4,000 people). In 1970, 71 percent of blacks lived in tracts that were more than 50 percent black, 38 percent in tracts that were more than 90 percent black. The concentration had become slightly more extreme between 1960 and 1970, and it is hard to believe that there has been much improvement since 1970. The West is the most integrated region, the Northeast next. North Central and South are rather similar on this measure, but segregation is even greater in the North Central region, where almost half of blacks lived in tracts that were more than 90 percent black, than in the South. No measure is perfect, of course. Perhaps the reason the South shows less segregation than the North Central region is that the South still has large pockets of rural blacks in newly suburban areas that were once rural. But the overall fact is clear: Despite changes in law, in attitudes, and in income and education of blacks, segregation remains remarkably high, and by some measures (without going into the complex details of how we measure integration) has increased.

There are three major explanations for the pattern of residential segregation.

(a) Economic. Blacks, who on the average have a household income three-fifths that of whites, simply cannot afford to live in many of the more desirable neighborhoods and therefore must be concentrated in poorer neighborhoods.

(b) Discrimination. Owners of rental housing, real estate agents, developers and builders, and individual owners all discriminate. They maintain areas as all white, or, if blacks do begin to move in, by their actions rapidly turn it to all black.

(c) Preference. Most groups (racial and ethnic) prefer to live among their own kind. While this may look like and have the same effects as prejudice, it really is different. For one thing, it may affect blacks in the same way as whites. For another, the housing decision is not one based on prejudice against a specific group—it may not be, for example, to avoid blacks as such, but rather to select a neighborhood that is more than 50 percent Jewish, or one that has Catholic churches or schools.

Do we know much about how these three factors operate? It appears that the economic factor is only partial explanation of the distribution patterns. While blacks generally are poorer than whites, there are enough of them at every income level, in almost every metropolitan area, to make possible much fuller integration than exists. And indeed, more prosperous blacks, who have greater choices, tend to be better integrated —but still far less so than if income alone determined where they live.

What about discrimination? The actual degree of existing, persisting discrimination is not easy to determine. It is never easy to delineate the dimensions of a practice that is illegal, for people doing illegal things will not usually acknowledge it openly. Recently the Department of Housing and Urban Development made public a study in which matched pairs of blacks and whites tried to rent or buy housing. It showed that many blacks will find discrimination. In asking about rental housing, whites are favored 28 percent of the time, blacks 12 percent of the time, and treatment was equal 60 percent of the time. In trying to purchase a house, whites were favored 52 percent of the time in the number of houses the agent suggested they look at, blacks 25 percent of the time. The North Central states were the most discriminatory: there was twice as much discrimination as in the South or West, three times as much as in the Northeast (*Washington Post*, April 17, 1978, pp. A1, A2).

Does this explain the segregated patterns of suburb and city? It is cer-

tainly a good part of the story. But when we see how often the black interested in renting or buying was *not* discriminated against, it seems there
is still a lot to be explained.

And so we come to the third and most elusive factor, individual preference. When people look for housing, they are limited by their economic
situation, they are concerned over whether they will meet prejudice, but
they also act out of preference—for neighbors of the same race or ethnic
group, for a neighborhood with institutions that serve a group, for a
location convenient to their work, for an old suburb or a new one, for
apartment houses, two-family houses, or single-family homes. Preference is a reality, affecting the choices of blacks as well as whites. But of
course it does not explain why so often blacks live in entirely black neighborhoods, whites in entirely white neighborhoods. The preferences of
white ethnic groups have not generally led to the creation of neighborhoods comprised almost exclusively of that group. Jews, Italians, Poles
have preferences which lead to concentrations, but they do not create, as
often as in the case of blacks, close to 100 percent neighborhoods.

In recent years, however, we have begun to learn that relatively mild
preferences for one's own group—or against another group—create a
dynamic process that leads to segregation. Only a slight amount of preference or prejudice leads to people's moving into or out of a neighborhood at such rates as to create high concentrations that hardly anyone
individually wants.

This was first demonstrated in an elegant theoretical article by Thomas
Schelling (1971). He suggests the following exercise. Take, he says,

> a roll of pennies, a roll of dimes, a ruled sheet of paper divided into
> one-inch squares, . . . and find some device for selecting squares at
> random. We place dimes and pennies on some of the squares, and
> suppose them to represent the members of two homogeneous groups
> —men and women, blacks and whites, French-speaking and English-
> speaking . . . We can spread them at random or put them in con-
> trived patterns. We can use equal numbers of dimes and pennies or
> let one be a minority. And we stipulate various rules for individual
> decision.
>
> For example, we could postulate that every dime wants at least
> half its neighbors to be dimes, every penny wants a third of its
> neighbors to be pennies, and any dime or penny whose immediate
> neighborhood does not meet these conditions gets up and moves.
> Then by inspection we locate the ones that are due to move, move
> them, keep moving them if necessary, and when everybody on the
> board has settled down, look to see what pattern has emerged.

The result in every case is "segregation"—all the pennies (or dimes, whichever is used to represent the minority) in one area of the board. Although one can use a computer to figure out what happens, the pattern can be demonstrated by simply going through the manual operations. And when one thinks about it, it makes sense. Most whites may consider an 11 percent black neighborhood (the average percentage of blacks nationwide) too black; many blacks may consider 11 percent not black enough. In the literature on school desegregation 11 percent black—two or three in a classroom of twenty-five—is often considered barely integrated, or not integrated enough. Many blacks argue for larger proportions if they are to feel comfortable and not like exposed and isolated tokens.

The point was first demonstrated theoretically or anecdotally. (In 1957 a study by Sklare and Vosk showed that a group of Jews surveyed in a small city felt that 50 percent Jewish in a neighborhood was just right; but would the Gentiles in such a neighborhood feel the same?) Now survey evidence demonstrates the same point. The University of Michigan Population Studies Center showed people in Detroit a schematic drawing of a neighborhood—fifteen boxes, of which some were white and some were black—and asked: "If you lived in this neighborhood, how would you feel about the mix of black families and white families in your neighborhood?"

If we show white respondents a drawing of the neighborhood of fifteen houses, in only one of which a black lives, that does not bother many of them, even in segregated Detroit. Only 7 percent would try to move out. Only 27 percent would not be willing to move in. But suppose two more black families move in, so that the ratio is three out of fifteen. The number trying to move out now rises fourfold to 24 percent. The number who would not move in doubles, to 50 percent. We can see that even though only *some* whites oppose blacks moving in, if they move out and other blacks move in, the percentage of uncomfortable whites rises and the area is threatened with becoming all black.

Take the other side, black preferences. Hardly any black would choose a neighborhood that is all white, and not many more would choose one that is all black. They would prefer, overwhelmingly, neighborhoods that are about 50 percent black. But that is not what whites prefer. And if we put these two sets of preferences next to each other, we see an inexorable process by which areas—not all, but most—beginning with, let us say, only 7 percent black, go rapidly to higher proportions and become almost all black—something blacks do not prefer, and whites do not prefer, but which both are left with, owing to the process by which mild preferences aggregate to almost total segregation (Farley et al., 1978).

What do we do about it? If the process is as I have described it—and leading social scientists agree it is—then we cannot be optimistic about some of the favored approaches to achieving integrated communities. We can enforce the law most vigorously, but enough whites will always prefer neighborhoods with very few blacks, and enough blacks will always prefer neighborhoods with considerably more blacks, for this process leading to segregation to begin. Certainly we should enforce the law. Certainly no black should ever be denied housing because of racial discrimination. And certainly we *can* have integrated stable neighborhoods. But we will not have very many, and most blacks will still live in concentrated black neighborhoods.

We should try to foster as much integration as possible, and we know a good deal about what creates stable integration in neighborhoods. The proportion of blacks should be low. The social, economic, and educational status of blacks and whites should be pretty much the same. Their children should have similar educational orientations. There should not be a much higher proportion of blacks in local schools than in the population. And so on. But these conditions are hard to arrange through public policy and hard to maintain in a society such as ours, where there is a great deal of private residential building and freedom of movement. They do require strong doses of community management—to keep the proportion of blacks low, to see that a rough social and economic parity between incoming white and black residents prevails, to recruit new white residents—because the kind of integrated stable neighborhood I have described will always be more attractive to blacks than to whites, and without management its black proportion will rise to create the kind of neighborhood both groups would prefer not to have. One thing that does seem hopeless is to try to implement simultaneous class integration and racial integration. Bringing together groups far apart in income—and all that accompanies income in this country—is in any case very difficult. It is foolish to try to create an abstract utopia that mixes poor and well-off, white and black; it will only create endless problems, unhappy communities, and new ghettos.

Does this mean we give up our hope for an integrated society? Not at all. Our society is increasingly integrated in its economic activity, its political life, its culture, its higher education. In two important areas we do find resistance to integration: in residence, and in elementary and secondary education. It is hard enough to create stable integrated schools by moving children around. It will be much harder to create them by moving families around. And just as banning segregatory acts in school assignments does not produce integration across the board, neither will policing vigorously against segregation in housing produce integrated housing across the board. This will change in time as integrative experiences in other spheres of life become more common and the two races are drawn closer together by shared experiences, interests, and values. That, at any rate, is my conviction.

References

Farley, Reynolds, Howard Schuman, Suzanne Bianchi, Diane Colasanto, and Shirley Hatchett. 1978. Chocolate city, vanilla suburbs: will the trend toward racially separate communities continue? *Social Science Research* 7:319-344.
National Advisory Commission on Civil Disorders (Kerner Commission). 1968. *Report*. Washington, D.C.: Government Printing Office.
Schelling, Thomas C. 1971. On the ecology of micromotives. *Public Interest* 25: 61-98.
———. 1978. *Micromotives and Macrobehavior*. New York: W. W. Norton.
Schnare, Ann B. 1978. *The Persistence of Racial Segregation in Housing*. Washington, D.C.: Urban Institute.
Sklare, Marshall, and Marc Vosk. 1957. *The Riverton Study: How Jews Look at Themselves and Their Neighbors*. New York: American Jewish Committee.

PART THREE

Approaches for the 1980s

8   Increasing the Effectiveness of School Desegregation: Lessons from the Research

WILLIS D. HAWLEY

Until very recently school desegregation was seen in relatively straight-forward terms.[1] Its purpose was to end discrimination manifest in overt or indirect exclusion of racial minorities from public schools. It was justified because it achieved this goal. But as desegregation has moved North and West, the moral imperative from which it drew its momentum has dissipated. It has become increasingly respectable to doubt that desegregation is a desirable social policy; indeed, such doubts are expressed not only by whites, but also by many blacks, Hispanics, and other minorities. Increasingly one hears—seemingly from all sides—concern about the costs of desegregation to children and to society, in terms of other educational and social objectives. To be sure, overt discrimination is not to be tolerated; but how far, it is asked, must society go to provide remedies for past discrimination or "accidental" or "coincidental" racial isolation?

Certainly school desegregation has not fulfilled its advocates' hopes that it would end prejudice and eliminate the achievement gap between whites and minorities. Still, at this time of increasing cynicism about the effectiveness of desegregation, it is important to recognize that: (1) generally speaking, the research shows that desegregation has positive consequences for children; and (2) the available research evidence provides a basis for developing desegregation plans and in-school strategies that will improve the quality of education for young people of all races. This chapter identifies what the research can tell us about the effects of school desegregation and suggests, in general terms, how educational programs might be designed to secure more effective integration. A serious constraint on the positive consequences of school desegregation is the decreasing social and racial heterogeneity of many school systems. Separate attention is given to this matter. In discussing each of these issues, I draw

attention to some of the more serious gaps in our knowledge about desegregation.

With the support of the Ford Foundation and the National Institute of
Education, the Center for Educational Policy at Duke University has
brought together a group of well-known scholars to form the National
Review Panel on School Desegregation Research. The central purpose of
the National Review Panel is to assess, as systematically and objectively
as possible, the effects of desegregation on a range of outcomes. This
chapter draws heavily on the analysis conducted by these scholars.[2]

The Effects of School Desegregation

Many of those who review the research on school desegregation conclude
that little is known about its effects. To be sure, we could know much
more, and some of the most serious gaps in our knowledge are noted in
this chapter. On a number of significant issues, however, there is enough
evidence from which to generalize with some certainty about the factors
that influence the effectiveness of school desegregation. Moreover, when
the research findings on desegregation are placed within the context of
other research and theory dealing with cognitive learning and social behavior, they fit well. The research does provide useful guidance to policy
makers and others concerned with making school desegregation more effective. It should be noted that there is very little research on the effects
of desegregation on minorities other than blacks; the generalizations
below are limited by this fact.

There are five primary objectives of desegregation:
  (1) Ending racial isolation among and within schools;
  (2) Increasing racial tolerance and understanding among children and
      adults of all races;
  (3) Improving the academic performance of low achievers;
  (4) Enhancing the self-concept and aspirations to achieve among
      minorities;
  (5) Increasing social equality through increased access for minorities to
      higher education, higher status jobs, and higher incomes.
What we know about the effects of desegregation on each of these desired outcomes is outlined below. Important conditions under which
these propositions are least likely to hold are also specified, as are issues
about which it seems most important to develop further evidence.

Ending Racial Isolation in Public Schools
From 1968 to 1976 segregation between minority groups and whites declined by 50 percent (Taueber and Wilson, 1979). Almost all of this de-

cline reflects changes in the level of segregation among black and white students. Hispanics, Asian Americans, and Native Americans have experienced relatively little desegregation with whites nationwide, though in most areas they were less segregated than blacks to begin with. It appears that Hispanics, perhaps because of recent immigration to this country, are becoming increasingly segregated at the high-school level, especially in certain areas of the West and Southeast.

The greatest progress in desegregation has been in the South, where changes have been dramatic and lasting. Indeed, the South is now the least segregated section of the country. While the rate of desegregation has slowed, it has not halted. In the North, the greatest progress has been made in larger districts although racial isolation remains a problem in many of these cities.

Minority groups are less segregated from each other than before, in part because school boards have sometimes sought to avoid black-white desegregation by classifying Hispanics as white and mixing them with blacks. Not surprisingly, racial isolation has been reduced most noticeably when courts have ordered desegregation, but desegregation imposed by the Office for Civil Rights and state agencies has also reduced racial isolation substantially.

The key point is that serious attempts to desegregate public schools do put an end to racial isolation. Even where desegregation results in substantial white flight, the amount of interracial contact has doubled and tripled over the period preceding desegregation. The reason minority students remain racially isolated in many school systems is that those systems have not undergone the desegregation process.

The difficulty of ending racial isolation in the public schools is, of course, substantially exacerbated by declining white enrollments, especially in nonsouthern cities, that have resulted from lower birth rates, suburbanization, and flight from desegregation itself. The white-flight issue is discussed at greater length later in this chapter.

Many school systems experience resegregation because of two factors: (1) changing residential patterns within the school district, often caused by the housing choices of new residents; and (2) separation of the races within schools because of dropouts, pushouts, special-education programs, and tracking.

Resegregation because of changing residential patterns within the school district is probably accelerated by community uncertainty about the commitment of leaders to desegregation and by initial pupil assignments that move relatively small numbers of minority students to schools in white neighborhoods. With respect to pushouts (whereby school officials explicitly or implicitly force or encourage minority students to leave school) or inappropriate assignments to special-education classes (such as remedial classes or programs for the "educable mentally retarded"), not much can be learned from the research. Minority leaders believe that these practices are widespread. No doubt research is needed on how teachers can more effectively respond to students whom they see as low achievers or disruptive influences. It may be, as some opponents of desegregation have charged, that school desegregation has led to an increasing number of minority pushouts or dropouts. But those who make these arguments must then explain the dramatic 50 percent decline in the dropout rate of black students from 1967 to 1977, the period during which desegregation had its greatest impact. By comparison, the dropout rate of Hispanic students has remained relatively constant since 1971, at 34 to 35 percent, compared to 21 to 22 percent for blacks, in a period when Hispanics have become more racially isolated.

School Desegregation and Race Relations

EFFECTS ON STUDENTS   Despite the fact that better race relations have always had a central place in the justification for school desegregation, there are remarkably few scientific studies of the impact of desegregation on prejudice and discriminatory behavior. On the basis of the available evidence, we can feel reasonably confident about the following propositions.[3]

School desegregation increases interracial contact, and that contact more often than not is friendly—or at least neutral—in character.

School desegregation does not lead to significant increases in school violence, although tension and incidents are more likely to occur in the first few months of desegregation. Busing children does not in itself contribute to the magnitude of disorders.[4]

Where any given racial group constitutes a very small percentage of a school or classroom (the actual proportion is uncertain), the individuals in that group may be racially isolated and develop defensive and negative feelings toward the dominant group.

In almost all cases blacks are found to be less prejudiced than whites, and desegregation may decrease the prejudice of blacks more than of whites.

The organization of schools and classrooms and the behavior of teachers toward students are critical factors in determining the effects of desegregation. Better race relations are likely when:

(1) Interracial interaction within classrooms and schools is encouraged in learning and play situations, as well as through seating patterns.
(2) Teachers are unprejudiced.
(3) Achievement grouping and tracking do not result in substantial racial isolation within schools.
(4) Positive social goals (such as good race relations) are emphasized by teachers and principals.
(5) Efforts are made to equalize the status of different races with respect to the particular tasks being pursued (leadership is shared, information and experience are equal, and so on).

The first of these factors seems to be the most important. Indeed, it may be that without substantial interracial contact other approaches to improving race relations—such as teacher workshops, class discussions, or curriculum revision—will have unimportant consequences.

Perhaps the most difficult question to resolve with respect to race relations is the alleged trade-off between the perceived need to group students so as to enhance their academic achievement and the fact that such grouping reduces interracial contact in most schools. The research results suggest that racially balanced classes are superior to imbalanced ones in producing unprejudiced behaviors, but tracking by itself may not be a totally negative practice from the standpoint of improving race relations. Schofield and Sagar (1977) found that in the magnet school they studied there was less friendly interracial behavior in the eighth grade, where there was tracking on the basis of academic interests (which created predominantly white or black classes), than in the seventh grade, where students were not tracked and the classes were racially heterogeneous. In their study of a number of northern and southern high schools Slavin and Madden (1979) found that tracking was not related to interracial attitudes and behavior. Since, however, Schofield and Sagar found that amicable interracial behaviors increased over time even in the tracked grade of their school, it might be that tracking is not an important detriment to race relations among older children as long as it does not lead to complete racial isolation and as long as mechanisms for contact are available within and outside the classrooms.[5]

In any case all researchers agree that stable forms of ability grouping and tracking reduce opportunities to improve race relations, even if they do not preclude improvement. Moreover, a considerable amount of effort has been directed at developing effective educational strategies that involve students of substantially different achievement levels. Research on these developments suggests that they can be very effective, at least with younger children, in terms of improved achievement, race relations, and, probably, self-esteem (Slavin, 1977; Lucker et al., 1977; and Garibaldi, 1977).

ADULT ATTITUDES AND COMMUNITY CONFLICT[6]   Desegregation has occurred at the same time that there have been dramatic reductions in racial intolerance, as measured by opinion surveys. Although opinion surveys surely understate the degree of prejudice people feel and experience, there is reason to believe that race relations are substantially better now than before the desegregation process began.

It appears that community-wide tension over the implementation of desegregation seldom affects interracial interaction over time with respect to education or other aspects of community life (work, sports and social events, or religious gatherings). Even where tension resulting from desegregation has resulted in violence, as in Boston and Louisville, interpersonal hostility among whites and minorities appears not to play a determining role in political campaigns. Interestingly, parents of children who are involuntarily bused consistently reflect more positive attitudes toward desegregation than do both parents whose children are not bused and other citizens.

SOME SIGNIFICANT UNRESOLVED ISSUES   Aside from the need to know more about how school and classroom practices and teacher behavior affect race relations, there are important questions about which we know very little.

(1) Under various conditions of social-class composition, are there some mixes of black, white, Hispanic, or Native American children that enhance race relations more than others?

(2) Are there approaches to ability grouping, other than rigid tracking, that would enhance both positive racial interaction and achievement?

(3) What are the effects of black-white desegregation on relations with Hispanic and Native American students?

(4) What factors influence teacher willingness and ability to promote positive interracial interaction?

Effects of Desegregation on Academic Achievement
There are hundreds of studies of the effects of desegregation on academic achievement. Many, however, are not scientifically creditable, and many

purporting to deal with desegregation actually deal with the impact of different school or class racial compositions on students, without regard to how racial mixing occurred. Nonetheless, it seems reasonable to make the following generalizations.[7]

White children almost never experience declines in performance on standardized achievement tests as a result of desegregation.

Minorities benefit academically from desegregation much more often than they experience negative effects.

The earlier minority children experience desegregation, the more likely desegregation will have positive effects. Most studies with negative outcomes deal with older students who have only recently experienced desegregation.

The more carefully and comprehensively a school district prepares for desegregation, the more likely it is that school desegregation will have positive effects on achievement. It is interesting to note in this regard that court-ordered desegregation seems more likely than voluntary desegregation to result in positive academic outcomes for minorities.

SIGNIFICANT UNRESOLVED ISSUES   While the balance of the evidence is clearly that school desegregation can lead to increased achievement for minorities, it is not evident why this is so. There is no conclusive evidence supporting one theory over another or identifying the effects on achievement of different factors in racially mixed schools. Because of their implications for the racial composition of a school, the theories that low achievers emulate their higher-achieving peers or are treated differently by teachers when there are a number of high achievers in the classroom are particularly important. If either of these theories is correct, it might follow that high achievers would perform less well in environments heavily dominated by low-ability students. What is striking about the research findings, however, is that there is so little evidence that desegregation lowers the achievement levels of whites, despite the fact that school desegregation often reduces the average academic achievement level of some schools and some classrooms. Teachers may focus on higher-achieving students in ways that establish high achievement as the dominant classroom value, even though a majority of students are low achievers. There is evidence that a classroom dominated by low achievers can adversely affect performance of children of the same race, though very high achievers seem less vulnerable—perhaps because of home support or teacher attention—than students of middle achievement (Summers and Wolfe, 1975). There is also reason to believe that whites are less influenced by the motivational levels of blacks than blacks are by whites, perhaps because many whites do not consider blacks a reference group (Hawley, 1976).

Effects of Desegregation on Self-Esteem and Racial Identity
One of the major justifications for ending publicly sanctioned desegregation was that racial isolation in schools resulted in psychological damage to minorities. The research on the effects of desegregation on self-esteem and racial identity (pride) is difficult to synthesize, partially because the measures used are so varied and alternative explanations (such as teacher behavior) for the findings are, when considered at all, so poorly tested. Nonetheless, it seems reasonable to conclude that:[8]

   Desegregation results in some increase in short-run anxiety and self-doubt among minorities, especially low achievers, but this is usually resolved over time.

   On general measures of self-esteem and aspirations, black children seem to have higher self-esteem than white children of the same social class or achievement level.

   The crucial determinant of the effects of desegregation on self-esteem is supportive and nondiscriminatory behavior of teachers.

   Rigid tracking systems on the one hand or highly competitive environments on the other probably weaken the academic self-image of low-achieving minorities. These negative effects may be greater for younger than for older students.

   The racial identity of whites and blacks does not appear to be negatively affected by school desegregation, though blacks may become more race conscious (but usually not more prejudiced).

We know almost nothing about the impact of desegregation on the self-concept and ethnic identity of Hispanics. This issue is especially important because bilingual programs, seen by many Hispanics as important to ethnic identity, can complicate desegregation plans.

Many educators believe that low-achieving adolescents will experience a diminution of self-concept if forced to compete in language arts and math with high achievers. If this conclusion—which is based on the observation that younger adolescents are both more unsure of themselves and more vulnerable to the disapproval of peers—is correct, it would have important implications for desegregation strategies, especially in junior and senior high schools.

In order to understand the impact of desegregated schools on different aspects of self-concept and racial identity, including notions such as "external and internal control," on achievement, and on behavior toward others, there is a critical need to identify the conditions that foster self-confidence with respect to academic achievement and the capacity to effectively pursue one's objectives in an interracial society. It is also important to learn how these conditions vary by the sex, age, or socioeconomic background of students.

Effects of Desegregation on Post-High-School Experience[9]

From the limited research on the effects of desegregation on employment and post-high-school educational attainment, there is reason to believe that:

　Students who have attended desegregated secondary schools are more likely to acquire higher-status jobs than those from segregated schools (this finding is very tentative).

　Whether or not one attends a desegregated school seems to have little effect on college attendance, including length of attendance.

　Minority students who attend a desegregated high school, especially if they attended a racially mixed elementary school, are more likely to attend and to persist in predominantly white (desegregated) colleges.

　Since access to higher-status jobs seems to be significantly affected by interpersonal contact, attending a desegregated college may be an important source of social mobility for minorities.

More research is needed on the effects of desegregation on post-high-school experience. For example, no work has been done on how differences in the educational experiences of students within segregated and desegregated environments affect post-high-school opportunities. It is also important to compare the effects of attendance in predominantly white and black colleges on long-term income and employment.

The Characteristics of More Effective Desegregated Schools

As any educator will observe, the best schools make the best desegregated schools. Both because they recognize the validity of this observation and because they are obliged to respond to court orders or to reassure parents and school personnel about the effects of desegregation, many desegregated school systems have adopted improved educational practices they might not otherwise have accepted. The idea that schools with all the characteristics of educational excellence will be effective when they are desegregated has led to exhaustive prescriptions for "making school desegregation work"[10] that are vague about priorities and at the same time so comprehensive that to most educators they probably do not seem feasible.

Based on pertinent research, certain school and classroom practices seem particularly important to achieve more effective school desegregation. The proposals listed below reflect especially the common conclusions of four recent efforts to identify the characteristics of more effective desegregated public schools (Orfield, 1975; Forehand and Ragosta, 1976; Systems Development Corporation, 1976; and Chesler, Crowfoot, and Bryant, 1978).

Desegregated schools seem most likely to improve race relations, enhance achievement, increase self-esteem, and improve students' "life chances" if, in addition to having the characteristics that generally foster school effectiveness, they follow the policies indicated below. Too often schools focus on only one goal or one strategy to achieve effective desegregation. It is important to stress the value of developing comprehensive plans and strategies; the policies described here should, therefore, be implemented simultaneously, if possible.

Assign students so that schools and classrooms are neither predominantly white nor predominantly black. When children of any race find themselves in a distinct minority, they may withdraw or be excluded so that little racial contact occurs. Moreover, if the minority has special needs, teachers and faculties may not be responsive to those needs. The number of children necessary to create this "critical mass" is unknown, but it probably is between 10 and 20 percent depending on the needs and backgrounds of the numerical minority and the predisposition of the dominant racial group and the school staff to interact across racial lines. This proposition, which has important implications for pupil-assignment plans, raises questions about achieving effective desegregation through interdistrict and other voluntary plans that involve moving small numbers of children to predominantly single-race schools.

Assign to each classroom a sizable number of children who perform at or above grade level. One explanation for the positive impact of desegregation on academic achievement is that desegregation generally increases the number of higher-achieving students to whom low achievers and their teachers are exposed. Pupil-assignment plans that look only at race, without considering additional assignment criteria, probably miss opportunities to create more productive learning environments.

Encourage substantial interaction among races both in academic settings and in extracurricular activities. There is no better way to improve race relations than to increase interracial contact. Such contact is not the automatic result of desegregation, but requires careful structuring and encouragement by teachers and administrators. Moreover, it is most effective when students of different races are placed in cooperative, interdependent, and mutually supportive situations. Several strategies developed to foster such interaction not only improve race relations, but usually enhance achievement as well (Slavin, 1977).

Eschew academic competition, rigid forms of tracking, and ability grouping that draws attention to individual and group achievement differences correlated with race. Students should be encouraged to compete with goals rather than with one another. Evidence on the effects of "ability grouping" suggests that it is most harmful among younger children. School practices that draw attention to racial differences in performance will probably impede improved race relations. This does not mean that when achievement is correlated with race ability grouping should never be used but, rather, that it should be limited to those situations in which it is educationally necessary. Student movement among groups should be possible, and if ability grouping is used in certain classes, special efforts should be made to provide for interracial contact in other settings.

Recruit and retrain teachers who are relatively unprejudiced, supportive, and insistent on high performance and racial equality. What teachers do in classrooms is the single most important determinant of effective education. Racially biased teachers cannot be good teachers of the children against whom they are prejudiced. Few school systems have strategies for detecting teacher bias or identifying and rewarding positive teacher behaviors that foster desegregation. Moreover, existing efforts to deal with teacher bias usually are limited to workshops on "cross-cultural differences" and similar efforts to sensitize teachers to the need for better "human relations" attitudes. It seems more effective to focus training efforts on teacher behavior rather than on attitudes, and to demonstrate to teachers how they can structure classrooms, provide evaluation and feedback, and deal with discipline so as to improve race relations and their effectiveness as teachers. Because of the importance of teacher commitment to the desegregation process, it is critical that teachers be involved in planning for and evaluating desegregation. Few school systems have involved teachers in a meaningful way in the design of strategies and practices.

Recruit and retrain principals who are supportive of desegregation and exert leadership in that direction. Students of desegregation agree that principals play a key role in the effectiveness of desegregated schools, although there are no systematic studies of how variations in the actual behavior of principals account for variations in the results of desegregation. Few school systems, however, provide much desegregation-related training to principals, and the topic of desegregation gets short shrift in most college and university educational-administration programs.

Involve parents at the classroom level in actual instructional or learning activities. School desegregation often increases the discontinuity between home and school environments, making it difficult for parents to participate in school activities. Community-wide parent advisory committees are no answer, and parent committees at the school level may not be effective either. Involving parents in the education of their own children so that the responsibility for defining and meeting a child's needs is shared by home and school seems to hold the greatest promise of increasing the effectiveness of desegregated schools. This will require active outreach efforts by the school and especially by teachers, whose time would be well spent in such activities as visiting homes and holding parent-teacher conferences in neighborhood facilities, such as churches.

Initiate programs of staff development that emphasize the problems relating to successful desegregation. A continuing staff development effort focused on desegregation is important; when possible, it should be designed and conducted by teachers and principals themselves. Too often, staff development is planned in the central office and is seen as a two-day-a-year enterprise. Such programs are usually a waste of time and money.

Maintain a relatively stable student body over time. One difficulty of school desegregation is that it requires many students to adjust to unfamiliar environments. The more often students are moved, the more difficult it is to make desegregation effective. Some school systems have designed plans that require frequent movement for individual children in order to mollify parents who object to busing. Other systems have adopted racial-balance requirements that necessitate frequent redrawing of pupil-assignment plans. There are a number of reasons frequent movement may be necessary, but once racial isolation is ended, the goal should be stability of student-student and student-teacher relationships.

Desegregate students early, in kindergarten if possible. If there is one thing about desegregation that can be said with certainty, it is that the younger the student is when first desegregated, the better the outcome. Paradoxically, parents often fear most for their youngest children and resist plans to desegregate primary grades. As a result, we have desegregated many school systems first—and in some cases only—in the upper grades, where the difficulty of achieving effective desegregation is greatest.

Obviously this prescription for effective desegregated schools is not a definitive or complete set of strategies and tactics. More research and experimentation are needed to understand how the effects of these policies and practices vary in different school contexts, and to increase the confidence with which they can be adopted and implemented.

There are at least two other conditions that almost all advocates of desegregation find important: a multiethnic curriculum and a desegregated faculty. Although steps to attain these goals seem worthwhile for many reasons, there is little research to show that they make a substantial difference in securing the goals of student desegregation. Moreover, two warnings are in order. First, multiethnic materials in themselves are not enough: they must be used so that they foster interaction across racial lines and get to issues that divide youngsters from different backgrounds. Too often multiethnic materials have a blandness that does not begin to provide understanding of stereotypes and subtle biases, many of which may be rooted in local history and conditions. Second, if racism is a cause of faculty segregation or shortage of minority teachers and administrators, it may also lead to the assumption by school administrators that minority educators need not be carefully selected or that they will not benefit from further professional development.

These policies are most likely to improve the education of elementary students. Findings about the impact of desegregation on junior-high students are less certain. Early adolescence under any circumstances is a tough time for most youngsters. Nonetheless, it seems safe to say that all types of schools undergoing desegregation are more likely to be effective if they adopt the programs discussed above.

Desegregation and the Heterogeneity of Cities and Schools[11]

School desegregation can affect the overall racial and social heterogeneity of public schools and communities if it causes people to move their children to private schools or their residences to other school districts. School systems in which students are almost all of one race obviously cannot benefit from desegregation.

There is now no debate among major researchers on whether desegregation leads to white flight. In almost all cities white flight during the first year of desegregation exceeds the normal rate of white and middle-class suburbanization. Except in school systems with high proportions of minority students (more than 30 or 35 percent black), desegregation nonetheless seems to have a negligible long-term effect on a community's racial composition. It is often claimed that mandatory desegregation will cause so much white flight that not enough whites will remain to achieve meaningful desegregation. Yet even where considerable white flight occurs, mandatory desegregation increases interracial contact among students over the long term (as much as five years). Without even the limited increase in racial contact provided by desegregation, what processes *would* reduce racial intolerance to the point where whites would not flee from desegregation?

What can and should be done? We have more questions than answers. Some suggest that voluntary plans are the answer. However, these programs seemingly have limited impact on racial isolation in cities with large minority populations, even where special (magnet) schools are extensively used to promote desegregation (Rossell, 1979). There are some approaches that appear to have promise for minimizing white flight while desegregation is pursued. For example, whites are twice as likely to flee desegregation if they are being sent to formerly black schools than to others, and they are less likely to take flight when being desegregated with Hispanic than with black students. Of course, "one-way busing" asks minorities to bear a heavier burden than whites.

It may be that the racial stability of school systems will be encouraged by plans that leave portions of the system predominantly black or Hispanic. It is already the case that in some systems a reasonable degree of school desegregation can be achieved *only* by leaving some schools racially isolated. Racial stability of schools might also be enhanced if guarantees were given to parents that the racial balance of a school, perhaps at a 50-50 level, would be maintained even in the face of district-wide changes in racial composition.

Some voluntary elements, coupled with mandatory provisions, might be included in desegregation plans. But magnet schools are more likely to attract white students if they are included within a mandatory plan than if they are totally voluntary. Phasing in desegregation, rather than implementing it all at once, seems to increase white flight.

Metropolitan-wide plans apparently restrict white flight in most areas to relatively minor losses to private-school enrollment. Flight to private schools is subject to reversal and is limited by the availability over time of educationally sound options. On the basis of studies in Florida and four other areas, it appears that as much as half of the white flight from desegregation is to private schools rather than to new public-school districts. If this is true generally, there are substantial opportunities to attract parents back to the public schools. This means that school systems could maintain contact with those who leave for private schools, identify the concerns of these individuals, and try to respond to them.

While there are a number of other ways that the problem of white (and middle-class minority) flight from desegregation might be addressed, they probably require supporting action by state and federal governments. Some strategies that seem to hold promise are integrated housing, interdistrict transfers, financial incentives for parents who send their children to desegregated schools, smaller schools and classrooms, and increased information for parents about the characteristics of private schools (Rossell and Hawley, 1980).

In any event, scholars disagree about the reasons white flight occurs. More research is needed on how and why whites respond to various elements of desegregation plans, along with evaluation of various experimental programs.

Conclusion

Cynicism about the past and future consequences of school desegregation is unsupported by available evidence. To be sure, desegregation has fallen short of the goals its advocates have held for it. And, more than twenty-five years after the U.S. Supreme Court's decision to end legally sanctioned racial isolation in the public schools, many children, especially outside the South, attend racially identifiable schools.

But wherever schools have been purposively desegregated, interracial contact has increased. More often than not, desegregation has resulted in benefits for the children involved. Research and experience provide the basis for developing programs that enhance the positive effects of school desegregation, reducing its costs, and accumulating further knowledge. The most worrisome aspect of desegregation clearly is the impact it has on residential white flight in some cities. It is hard to believe that more knowledge, commitment, and imagination would not lead to more satisfactory resolutions of this vexing problem. Effective desegregation will also require that old myths and ideologies be put aside and that desegregation be seen as involving a range of strategies whose appropriateness will vary with local conditions. This should allow more attention to be focused on the objectives that people of all races share. Desegregation is not a zero-sum game.

Notes

1. I am grateful to Dennis Encarnation and Marianne Toms for their assistance in the preparation of this paper.

2. Members of the National Review Panel on School Desegregation Research are Mark Chesler, University of Michigan; Robert Crain, Rand Corporation and Johns Hopkins University; Edgar Epps, University of Chicago; John McConahay, Duke University; James McPartland, Johns Hopkins University; Gary Orfield, University of Illinois; Peter D. Roos, Mexican-American Legal Defense Educational Fund; Christine Rossell, Boston University; William Taylor, Catholic University; and Mark Yudof, University of Texas. Betsy Levin and I codirect the panel.

3. Except as otherwise noted, these propositions are derived primarily from careful analytical studies by John McConahay (1978) and Robert Slavin and Nancy Madden (1979).

4. These conclusions rest on the findings of the Safe Schools Study (National Institute of Education, 1978) and Robert Crain's unpublished analysis of 1973 data from 555 desegregated southern school districts. Obviously, interracial incidents cannot occur in segregated schools.

5. This analysis is derived from an unpublished paper by John McConahay, "Reducing racial prejudice in desegregated schools," prepared for the October 1979 meeting of the National Review Panel on School Desegregation Research.

6. The conclusions in this subsection are based largely on a review of relevant research by Christine Rossell (1978).

7. These conclusions rest largely on a careful review of the achievement literature prepared by Robert Crain and Rita Mahard (1978).

8. These conclusions are based largely on analyses by Edgar Epps (1978).

9. These conclusions are derived from James McPartland (1978) and Braddock and McPartland (1979).

10. See, for example, Smith, Downs, and Lachman (1973); U.S. Commission on Civil Rights (1976); and U.S. Office of Education and the Council of Chief State School Officers (1977).

11. This section draws heavily on Rossell's 1978 review of the relevant research. It also takes into account a more recent study by David Armor (1979).

References

Armor, David. 1979. White flight and the future of school desegregation. In *Desegregation: Past, Present and Future*, ed. Walter G. Stephen and Joe R. Feagin. New York: Plenum Publishing Corp.

Braddock, Jo Mills, and James McPartland. 1979. The perpetuation of segregation from elementary and secondary schools to higher education. Paper presented at the annual meeting of the American Education Research Association.

Chesler, Mark, James E. Crowfoot, and Bunyan I. Bryant. 1978. Institutional contexts of school desegregation: alternative models for research and program development. *Law and Contemporary Problems* 42(2):174-213.

Crain, Robert L., and Rita E. Mahard. 1978. Desegregation and black achievement: a review of the research. *Law and Contemporary Problems* 42(3):17-56.

Epps, Edgar. 1978. Impact of school desegregation on self-evaluation and achievement orientation. *Law and Contemporary Problems* 42(2):57-76.

Forehand, Garley A., and Marjorie Ragosta. 1976. *A Handbook for Integrated Schooling.* Washington, D.C.: U.S. Office of Education.

Garibaldi, A. M. 1977. Cooperation, competition, individualization and black students' problem solving and attitudes. Paper presented at the annual convention of the American Psychological Association.

Hawley, Willis D. 1976. Teachers, classrooms and the effects of school desegregation on effort in school: a second-generation study. Working paper of the Institute of Policy Sciences and Public Affairs, Duke University.

Lucker, G. W., D. Rosenfield, J. Sikes, and E. Aronson. 1977. Performance in the interdependent classroom: a field study. *American Educational Research Journal* 13:115-123.

McConahay, John. 1978. The study of the effects of school desegregation upon race relations among students. *Law and Contemporary Problems* 42(3):77-107.

McPartland, James. 1978. Effects of elementary-secondary school desegregation on post-high-school education and occupational opportunities. *Law and Contemporary Problems* 42(2):108-132.

National Institute of Education. 1978. *Violent Schools—Safe Schools: The Safe School Study Report to the Congress*, vol. 1, p. 132. Washington, D.C.: Government Printing Office.

Orfield, Gary. 1975. How to make desegregation work: the adaptation of schools to their newly-integrated student bodies. *Law and Contemporary Problems* 39:314-334.

Rossell, Christine. 1978. The community impact of school desegregation: a review of the literature. *Law and Contemporary Problems* 42(2):133-183.

———. 1979. Magnet schools as a desegregation tool: the importance of contextual factors in explaining their success. *Urban Education* 14:303-320.

——— and Willis D. Hawley. 1980. The causes of white flight from school desegregation and some policy options. Working paper of the Center for Educational Policy, Duke University.

Schofield, Janet, and Andrew Sagar. 1977. Peer interaction patterns in an integrated middle school. *Sociometry* 40:130-138.

Slavin, Robert E. 1977. Student team learning techniques: narrowing the achievement gap between the races. Report no. 228, Center for Social Organization of Schools, Johns Hopkins University, Baltimore.

——— and Nancy Madden. 1979. School practices that improve race relations: a reanalysis. *American Educational Research Journal* 16:169-180.

Smith, Al, Anthony Downs, and M. Leanne Lachman. 1973. *Achieving Effective Desegregation.* Lexington, Massachusetts: D. C. Heath.

Summers, Anita A., and Barbara Wolfe. 1975. Equality of educational opportunity quantified: a production function approach. Philadelphia Federal Reserve Bank Research Papers.

Systems Development Corporation. 1976. *An In-Depth Study of Emergency*

School Aid Act Schools: 1974-1975. Santa Monica, California.

Taeuber, Karl E., and Franklin D. Wilson. 1979. Report on the impact of the type and character of desegregation programs on school desegregation. Madison: Institute for Research on Poverty, University of Wisconsin. (Unpublished.)

U.S. Commission on Civil Rights. 1976. *Fulfilling the Letter and Spirit of the Law: Desegregation of the Nation's Public Schools*. Washington, D.C.: Government Printing Office.

U.S. Office of Education and the Council of Chief State School Officers. 1977. *Take a Giant Step: Recommendations of a National Conference on Successful Desegregation*. Washington, D.C.: Government Printing Office.

9   The Case for Metropolitan Approaches to Public-School Desegregation

THOMAS F. PETTIGREW

Three basic factors commend metropolitan approaches to public-school desegregation in urban America. The first is widely understood: the racial demography of many of the nation's cities demands a metropolitan perspective on the process. The second factor is related to this one: metropolitan approaches deter resegregation. Finally, a range of desirable goals for an effective school desegregation program—such as furthering genuine integration, cost and transportational efficiency, equity, and parental choice—can all be more effectively advanced within a metropolitan context. Yet misconceptions abound concerning this view of school desegregation. Consequently, this chapter considers each of the three reasons for metropolitan solutions to public-school segregation and discusses the misconceptions about them.

Urban Demography Necessitates Metropolitan Approaches

The most obvious reason for adopting a metropolitan perspective concerns the racial composition of many of the nation's central cities. Among the twenty largest cities, only five—Indianapolis, Jacksonville, Milwaukee, Phoenix, and San Diego—currently have public schools with a white, "Anglo" student majority. Recent public-school student enrollments have dipped to 22 percent white in Chicago, 19 percent in Oakland and New Orleans, 18 percent in Detroit, 15 percent in Atlanta, and just 4 percent in Washington, D.C.

These large-city enrollment data reflect in part white attendance at private schools, but even more the residential distribution of blacks and whites within metropolitan areas. First, blacks live in metropolitan areas more than whites (76 percent versus 67 percent in 1974). Second, they are more likely to live in the very largest metropolitan areas. Thus, in 1975, blacks constituted 27.6 percent of the central-city populations of Stand-

ard Metropolitan Statistical Areas (SMSAs) of more than one million
and only 16.8 percent of the central cities of smaller SMSAs. Finally,
black Americans are more likely to be living inside central cities than in
the metropolitan rings. In 1974, 77 percent of metropolitan blacks re-
sided in central cities (down slightly from 79 percent in 1970) compared
to only 38 percent of metropolitan whites (down from 41 percent in 1970)
(U.S. Department of Commerce, 1975, pp. 9, 14, 15; and 1979, p. 15).
This proportion of blacks in the core cities, twice that of whites, is the
basic condition underlying the maldistribution of the races in the nation's
SMSAs; it alone is the major reason for the vast separation of black and
white citizens both residentially and educationally.

Care must be taken not to overgeneralize these big-city data. Many
smaller cities in the United States—from Portland, Maine, to Eugene,
Oregon—have overwhelmingly white school districts and do not require
metropolitan efforts in order to desegregate completely and easily. Pro-
totypical of these cities is Des Moines, Iowa, with only a ninth of its approximately 40,000 pupils black. Attention to the largest cities often
obscures the significant amount of easily correctable segregation that remains in Des Moines and similar cities. However, this discussion focuses
on the medium and large urban districts that require some degree of
metropolitan cooperation to solve their problems of school segregation.

There is wide agreement that metropolitan approaches are necessary to
achieve urban desegregation in a variety of American cities, ranging from
Richmond, Virginia, to Los Angeles. But agreement ends when the policy implications of this phenomenon are drawn. Proponents of court-
ordered school desegregation view this fact as an obvious call for metropolitan initiatives. Opponents regard virtually any form of metropolitan
solution as either impossible to achieve or highly undesirable. Their view
of the impossibility of the effort ignores the fact that metropolitan desegregation is already successfully operating in a growing number of SMSAs,
ironically most of them in the South—for example, Miami, Fort Lauderdale, Jacksonville, Tampa, Charlotte, Nashville, Louisville, Las Vegas,
and most recently, Wilmington, Delaware. Their view of the undesirabil-
ity is often based on the misconceptions of metropolitan approaches that
will be considered later in this chapter. However the policy implications
are argued, the stark fact remains that *urban school segregation will not
only remain but worsen without metropolitan remedies in central-city
districts that provide public instruction to roughly half of America's
black elementary and secondary students.*

There is also some disagreement about the causal factors underlying the patterns of racial demography that make metropolitan remedies necessary. Few social scientists, however, would join Justice Potter Stewart in his remarkable observation in *Milliken* v. *Bradley* that these factors are "unknown and perhaps unknowable."[1] The great majority of social scientists who have studied the subject, particularly specialists such as Karl Taeuber and the late Charles Abrams (Taeuber and Taeuber, 1969; Abrams, 1975; Pettigrew, 1975a), believe that structural barriers erected by public policies shaped and determined today's dual racial housing markets. These governmental policies clearly constitute "state action" under the Fourteenth Amendment, the worst offender being the federal government itself. Consider this assessment by Abrams: "The federal government, during the New Deal period, not only sanctioned racial discrimination in housing, but vigorously exhorted it. From 1935 to 1950, discrimination against Negroes was a condition of federal assistance. More than 11 million homes were built during this period, and this federal policy did more to entrench housing bias in American neighborhoods than any court could undo by a ruling. It established . . . federally sponsored mores for discrimination in the suburban communities in which 80 percent of all new housing is being built and fixed the social and racial patterns in thousands of new neighborhoods" (Abrams, 1975, p. 47).

Since 1950 one federal housing program after another—public housing, mortgages from the Federal Housing Administration and the Veterans Administration, urban renewal, Model Cities, even taxation policy —have exacerbated this trend (Lowi, 1970). Within this national structure, of course, the many discriminatory practices of the banking and real estate industries cemented housing segregation by race at the local level. Over four decades of dual housing markets for black and white Americans have inevitably influenced the racial and housing attitudes, expectations, and behavior of both races (Pettigrew, 1975a, pp. 92-126). At this late date, then, it is a gross confusion of the historical sequence and causal order to argue that unfettered housing choices by black and white citizens created "naturally" today's patterns of residential segregation independent of state action. Such an "unfettered choice" thesis, advanced by a few nonspecialists, simply ignores the fact that these so-called choices are derivatives of the dual housing markets. And it ignores the vast evidence for the massive and intense degree of housing discrimination against black Americans, an intensity unmatched by

housing discrimination against any other race or ethnic group in the
United States.

Metropolitan Approaches Deter Resegregation

Also in contention has been the importance of court-ordered school desegregation as a factor in creating increasingly black core cities and white
suburban rings (Coleman, Kelly, and Moore, 1975; Farley, 1975; Lord,
1975; Rossell, 1975-1976; Pettigrew and Green, 1976a and b; Lord and
Catau, 1976; Coleman, 1976; Fitzgerald and Morgan, 1977; Farley,
Richards, and Wurdock, 1978). The "white-flight" thesis is that these
court orders have been self-defeating in that they drive out of central-city
public-school systems white children who would have remained had there
been no court orders. This contention argues for continuation of present
segregation on the grounds of the dangers of possible resegregation and
rejects the possibility of metropolitan desegregation. And, like the unfettered choice thesis, the white flight thesis reverses the time sequence; for
the racial trends of urban demography that now necessitate metropolitan
efforts were already deeply established prior to court-ordered school desegregation in most southern and virtually all northern cities.

Several points must be made about the much-debated white-flight
phenomenon in order to see how it provides yet another reason for metropolitan approaches to school desegregation. First, the school desegregation process came to most central cities at precisely the time that student enrollments were already beginning to decline rapidly. Elementary
and secondary education was a growth industry between 1946 and 1970.
But birth rates began to decline in 1957 (earlier and faster for whites than
blacks), and the lagged time effect of this basic trend means that public
education has had steadily declining enrollments since their peak in 1971.
Adding to this national trend, net migration into the larger metropolitan
areas began to reverse itself into a net outflow; now it is the more sparsely
populated rural areas that are starting to grow swiftly (U.S. Bureau of
the Census, 1977). The coincidence of these two trends with urban desegregation made it appear to much of the interested public that the two
were inextricably and causally related. For our present concerns it is important to observe that these trends are not changing—indeed, they are
likely to become stronger in the future and continue to lower pupil enrollments in the metropolitan rings as well as in the central cities. We shall
later note that these trends lend economic incentives for metropolitan
cooperation.

Second, white-flight researchers agree that the loss of white students is far more related to the proportion of black enrollment than to school desegregation itself. The school systems of Chicago, St. Louis, and Newark all had majority black enrollments in 1968 and experienced heavy losses of white students from 1968 to 1973 without any program of school desegregation whatsoever (Pettigrew and Green, 1976a, pp. 35-37). Only metropolitan approaches can overcome this condition.

Third, in addition to these more critical and basic phenomena, there is often a larger-than-usual loss of white students during the first year of school desegregation. Most studies find these losses to be limited to the initial years of desegregation (Coleman et al., 1975, p. 79; Farley et al., 1978). Sometimes the losses can be substantial (Atlanta, Memphis); sometimes they are moderate (Dayton, Minneapolis). And they tend to be least in desegregation programs of metropolitan scope—the critical point to emphasize.

Fourth, there is some question about the meaning of these losses. Farley points out that white enrollment may decline from one year to the next for four reasons (Farley, 1978). White high-school graduates can outnumber the entering white first-graders. This factor has been and will continue to be a major one, given declining fertility rates. The number of white students whose families move into the district may decline for many reasons, most of which are unrelated to the schools. In addition, racial and ethnic identities become salient at the time of desegregation, and students with varying degrees of Hispanic, Asian, or Native American ancestry may be recorded as white one year but minority the next. This factor, never mentioned by enthusiastic advocates of the white-flight thesis, is believed to have been especially significant in the Southwest and California.

Finally, white enrollment may decline because parents move out of the district or place their children in private schools. Much of this movement has nothing to do with desegregation or even with the schools at all. Some of the shift *is* related to desegregation, whether court-ordered or not. Just how much of this shift is caused by desegregation itself, however, is difficult to specify, given the paucity of relevant survey data. Furthermore, the assumption that the loss associated with desegregation is composed of white students who would not otherwise have been lost to the city school district at a later point is not supported by studies over time (Farley, 1975; Rossell, 1975-1976; Pettigrew and Green, 1976a; Farley et al., 1978). Instead, the phenomenon is more accurately viewed as a "hastening up" effect. The initial losses of white pupils do indeed speed resegregation; but over a five- or ten-year period they often constitute merely "fine tuning" around the far more critical factors of demographic trends and suburban housing discrimination against black citizens.

The "hastening up" effect is illustrated by Farley's projections for white, Anglo enrollment in the Los Angeles Unified School District (LAUSD) (Farley, 1978, p. 40). Given the low Anglo birth rate and the still-high Hispanic birth rate, together with the continued Hispanic immigration across the border, Farley estimates that the white, Anglo student proportion of the district will fall sharply from its 1977 percentage of 34. By 1982, his projections estimate an Anglo percentage of 23 if there is no white flight from desegregation whatsoever and 19 if there is a high rate of white flight. By 1987, his projections estimate only 14 percent Anglo pupils if there is no white flight and 12 percent if there is a high rate. In other words, the Anglo proportion of the LAUSD will probably decline swiftly over the next decade from 34 to either 12 or 14 percent whether or not there is an extensive desegregation program in the LAUSD and whether or not white flight occurs as a consequence of school desegregation.

This reinterpretation does *not* mean that resegregation in our central-city school systems is not a serious problem, or that it is not important to deter the "hastening up" effect. Quite the opposite is the case. From this perspective it becomes all the more urgent to adopt metropolitan approaches because they alone have been found to be effective deterrents to the loss of white students. Especially is this the case for large central cities with high proportions of black students where the white student loss, however conceptualized, is greatest.

Even the few critics of court-ordered school desegregation within social science admit that white flight is minimal in metropolitan desegregation programs. The usual explanation is that metropolitan solutions allow no place for white flight save to expensive private education. Yet metropolitan solutions enhance other goals of effective desegregation, such as equity among families. And greater equity may play a role in the proven ability of metropolitan desegregation programs to impede white flight.

In any event, this proven ability of metropolitan approaches is beyond dispute. *No metropolitan program of public-school desegregation has experienced an extensive loss of white students.* The metropolitan programs of Miami, Fort Lauderdale, Tampa, Jacksonville, Louisville, Charlotte, Las Vegas, and Nashville have not experienced losses even comparable to those of some programs limited to the central city, such as those in Memphis, Atlanta, and San Francisco.[2] Tampa and Fort Lauderdale, both with county-wide districts, as is the case throughout Florida, actually gained white pupils between 1968 and 1973 while undergoing more extensive school desegregation than either Atlanta or San Francisco (Pettigrew and Green, 1976a, p. 35).

The most detailed study of this phenomenon was made of seven county-wide desegregating Florida school districts where residential relocation was impractical and transfer to private schools offered the only means of white flight (Cataldo et al., 1975, pp. 3-5; Giles, Cataldo, and Gatlin, 1975). The study found only a minimal loss of white students at the time of school desegregation in these large districts. Moreover, survey data of individual families revealed that white enrollment in private schools to avoid desegregation was *unrelated* to racial prejudice or to busing and was greatest among upper-status families and those whose children attended schools with more than 30 percent black enrollment. This last condition, schools with more than 30 percent black pupils, would be uncommon in the vast majority of metropolitan desegregation programs that could be designed.

Metropolitan Approaches Advance Other Desirable Goals of School Desegregation

In deterring the loss of white students, metropolitan approaches contribute significantly to the stability of desegregating programs. But stability is just one, albeit an important one, of the desirable goals of school desegregation. Among the most desirable of these goals are the following:

(1) *Optimal conditions for genuine integration and quality education.* Obviously, the principal goal of the entire process is to improve the educational experiences of all schoolchildren. To achieve this, genuine racial integration is necessary, not mere desegregation; that is, positive intergroup contact with cross-racial acceptance must evolve out of the mixing of children. Experience across the country has shown that the design of the desegregation efforts can greatly further this process of intergroup integration.

(2) *Cost efficiency.* Effective integrated education need not cost significantly more than segregated education—a critical point in the present political and economic climate. But it must be well planned to be cost efficient. Indeed, the process presents a rare opportunity to alter traditional procedures that have not proven to be cost effective in the past.

One important budget item for desegregation is student transportation, which raises the next consideration.

(3) *Efficient transportation*. Student desegregation needs to be maximized, while the busing of students needs to be minimized.

(4) *Equity*. No group or particular neighborhood should have to bear a disproportionate burden of disruption and transportation. Yet absolute equity is not possible, since special accommodations have to be made for concentrated housing patterns, language issues, and other distinctive problems.

(5) *Choice*. Increased choice for both students and parents is also highly desirable.

(6) *Stability*. Successful school desegregation requires stability in both the short and the long run. Issues of long-run stability were discussed in the previous section. Short-run stability is also important in order to develop the confidence and involvement of parents in the process.

Once these goals are made explicit, it can readily be seen that various parties in desegregation suits tend to focus on one or more of them to the exclusion of the others. Plaintiffs stress the conditions for integration and equity; defendants, costs and stability. And each party can in fact make a persuasive case for its particular emphases, for each of the six broad goals *is* highly desirable. Problems arise, however, because these goals often (though not always) conflict. There are important and necessary trade-offs to be made between them in any practical desegregation plan. And these trade-offs typically are not adequately addressed in desegregation cases because the adversary procedure itself militates against taking the broader view needed to consider them.

Metropolitan approaches are unique in that they frequently allow a particular desegregation plan to maximize all six of the desirable goals without the harsh trade-offs forced upon plans that are constrained by central-city boundaries. Consider each of the goals again in metropolitan perspective.

Optimal conditions for genuine integration and quality education
At least ten school conditions appear to maximize the evolution of successful integration: (1) equal access to the school's resources; (2) cultural fairness (respect for cultural traditions); (3) classroom—not just school—desegregation (McPartland, 1968); (4) avoidance of strict "test-score grouping"; (5) maintenance and improvement of services; (6) initiation of desegregation in the early grades (U.S. Office of Education, 1966, p.

331; Crain and Mahard, 1978); (7) consistent school feeder patterns that keep desegregated classes together; (8) interethnic staffs; (9) substantial, rather than token, minority student percentages; and (10) minimal association between race and socioeconomic class (Coleman et al., 1966, pp. 331, 333; Pettigrew, 1975a, pp. 236-237).

A number of these factors are easier to achieve with a metropolitan approach. For example, the "maintenance and improvement of services" is rendered more feasible by a broader tax base. Similarly, "substantial, rather than token, minority [and majority] student percentages" become possible. Many suburban school districts have only token numbers, if any, of minority pupils—a mirror reflection of the schools of some central cities. Metropolitanization, in pooling the enrollments, not only tends to lead to appropriate percentages of students by group, but often also stabilizes demographic trends. For example, the Richmond public schools have gone from a one-third-black to a more-than-three-fourths-black system in recent decades; yet the pooled public-school enrollment of the central city together with its two surrounding suburban counties has remained approximately one-third black throughout these same years.

Cost efficiency
Metropolitan approaches to public education are major means of achieving cost efficiency. This advantage becomes even greater in a period of low birth rates and declining school enrollments. Wasteful duplication across adjacent districts is common, and there are such anomalies as schools being closed only a few miles away from another district with overcrowded schools on double sessions. Not surprisingly, then, Florida has only county-wide school districts mainly for reasons of cost efficiency.

Efficient transportation
One of the ways in which metropolitan approaches contribute to cost efficiency is by minimizing pupil transportation while maximizing school desegregation. Hence, the metropolitan desegregation plan proposed for Richmond (but denied by the U.S. Fourth Circuit Court of Appeals), for example, would have thoroughly desegregated a two-county and central-city area *and* reduced student transportation significantly (Pettigrew, 1975b).[3] Likewise, in Charlotte-Mecklenburg, the county-wide plan approved by the U.S. Supreme Court completely desegregated the full county area and reduced the busing times that prevailed before desegre-

gation (Taylor, 1977, pp. 118-119). The efficiency advantage of metropolitan solutions would also hold for most urban areas in the North; but
there would not be, as in Charlotte, less busing than at present, because,
unlike in North Carolina, so few intradistrict desegregation programs are
already under way in the North. Efficiency would be especially maximized in long, narrow central-city school districts, such as those in Boston and Los Angeles, an optimal shape for cooperation with suburban
school districts (Pettigrew, 1978).

Equity

Metropolitan approaches can also contribute to greater equity for both
majority and minority families. Usually minority concentrations in the
core cities are nearer to majority concentrations in the suburbs than they
are to majority areas in the core city itself. Intradistrict plans, therefore,
often expand busing and school coordination unnecessarily. Why, for instance, should Anglo children in the far western reaches of the San Fer-
nando Valley of Los Angeles be paired with Hispanic children twenty-
five miles or more away in East Lost Angeles when ample Anglo children
live within ten miles of East Los Angeles in such suburbs as Burbank,
Glendale, South Pasadena, San Marino, and Temple City, where there is
little or no school desegregation? It is precisely such inequities of intradistrict plans that metropolitan approaches can eliminate.

Choice

This desirable goal can be enhanced in a carefully planned metropolitan
solution by a number of means. Specialized schools and programs that
attempt to act as voluntary "magnets" are more feasible under metro-
politanism for two reasons. The broader tax base allows for greater number and range of such schools and programs. And the much broader
enrollment base lends the possibility of greater viability to this approach
—an important point when one considers the general lack of success of
magnet schools in their intradistrict application.

    Choice can also be furthered through special exemptions designed to
promote stable integrated neighborhoods. These exemptions would allow
neighborhood school attendance for all majority schoolchildren in predominantly minority areas, for all minority children in predominantly
majority areas, and for all children in a stable integrated neighborhood.
Though it is usually too constraining on the total system to allow such
blanket exemptions when the desegregation program is confined to the
central district, these residential exemptions become feasible in most

metropolitan efforts. By allowing naturally mixed areas to utilize local schools without busing, choice is enlarged for families through residential rather than directly educational decisions. Hence, an overwhelmingly Anglo neighborhood that attracted new minority neighbors would become eligible for exemptions. Less likely to occur, but also eligible, of course, would be minority areas that attracted majority neighbors. Moreover, families of any racial group that moved to a mixed area would become eligible. An incentive is thereby provided for intergroup living, a rare phenomenon in the American housing market. And there have been indirect indications that such an incentive might well be substantial for generating change in racial residential patterns (Pettigrew, 1978, pp. 73-74).

Another advantage of this housing approach is that it extends parental choice without seriously limiting the attainment of the other desirable goals of an effective desegregation program. This is no small point, because most attempts to enlarge parental choice have tended to restrict severely such goals as attainment of the optimal conditions for integration, cost and transportation efficiency, and equity. For example, the 1978-79 desegregation plan of the Los Angeles Unified School District so extended parental choice that it proved less than ideal on virtually all other counts (Pettigrew, 1978, pp. 79-92). Still, choice through residential decisions coincides with most of the other goals. It would generally enhance the ten conditions that further the evolution of genuine integration. It would on balance aid cost and transportational efficiency (though it adds to busing time generally when administered within intradistrict plans). It would also advance stability. But it would involve some degree of inequity, in that majority neighborhoods and upper-status families of all groups would be more able than others to take advantage of this incentive made possible by a metropolitan approach. On balance, the trade-off seems to be one well worth making.

Stability
We have noted that metropolitan solutions help achieve long-term stability by deterring the "hastening up" of white flight. They also contribute to short-term stability. When citizens regard a social alteration as partial or temporary, they are understandably less willing to commit themselves to its implementation and success. Such is likely to be the case with an intradistrict plan for a core-city district without any prospect of later expansion to the suburbs.

Both long-run and short-run stability depend on affected families be-

ing certain about what to expect from the program. Over the past generation in America, at least as much resistance to public-school desegregation has been generated by uncertainty and fear as it has been by beliefs
that could fairly be labeled "racist." Metropolitan approaches, conducted properly, can allay such uncertainty and fear by allowing promises to be made to parents and children that can be kept in the future far
beyond those possible in a constrained, intradistrict plan.

Misconceptions about Metropolitan Approaches to School Desegregation

There are four persistent and interrelated misconceptions about metropolitan approaches to school desegregation. The basic misconception is
that such approaches necessarily entail one mammoth school district cov-
ering the entire SMSA and more. Premised on this mistaken notion are
the additional fears that such approaches invariably require massive
amounts of pupil busing and usurp all local educational authority. Finally, there is the misconception that the achievement of metropolitan
approaches is an all-or-none process, that there are no intermediate steps
of metropolitan cooperation that can be sought initially. Let us briefly
consider these points in turn.

Throughout this chapter we have referred to metropolitan "approaches" and "solutions"; no mention of a single, suprametropolitan
school district has been or needs to be made. All that is necessary to gain
the benefits of a metropolitan solution is to prevent the present, artificial
boundaries of the central-city districts from serving as an impenetrable
"Berlin Wall," shutting off cooperation between a predominantly minority system within and predominantly majority systems without. In systems terms, these district boundaries are currently acting as a powerful
constraint that prevents a rational, efficient, equitable, and stable solution to the problems of urban school segregation. Metropolitan benefits
flow from effectively eradicating this constraint.

This perspective differs sharply from popular misconceptions about
metropolitan education. Understandably, the successful metropolitan
school systems of Jacksonville, Miami, Tampa, Nashville, Charlotte, and
other areas have led the public and even a few social scientists to equate
metropolitan efforts with large-scale consolidation. Yet this is not at all a
necessary direction of metropolitan efforts. In the metropolitan plan for
the Richmond area, with which I was associated, seven individual districts were proposed, each *smaller* than the smallest of the three existing

districts. What made it possible for this plan to desegregate the entire area thoroughly with a reduction in student transportation was that the new, smaller districts crosscut the old district boundaries in strategic ways to allow efficient mixtures of black and white children.

It is important to correct this prevalent misconception of metropolitan efforts as necessarily leading to bigness. Many astute observers believe that central-city school districts are already too large today to be as responsive and efficient as they should be. From this vantage point, metropolitan efforts present a rare opportunity to create subregional districts smaller than the present-day core districts. A recently devised metropolitan design for the Los Angeles area, for example, envisages eight separate confederations of school districts, each of them significantly smaller than the present Los Angeles Unified School District (Pettigrew, 1978, pp. 109-137).

We have already seen that the far greater efficiency of student transportation made possible by metropolitan approaches modifies the fear of massive busing and of long rides across much of the SMSA. Likewise, the fear that all local education authority is necessarily lost can be at least partially allayed. When metropolitan solutions head toward smaller, more manageable subregional districts, a great variety of arrangements for governance and financing is possible. Many of these schemes allow for considerable input from present school boards. At a central level, of course, the state must have ultimate reponsibility for the smooth operation of the metropolitan subregional confederations. And, of course, any of these arrangements will constrain some of the present authority of local boards. But the fearful vision of a behemoth district with an impenetrable bureaucracy and no local control whatsoever clearly need not and should not be allowed to arise from metropolitan efforts.

Ironically, the often intense political problems raised by metropolitan approaches to public-school desegregation are partly eased by the current conservative movement for restricting local governmental expenditures. Proposition 13 in California, for example, has led directly to the state's having to assume an increased proportion of the cost of elementary and secondary public education. Such a trend toward central financing of public education tends both to equalize per capita costs across districts and to lessen the financial difficulties inherent in establishing metropolitan approaches.

Finally, metropolitan efforts need not be total in their scope. A larger number of urban areas have cross-district cooperation for limited school desegregation than have full-scale metropolitan programs. In the 1960s many urban areas began programs of voluntary one-way busing of inner-city black children to white suburban schools. The first such examples involved tiny numbers of students but nonetheless attracted considerable national attention. While some of these early programs were later eliminated, several of them have grown into relatively large projects, encouraged by state governments with aid from the federal government. The best known, perhaps, is the Metropolitan Council for Educational Opportunity (METCO), operating in the Boston and Springfield areas of Massachusetts. This program now arranges for about 3,200 black youngsters to receive their education in one of more than 200 schools in forty-one cooperating suburban districts.[4] Applications of children wishing to participate typically number two or three times the available spaces, so a sizable waiting list is maintained. Over the past thirteen years of operation, the spaces available and the number of voluntarily cooperating communities have climbed steadily. Sharp debates sometimes break out over the issue in suburban town meetings; and, in turn, black-administered METCO sometimes rejects a community's application when the suburb is regarded as "not ready yet" for genuine integration. Significantly, however, METCO has come to be regarded as a permanent fixture of public education in the state, and its state financial support has remained secure throughout Boston's stormy school desegregation process.

Connecticut's Project Concern began in the 1960s as a small program transporting black students in Hartford to a number of participating suburbs. Once significant funds were made available, Project Concern was able to spread to New Haven, Bridgeport, and other Connecticut cities.

Relatively successful and publicized projects, METCO and Project Concern have served as models for other states. The most notable recent effort along these lines has occurred in Wisconsin. Concerned with the problems raised by a federal court order to desegregate schools within Milwaukee,[5] the Wisconsin state legislature in 1975 created an interesting program (Chapter 220 of Wisconsin's laws of 1975, popularly known as the Conta bill after its originator and driving force, Dennis J. Conta) (Conta, 1978). In its initial year of operation, 1976-77, this statute supported with $8 million 14,000 intradistrict and 360 interdistrict voluntary transfers that aided school desegregation in both Milwaukee and Racine. Two principal mechanisms are featured. One provides substantial economic incentives to *both* the sending and receiving school districts for transfers that further school desegregation. All transportation costs of the transfers are assumed by the state; and state funds are available to help any school desegregation program mandated by a court. A second mechanism of the law requires the establishment of seventeen joint educational councils between each of the suburban school districts of Milwaukee County and the Milwaukee City school district. Each council annually must submit a transfer plan; however, each school district retains veto power over these plans.

Interdistrict cooperation has been initiated by other states, from Rhode Island to Washington, frequently for reasons of savings through economies of scale. Often state incentives are provided to two or more school districts to conduct various educational programs jointly. Though neither necessarily racial nor metropolitan, such statutes provide important precedents and incentives for metropolitan cooperation that facilitates later interdistrict desegregation efforts.

I do not cite these examples here to hold them up as ideal programs to be emulated but, rather, to point out that there are initial metropolitan efforts intermediate in scope between a strictly intradistrict plan and a complete metropolitan plan. Discussions about "how to get there from here" need to be informed about such intermediate steps. The one common element is the important role of the state government. Public education is, after all, the responsibility of the state; and boundary lines that create and perpetuate segregated schools are the creation and responsibility of the state. Not inappropriately, then, Massachusetts, Connecticut, and Wisconsin, together with a few other states, have made at least tentative efforts toward easing the burdens of racial segregation made worse by the Berlin Walls erected between inner-city and suburban school districts.

Yet it must be candidly stated that there are serious problems with these projects. The METCO and Project Concern programs are one-way busing schemes; those whose constitutional rights have been violated are the ones who bear the full burden of the remedy. Moreover, the relatively small numbers involved do not significantly affect the core-city problem of educational segregation. And these small numbers typically mean that black pupils are represented only in token numbers in their suburban schools. In METCO, for instance, black children constitute less than 5 percent of every school system save one in which they participate; and some of the host systems do not have a single black staff member.

Why, then, do black parents eagerly sign up their offspring for these programs? Why do they even wait years on a reserve list in order to have their children participate? The answer is simple. These suburban busing

schemes offer one of the few options available for black parents with
ambitions for better lives for their daughters and sons. These parents are
generally aware of the costs of the programs, psychological and other,
to their childen and themselves. Nevertheless, in full "black flight" from
segregation and with little access otherwise to the networks of opportunity, the benefits of even token school desegregation under less than ideal
conditions outweigh the alternatives.

As a means of broadening the options of minority parents in a severely
limited situation, these programs are certainly justified. And some of
their current problems—such as only token numbers of students and the
lack of black staff—are correctable. Furthermore, METCO and similar
projects present useful models of interdistrict cooperation that may in
time allay suburban fears and prepare the ground for the full metropolitan measures that are needed. But those who advocate such programs as
the final and complete answer to urban school segregation, as all that
white America can and will tolerate, are in fact urging the continued racial segregation of the nation's urban schools.

Summary

The case for metropolitan approaches to urban problems of school segregation emphasizes three points. First and foremost, urban racial demography requires such approaches. Second, metropolitan approaches
deter resegregation. Whether conceptualized as white flight or a "hastening up" effect, losses of white students in urban school districts have
been consistently limited by metropolitan approaches. Third, metropolitan approaches advance other desirable goals of effective desegregation.
With minimal trade-offs, such solutions further the attainment of optimal conditions for genuine integration, cost and transportational efficiency, equity, choice, and both short-term and long-term stability. By
contrast, these goals are often in conflict in intradistrict plans, and harsh
trade-offs among them must be made.

Arguments against metropolitan approaches are often based on a
number of misconceptions, central among them the belief that such efforts require one enormous school district spread over the whole SMSA
and beyond. Related to this specter are fears of massive student busing
and the loss of all local educational authority. Actually, there is a great
range of efforts possible within a metropolitan perspective and no necessity whatsoever for one suprametropolitan district. As long as the
essential requirement of strategically cutting across present city-suburban

boundaries is met, metropolitan designs can feature multiple subregional districts that are smaller than the current central-city and some suburban districts. Moreover, metropolitan plans are maximally efficient for limiting student transportation as a function of the amount of school desegregation achieved. Fears of massive busing crisscrossing the entire SMSA can be allayed. Likewise, fears of the loss of all local control of public education can also be allayed by careful planning of the form of governance desired.

In addition, there is a range of efforts of intermediate scope with which to initiate metropolitan designs. These efforts, which have typically involved one-way voluntary busing programs of black pupils from the city to white schools in the suburbs, have generally suffered from their small numbers of students, lack of black staff in suburban schools, and assignment of the full transportational burden to blacks alone. Yet they widen the options available to black families and furnish useful precedents for more extensive interdistrict cooperation. They can never serve, however, as the complete answer to the nation's embedded problem of urban school segregation.

I conclude from these considerations that without metropolitan remedies school segregation not only will remain but will worsen in many central-city districts. There are various metropolitan approaches to fit different urban situations. To argue against *all* such metropolitan forms is to argue directly for the perpetuation and entrenchment of racial segregation of the public schools throughout much of urban America into the far-distant future.

Notes

1. Milliken v. Bradley (Milliken I), 418 U.S. 717, 756 n.2 (1974) (Stewart, J., concurring).

2. There are three factors that may explain why metropolitan approaches have been most prevalent in the South: (1) cost efficiency traditionally has been a prime factor in southern education, though in the lean 1980s it may become more important throughout the nation; (2) the South has been under more intense HEW and federal court pressure to desegregate its public schools for a longer time than the North and West; the Charlotte, Nashville, Louisville, and Wilmington metropolitan plans were all intimately related to federal court action; and (3) because the South's suburban development typically lags a generation or so behind that of other regions, the suburban structure and its resistance to involvement with the city are less deeply entrenched than in the North.

3. Bradley v. School Bd. of Richmond, 338 F. Supp. 67 (E.D. Va. 1972).

4. These data for the 1977-78 school year were kindly supplied by Jean

McGuire and J. Marcus Mitchell of METCO.

5. Federal court orders for a central-city district led to Wisconsin's funding of largely voluntary metropolitan efforts. This sequence underscores once again the impracticality of the position taken by some observers who would oppose such court orders and rely upon voluntary schemes entirely.

References

Abrams, Charles. 1975. The housing problem and the Negro. In *Racial Discrimination in the United States*, ed. Thomas F. Pettigrew. New York: Harper & Row.

Cataldo, Everett F., Michael W. Giles, Deborah Athos, and Douglas Gatlin. 1975. Desegregation and white flight. *Integrated Education* 13:3-5.

Coleman, James. 1976. Response to Professors Pettigrew and Green. *Harvard Educational Review* 46:217-224.

———, Ernest G. Campbell, Carol J. Hobson, James McPartland, Alexander M. Mood, Frederic D. Weinfeld, and Robert L. York. 1966. *Equality of Educational Opportunity*. Washington, D.C.: U.S. Department of Health, Education and Welfare, Office of Education.

———, Sara D. Kelly, and John Moore. 1975. *Trends in School Segregation: 1968-1973*. Washington, D.C.: Urban Institute.

Conta, Dennis J. 1978. Fiscal incentives and voluntary integration: Wisconsin's effort to integrate public schools. *Journal of Education Finance* 3:279-296.

Crain, Robert L., and Rita E. Mahard. 1978. Desegregation and black achievement: a review of the research. *Law and Contemporary Problems* 42(3): 17-56.

Farley, Reynolds. 1975. Racial integration in the public schools, 1967 to 1972: assessing the effects of public policy. *Sociological Focus* 8:3-26.

———. 1978. Report to the Honorable Judge Paul Egly. Los Angeles County Superior Court, Pomona, California.

———, T. Richards, and C. Wurdock. 1978. School integration and white flight: a resolution of conflicting results. Population Studies Center, University of Michigan, Ann Arbor. Unpublished.

Fitzgerald, M., and D. Morgan. 1977. School desegregation and white flight: North and South. *Integrated Education* 15:78-81.

Giles, M., E. Cataldo, and D. Gatlin. 1975. Desegregation and the private school alternative. Paper presented at the Symposium on School Desegregation and White Flight, Brookings Institution, Washington, D.C., August 15.

Lord, J. Dennis. 1975. School busing and white abandonment of public schools. *Southeastern Geographer* 15:81-92.

——— and J. C. Catau. 1976. School desegregation, busing and suburban migration. *Urban Education* 11:275-294.

Lowi, Theodore J. 1970. Apartheid U.S.A. *Transaction* 7(4):32-39.

McPartland, James. 1968. The segregated student in desegregated schools: sources of influence on Negro secondary students. Report no. 21, Center for Social Organization of Schools, Johns Hopkins University, Baltimore.

Pettigrew, Thomas F., ed. 1975a. *Racial Discrimination in the United States.* New York: Harper & Row.

―――. 1975b. A sociological view of the post-Bradley era. *Wayne Law Review* 21:813-832.

―――. 1978. Report to the Honorable Judge Paul Egly. Los Angeles County Superior Court, Pomona, California.

――― and R. Green. 1976a. School desegregation in large cities: a critique of the Coleman "white flight" thesis. *Harvard Educational Review* 46:1-53.

――― and R. Green. 1976b. A reply to Professor Coleman. *Harvard Educational Review* 46:225-233.

Rossell, Christine. 1975-1976. School desegregation and white flight. *Political Science Quarterly* 90:675-695.

Taeuber, Karl E., and Alma F. Taeuber. 1969. *Negroes in Cities.* New York: Atheneum.

Taylor, William L. 1977. Metropolitan remedies for public school discrimination: the neglected option. In *School Desegregation in Metropolitan Areas: Choices and Prospects.* Washington, D.C.: U.S. Department of Health, Education and Welfare, National Institute of Education.

U.S. Department of Commerce, Bureau of the Census. 1975. *Current Population Reports*, ser. P-23, no. 54.

―――. 1977. *Current Population Reports*, ser. P-25, no. 709.

―――. 1979. *Current Population Reports*, ser. P-23, no. 80.

10   The Role of Incentives
in School Desegregation

JAMES S. COLEMAN

Since the *Brown* decision of 1954, there have been sharp changes in both
the goals of school desegregation and the means used to achieve these
goals. Yet many discussions of school desegregation ignore these changes,
which are of obvious importance in informing future desegregation policies. This inattention to the past is especially disorienting because ends
and means have moved in opposite directions. That is, ends have moved
away from those having a constitutional justification through the Fourteenth Amendment on equal protection toward those that have weaker
justification. At the same time, means of desegregation have come to be
considerably more coercive, possibly appropriate to constitutionally justified ends but not to those with lesser justification.

It is useful (even if somewhat oversimplified) to think of the history of
school desegregation since 1954 as comprising two periods: the first
stage, from 1954 to the late 1960s; and the second stage, the period since
then.

The Ends in *Brown* and the Period Following

In the first stage, that is, at the time of the *Brown* decision and for a
number of years after that, the sole end of desegregation (indeed, the
very *meaning* of desegregation) was abolishing state-created segregation
of the schools in order to provide blacks the same range of educational
opportunity available to whites. This meant eliminating the dual school
systems in the South and creating unitary systems. At first, this had no
relevance at all for schools in the North, which had not had a history of
dual systems; but a sufficient number of segregating actions by school
boards in the North were found to show that some desegregating actions
were necessary there as well. However, since these latter findings arose
during the second stage of school desegregation, there has been a confusion about the ends of desegregation, both in the courts and outside.

But this gets ahead of the story. Let us turn to the second stage of school desegregation, beginning in the late 1960s.

The Ends of School Desegregation since about 1970

In the late 1960s there emerged a new set of ends of desegregation and, as a result, an almost unnoticed redefinition of desegregation. The clue is provided by a term that appeared at about that time, "affirmative integration." There was a move away from the goal of eliminating state-imposed segregation to eliminating all segregation, whether it resulted from individual actions of families or from state action. Stated differently, the goal shifted from eliminating state-imposed segregation to instituting state-imposed integration, by creating a numerical racial balance throughout the school system.

What brought about this curious change? It is a change, of course, that was not agreed to by all, but a change initiated by desegregation protagonists and then to a considerable extent accepted by the courts. Because the issues were shaped by the protagonists (for it was they who brought the cases and designed the arguments contained in the briefs), their redefinition came to shape the course of desegregation policy.

There are at least two causes for the transition from first-stage ends to the more encompassing second-stage ends, one somewhat more justifiable than the other.

The first and less justifiable cause can be termed organizational preservation. This process can be illustrated by an organization in which it was studied in detail, the March of Dimes (Sills, 1957). The original goal of the March of Dimes organization had been to eliminate polio. But with the advent of the vaccine, polio *was* virtually eliminated. So what could the March of Dimes do with the experience and momentum of its enormous volunteer staff and small full-time staff? It did not go out of business when its goal was accomplished. Rather it found a new goal, which allowed it to remain in operation: elimination of birth defects.

The point is that when the original *Brown* goal was achieved (as it essentially was in 1970, except in some large cities in the South), the organizations that had carried the desegregation fight forward found it necessary to take on a new goal, just as the March of Dimes did when polio was eliminated. The goal was that of eliminating all segregation, not merely that resulting from state action.

The second cause for the shift indicates why the new goal was not wholly unreasonable. To indicate what that cause is requires examining briefly the origins of American public education. Public education in America has a history unlike that in any country in Europe. European education was, from the outset, two-tiered: one set of schools for the elite, another for the masses. This dual school system took different forms in England, France, Germany, and elsewhere. But everywhere, whether in the lycée, gymnasium, grammar school, or other form, it was marked by richer, more academic, and more intensive curricula and a longer period of schooling for children of the elite.

American public education was, however, from its beginning a single system, founded on the ideology of a single "common school" that children of all economic levels and all groups would attend. Only in the South was there a parallel to the dual school systems of Europe, and that duality depended on racial distinction. Everywhere else there was a single system, with only minor aberrations. For example, the East Coast, mimicking Europe and always less egalitarian than the rest of the country, maintained and still maintains a number of private schools for the elite; throughout other parts of the country private secondary academies were numerous seventy-five years ago, but vanished when public secondary schools came into being. Another aberration has been the religious schools, primarily Catholic. But because Catholics have seldom been an economic elite in American communities, Catholic schools have not constituted a separation of the elite from the masses. And finally, the ideal of the common school was always realized more fully in towns, small cities, and rural areas than in large cities.

The general idea of the common school did not mean, of course, that schools were fully egalitarian. Within the school, children from lower socioeconomic groups were likely to fare less well; the general social structure of the community impressed itself on the functioning of the school. Nevertheless, the difference between these schools and the class-stratified schools of Europe was marked, just as the general assumption of equal opportunity of America was markedly different from the European assumption that every man had his station.

However, there have been changes, economic and technological, that undermine the idea of the common school and the underlying idea of equal opportunity through education. The technological changes have been in transportation, principally the automobile, whose existence has made possible the physical separation of work and residence by rather long distances. The economic changes have stemmed from a general increase in affluence, which allows families (given that the car frees them from living near work) to choose where they will live and to repeat that choice several times during their lifetimes as their economic conditions change. The result has been communities far more economically homogeneous than before World War II, and suburbs that differ sharply in economic level from one another as well as from the central city. Racial segregation by residence has also become more feasible than in the past and maintains itself despite sharp reductions in racial prejudice and discrimination in all walks of life.

The effect of this residential fractionation along economic and racial lines is felt in the schools. Although residence and workplace are no longer tied together for the adult members of the family, residence and schooling are tied together for the family's children. This is in part because of the naturally smaller radius of movement that young children have—making the "neighborhood school" a likely institution, while the "neighborhood office" or the "neighborhood factory" is not—and it is in part because of school policies. These policies characteristically limit the child to attendance at a particular school within the school district, the one into which he is zoned by his residence. This is often the closest school (his "neighborhood school"); if not, it is at least one of the closest.

With families sorting themselves out residentially along economic and racial lines, and with schools tied to residence, the end result is the demise of the common school attended by children from all economic levels. In its place is the elite suburban school (in effect a homogeneous private school supported by public funds), the middle-income suburban·school, the low-income suburban school, and central-city schools of several types —low-income white schools, middle-income white schools, and low- or middle-income black schools.

The effect on racial segregation in the schools of this reduction of economic and technological constraints on residence has been great. The existence of black ghettos in large cities has meant all-black schools in those ghettos, a segregation not imposed by the state but by the residential choices of white families with the money to implement their preferences. And, as Thomas Schelling shows, it requires only a very small preference for same-race neighbors to produce a high degree of residential segregation, if there are no economic or other constraints on moving (Schelling, 1978, ch. 4).

It is this situation that desegregation protagonists, having largely overcome state-imposed segregation, began to attempt to undo in the late 1960s. An indication of the new philosophy can be seen in the legal arguments used for the first time in the city-wide busing cases such as Charlotte-Mecklenburg and Denver. These were cases in which there was obviously affirmative integration, designed to overcome much more than state-imposed segregation. One element in the legal arguments that won these cases was that black children learned better in schools that were majority white schools, an argument that had not been used during the first stage of school desegregation, and one that bears no relation to removal of state-imposed segregation.

Are the Second-Stage Ends Wrong?

In the case of the March of Dimes, the new goal taken on by the organization (elimination of birth defects) was no less meritorious than the old one (elimination of polio), though it commanded considerably less public attention and support. What can be said about the new goal of desegregation action that arose in the second stage?

I believe the situation is similar. The new goal of overcoming the segregation that results from unconstrained residential choice is based on the same foundations as the goals behind the early American ideal of the common school for all—the creation of a single, unified nation by bringing together its children in school, regardless of race, religion, ethnicity, or class.

There is, however, a difference between the first-stage goal and the second-stage goal that is fundamental for the means used to achieve them. The first-stage goal concerns protection of the individual against discriminatory actions by the state and its agencies. It is not a goal designed to produce a particular social configuration in the schools, but rather one directly related to constitutional guarantees provided to all citizens. The second-stage goal, in contrast, *is* designed to produce a particular social configuration in the schools. It does not derive from constitutional guarantees, but from a sense of what a "good society" should be like. It may be more important in achieving the good society than is the narrower constitutional goal of the first stage. But somewhat different means are required to achieve it. And it is not, and never has been in American society, an overriding goal to be achieved at any expense. The common school of the American ideal had to compete with other goals in society: the right of people to live where they wish, schools as an integral part of the communities they serve, and others.

Means Appropriate to Second-Stage Ends

One can say, as a constitutional lawyer would, that when the goals change from those involving constitutional guarantees to those involving social configurations that can help bring about the good society, the appropriate locus of action shifts from the court to other arenas. Those arenas may be the legislature, the school board, the city council, or nongovernmental groups (for example, groups that establish integrated private schools for the socialization benefits they bring to black and white children). But the court is not one of them.

There is a more fundamental reason different means are necessary to reach this new, more encompassing goal. If a social arrangement (such as dual school systems before 1954 in the South) is the result of an action of an agency of the state, then that agency may be the defendant in a court case, and, if the case is won by the plaintiff, the defendant may be ordered to undo its offending action. Since there is a particular offending action, or set of actions, the court may oversee or police the undoing.

When the social arrangement is not the result of state action, but is the joint result of a multitude of individual residential decisions, each wholly legal, and many taken for admirable reasons (such as the decisions by many—civil rights leaders and desegregation fighters included—to move to a location where their children can attend a good school), then there is no proper defendant for a court case, nor even the basis for a court case. When a court case *is* initiated to overcome such segregation, with the city school system as defendant, as has occurred in many cities since about 1970, the results are peculiar. If the city loses the case, it is ordered to undo the segregation that exists, ordinarily through compulsory busing to achieve racial balance. When it complies, the outcome is simple, straightforward, and predictable: the same elements that brought about the segregation in the first place, individual residential and private-school decisions, will do so again. Sometimes this process occurs through a rapid evacuation, as in Boston or Memphis, sometimes through a long and steady one, as in Denver and Dallas. Resegregation, of course, arises because the means used are wholly inappropriate to the goal: an agency of the state is required to undo actions not of its own, but of individual families—actions that are not subject to legal assault in the first place.

There are paradoxical consequences of this use of inappropriate means for achieving the second-stage goals. Legal action requires an agency of the state to be the defendant; that agency, if it is to be found guilty, must be the one responsible for students of both races (ordinarily a central-city school district). Those whose residential decisions brought about the segregation in the first place—individual white families—have a simple strategy in response. They need only move their residence or their children to a school district without responsibility for large numbers of black students—and thus one that cannot be found guilty of segregating actions. This is precisely what they do, and they do so in large numbers when the "remedies" imposed are severe, such as busing their children to a different part of the city.

One might ask just how the pursuit of desegregation arrived at such an incongruity between ends and means. The answer involves many details of the way desegregation was pursued in the South, the transition from desegregation in the South to desegregation in the North, and the openings provided by the courts to continue use of the original means to accomplish new ends. The story of that process of transition and development cannot be pursued here. Rather, it is important to ask what means are appropriate to the new ends when those that are in current use are self-defeating.

First, of course, is the question of whether the ends of the common school, the unitary socialization experience provided by the common school, and the contribution this makes to society's integration are important to pursue. Members of the society will disagree about this; but much of the disagreement arises because the means used intrude on other values that may be strongly held (such as individual liberty). There is little disagreement with the ends themselves, only with their position in a hierarchy of social goals. And one of the safeguards that exists when these ends are pursued by appropriate means is that, because their accomplishment necessarily implies the assent of parents and children, black and white, the means are themselves self-policing. If they intrude little on other deeply held values, they will be effective; if they intrude too much, they will be ineffective and self-defeating, as in the case of court-order-induced white flight.

To develop a general idea of the means appropriate to the second-stage goals, it is useful to consider a small book by Charles Schultze (1978), chairman of the Council of Economic Advisers, based on the Godkin Lectures he presented at Harvard University in 1976. While at the Brookings Institution several years ago, Schultze held a seminar devoted to the same topic as the lectures. The seminar, lectures, and book all grew out of his experience as director of the Office of Management and Budget during the Johnson administration, when it was still the Bureau of the Budget. The general thesis is this: Government policy often produces the opposite of what is intended because of a failure to recognize the simple fact that persons, or local governments, or business firms, on whom a policy has its impact, themselves have goals that are different from those of the government. When a new policy is instituted, they will continue to work toward their own goals, viewing the official policy as a constraint or obstacle to accomplishing them. Thus policies often result in an outcome far from, and in some cases even *opposite* to, that intended by the policy makers. An example Schultze gives is the 1972 Water Pollution Act regulating the discharge of effluents into streams. He writes, "The very nature of the controls discourages pollution-reducing technological change. The 1983 criteria base effluent limits on 'best available technology.' But will firms in polluting industries sponsor research or undertake experimentation to develop a new means of reducing pollution still further if its very availability will generate new and more stringent regulations? The entire approach," he continues, "provides strong and positive incentives for polluters to use the legal system to delay progress toward effective cleanup" (p. 53). In this way, Schultze suggests, policymakers can thwart their own intent by not recognizing that there is an active party at the other end of the policy. What Schultze describes can be summed up in what we might term Schultze's Law: If a social policy does not actively employ the interests of those on whom it has an impact, it will find those interests actively employed in directions that defeat its goals.

Unfortunately, school desegregation policy in large cities is a case that Schultze can add to his list. Two kinds of consequences of school desegregation policy have been examined in some detail. One is the effect of desegregation efforts *within* a school district on the degree of segregation *between* districts. For large cities desegregation within the central city seriously increases the segregation between city and suburbs. In a striking recent case, the city of Boston lost 16 percent of its white students in 1974 when a busing plan was put into effect, and 19 percent the next year when its "Phase II" went into effect. In 1978 extensive desegregation in Los Angeles led to massive white flight, that is, segregation between the city of Los Angeles and its suburbs. The segregation that occurs is long-distance residential segregation, deeper and more difficult to overcome than segregation within a city. This is no accident, for those who are escaping the consequences of a policy they do not like make sure they are more difficult to reach the next time. In Los Angeles and other large cities, school desegregation has helped bring about a ghettoization of the city. We have, then, a prime example of Schultze's Law. Desegregation policies have been made with the simplistic assumption that racial composition of schools can be fixed by school assignment—that children and families are like pawns on a chessboard, and will stay where they are put. They do not, and the result is a tragic confirmation of Schultze's Law.

Another example of Schultze's Law can be found in the effect of desegregation on achievement. In 1966, the National Center for Education Statistics in HEW produced a report titled *Equality of Educational Opportunity*. It showed that disadvantaged black children achieved better in schools that were predominantly middle-class (which meant in effect majority white) than in homogeneous lower-class schools. The implication was that desegregation should lead to higher achievement of black students.

Since then the effects on achievement of black students of the desegregation of the late 1960s and early 1970s have been examined. A large number of desegregated school districts have been studied. The most recent review of these studies, by Crain and Mahard (1979), reports nineteen studies showing increased black achievement, twelve showing reduced achievement, and ten showing showing no effect at all. Among the studies in northern districts, there were in fact *more* showing reduced achievement than increased achievement. These results were reported despite the fact that Crain and Mahard were themselves interested in showing how desegregation could be beneficial for black achievement. Another review carried out earlier by St. John (1975) shows roughly similar results. The precise numbers are unimportant; what is important is that the premise based on the research results reported in *Equality of Educational Opportunity*, that there would be *generally* beneficial effects on achievement, has not been realized.

I do not believe that this nullifies the earlier research results, which show the potential that desegregation has for increasing achievement of the disadvantaged. What it *does* show is that, *as it has been carried out* in the past ten years, school desegregation has realized that potential too seldom. Again we have an illustration of Schultze's Law: A policy intended to increase achievement for black students has, in a large number of districts (if we are to generalize from this sample), decreased it instead; in others it has had no effect on achievement.

Why? Why the difference from the results reported in *Equality of Educational Opportunity*? I believe that again there has been a failure to recognize that the consequences of policies depend on the goals—and in turn on the responses—of those who are affected by them. We know little, in this case, about what caused the decreases in achievement. We do know that in many cases desegregation was implemented with little attention to its possible consequences in increasing disorder, conflict, and absence from school. Instead, attention was concentrated on the right numbers of the right colored bodies at specified schools, in order to comply with a desegregation edict that addressed itself to numbers alone. And the school system, including teachers and other staff, has only a limited amount of attention to allocate. If that attention is focused primarily on compliance with a court's edict or HEW administrative orders, then it must be less focused on educational goals.

In both ways I have shown, the means used to bring about school desegregation have illustrated Schultze's Law by defeating ill-conceived policies. One must then ask, What kinds of policies in school desegregation would not be defeated by Schultze's Law? The first part of the answer is to recognize that the movement in the direction of the second-stage goal does not necessarily involve overcoming all segregation. "Elimination" of every all-black school in a city need no longer be the criterion for success of the policy. There is a place for integrated schools, for all-black schools, for all-Spanish schools, for all-Chinese schools, for all-white schools, under a single criterion: that every child has the full right and opportunity, unconstrained by residence or race or transportation costs, or by artificial school district boundaries, to attend the school of his or her choice. The principle that ought to hold is that a child and his family have the right of choice of school, within or outside the district of residence, but that the school does not have the right to exclude the child.

If the second-stage goal of school desegregation is, as I have suggested, good though not overriding, it should be encouraged. To encourage or increase racial integration of schools beyond that which free choice would bring about—that is, to move in the direction of the second-stage goals—it is important to attend to Schultze's Law, and actively employ the interests of all those on whom the policy has an impact. This means actively using the interests of school administrators, teachers, and both black and white parents and children. There are a number of current and proposed policies that engage the interests of one or more of these groups for their success, and the use of incentives is what Schultze's Law implies.

Incentives for Integration

Magnet schools and other increases in school attractiveness

One general class of incentives not usually seen as such is the creation of magnet schools, which have some special characteristics that others do not have, sometimes including extra funds. Some magnet schools have curricula that include offerings not provided at other schools, such as special programs in music or foreign languages. In many respects, although the term "magnet" is new, the idea is old, perhaps best realized in some of the specialized high schools of New York City. In some integration plans (Boston, for example), there is an attempt to combine compulsory racial balance with the incentives provided by magnet schools, by designating certain schools as magnet schools but requiring a certain racial composition of the student body.

Incentives to school districts or schools

One incentive system that has been used to facilitate transfers across school district lines includes a financial incentive to the sending district and one to the receiving district for students who choose to transfer across school district lines. This plan is employed in Wisconsin for cross-district transfers. In practice, it is used mainly for black students transferring from Milwaukee to suburban school districts. In this case, both the Milwaukee district and the suburban district receive a payment from the state for the child who is transferring.

When we consider the possibility of such transfers, it appears that both kinds of incentives are necessary. If the receiving district is not to have an extra burden, the state should pay the costs of the transferring child, which include both the state aid ordinarily provided on a per-pupil basis and the portion of expenditures that are provided from local taxes (since the entering child's family does not pay local taxes in the district). And if the sending district is not to suffer, it will need at least a portion of the state aid that would have come to the district if the student had continued in school within it.[1]

Incentives to schools in conjunction with voucher plans

Voucher plans, in which a child brings a voucher to the school he chooses to attend, can be accompanied by incentives of various sorts. One that has been suggested is to have the voucher from a child who is in a minority in the school redeemable by the school for a greater amount of money than the voucher provided by a child who is in the majority in the school. This would create an incentive for the principal (and for the teachers, if they could participate in the extra benefits) to have a school that is racially heterogeneous, since it would mean greater school resources. Such proposals have not progressed very far, because they depend upon the existence of choice of school by children and their parents through a voucher or entitlement plan, and no such plans have been adopted.

Conclusion

The incentives I have discussed do not, of course, exhaust the possibilities for policies that actively employ the interests of affected parties in bringing about their success. But I believe the principle is clear.

Policies in this class are highly constrained, both in the means they use and in the degree of integration they can bring about. Yet they are the only kind of policy compatible with the second-stage goals. They do not suffer the serious defect of the unconstrained policies designed to achieve instant racial balance through compulsory busing. That defect, of course, is in accord with Schultze's Law—unconstrained policies exacerbate the very problem they are designed to cure.

Note

1. There are two conflicting considerations that determine whether the sending school district is financially better off or worse off if it loses a child and the state aid that accompanies the child. One is that, because such transferring students are sparsely strewn throughout the district, loss of one or a few children from the school system affects costs very little, but reduces income by the amount of state aid for those students that is no longer provided. (State aid is, on the average, more than 40 percent of school expenditures, while federal aid is about 9 percent.) The opposing consideration is that there is a reduction in the number of pupils without a reduction of the local tax base, so that the same local taxes provide more money per pupil after the transferring children have left.

References

Crain, Robert, and Rita Mahard. 1979. Desegregation and academic achievement. In *New Perspectives on School Integration*, ed. M. Friedman, R. Meltzer, and C. Miller. Philadelphia: Fortress Press.

St. John, Nancy. 1975. *School Desegregation: Outcomes for Children*. New York: Wiley Interscience.

Schelling, Thomas C. 1978. *Micromotives and Macrobehavior*. New York: W. W. Norton.

Schultze, Charles. 1978. *The Public Use of Private Interest*. Washington, D.C.: Brookings Institution.

Sills, David L. 1957. *The Volunteers*. New York: Free Press.

11 Civil Rights Commitment and the Challenge of Changing Conditions in Urban School Cases

DERRICK BELL

Any child, white or black, who is compelled to leave his neighborhood and spend significant time each day being transported to a distant school suffers an impairment of his liberty and his privacy.

Justice Lewis F. Powell's suggestion that school desegregation plans might impair liberty and privacy seemed no more than a suspicious cloud in an otherwise bright sky when the Supreme Court finally issued its first northern school decision in 1973.[1] The Court's majority in the *Denver* case, speaking through Justice William J. Brennan, refused to find a constitutional violation based solely on the existence of racially isolated schools as civil rights lawyers had contended in earlier northern school cases.[2] But it found that plaintiffs' proof of intentionally caused segregation in a substantial portion of the school system "justifies a rule imposing on the school authorities the burden of proving that this segregated schooling is not also the result of intentionally segregative acts."[3]

Though the *Denver* standard was difficult to meet in some cities and counties where segregated schools were the result of a complex of factors with which school board policy was intricately intertwined, it seemed sufficient to obtain orders to desegregate school districts across the North and West.[4] *Denver* was a long-awaited breakthrough in what was then a two-decade-long battle to implement *Brown*. Compared with this breakthrough, Justice Powell's concurring and dissenting opinion balancing the convenience of whites against the rights of blacks appeared out of place, an inappropriate irrelevance in a long-sought victory.

Disagreeing with the majority, Justice Powell urged rejection of the de facto-de jure distinction as a "legalism rooted in history rather than present reality." Where public-school systems are substantially segregated, Powell would find a prima facie case of school board responsibility, and place on the boards the burden of proving that, despite the racial

194

segregation in their schools, "they nevertheless are operating a genuinely integrated school system." Powell was concerned that the de jure-de facto distinction would require southern school systems with their history of official segregation to undertake remedial steps that equally segregated school systems in the North and West could avoid in the absence of segregative intent that was more difficult to show. He would require all school authorities of segregated districts to "make and implement their customary decisions with a view toward enhancing integrated school opportunities."[5]

Justice Powell's standard for liability was thus broader than the majority's, but the scope of relief he would offer was significantly narrower. In his view an integrated school system was one that integrated faculties and administration, assured equality of facilities, and promoted integration in drawing attendance zones, locating new schools, closing old ones, and transporting students. But Powell felt that, in light of the residential patterns in most metropolitan areas, an integrated system need not mean "that every school must in fact be an integrated unit."

When segregation is found in metropolitan districts, Powell expressed "profound misgivings" about its correction through court-ordered large-scale or long-distance transportation of students. He extolled the values of the neighborhood school: "the greater ease of parental and student access and convenience"; the "greater economy of public administration"; and the educational benefits of the community school.[6] He equated the parental interest in neighborhood public schooling with the right to have foreign languages taught in the public school[7] and with the parental right to have children educated in parochial schools.[8] Alleviating public-school segregation, Powell suggested, might deserve lower constitutional priority than protecting parents' interests in controlling the schooling of their children. In addition to the burden suffered by innocent parents and children, Powell noted that the great cost of providing transportation would fall disproportionately on large, urban districts, already struggling financially, while districts with few minority students would experience little or no expense, disruption, or white flight. Finally, he noted that even discounting all school board violations, the problem of residential segregation would remain. Thus remedies that sought to correct all racial imbalance exceeded those required to remedy the constitutional harm.[9]

Justice Powell's opinion seemed neither novel nor impressive at the time, but the very next year its reasoning was to become a major consideration in Chief Justice Warren Burger's rejection of metropolitan-wide school desegregation remedies in the *Detroit* school decision.[10] It is interesting and disconcerting to note that in more recent opinions Justice Powell abandoned the broad view of liability he suggested in *Denver* and helped form a majority in a series of decisions in 1977 school case opinions applying a very strict standard under which school officials were liable only if they had intentionally segregated the schools in order to discriminate invidiously against minority children.[11] In one of these decisions involving the *Austin* case, Justice Powell, joined by Chief Justice Burger and Justice William Rehnquist, concurred with an opinion that reiterated concerns he had expressed in *Denver*, including the view that the busing remedy exceeded the constitutional harm.[12]

Thus, under the legal rubric of more stringent standards for proving entitlement to relief, Powell's concerns about the costs of racial balance remedies in urban school districts gained temporary support from the majority of the Court. In effect, the new majority seemed to be weighing the interests in racial balance remedies asserted by civil rights lawyers on behalf of minority children against the interests of white children and their parents in attending public schools of their selection. Only when proof of school board involvement in segregated patterns is serious and intentional are desegregation interests to be given priority. This is not the stance expected of a Court committed until recently to the full implementation of *Brown* v. *Board of Education*.[13] Indeed, the *Brown* decision itself rejected parental rights arguments not unlike those now given so much weight. The regression of priorities to those prevailing prior to *Brown* did not happen suddenly. The signals have been quite clear since the *Denver* decision in 1973 and, some might argue, were evident in the immediate aftermath of the *Charlotte* case in 1971.[14] And yet, civil rights policy makers have not altered their strategies. Effecting a rough racial balance in each school remains the primary goal of most desegregation litigation.

Many, including this author, felt that continued emphasis on racial balance remedies was a suicidal strategy for the civil rights movement, and that when the Court next reviewed school cases according to its more strict standard, it would seriously undermine the principles by which the *Brown* decision had been interpreted for twenty-five years. A silver anniversary seemed an inappropriate time for retreat from what many believe to be the most important decision in the Court's history. On the last day of its 1978-79 term, the Court handed down decisions in the *Dayton* and *Columbus* school cases approving, albeit by fairly slim margins, appellate court orders requiring racial balance desegregation orders as appropriate correctives for school board policies found responsible for large-scale and long-standing segregation in the two systems.[15]

Civil rights lawyers sighed with relief. One of them, in an obvious reference to those who had predicted the worst, suggested that "even Cassandra occasionally nods" (Taylor, 1979). But the victory was not without its ominous omens. In each case, only five justices were willing to affirm without reservations. Four justices dissented in the *Dayton* case, and two in *Columbus*, with two others writing reluctant concurrences. Cassandra nodding or not, on such slender foundations of victory major disasters can be built.

Justice Powell dissented in both cases. In *Columbus*, writing for himself in language that gained the support of the chief justice and Justices Rehnquist and Potter Stewart, he renewed his warning that public education would suffer further unless the Court returned to a "more balanced evaluation of recognized interests of the society in achieving desegregation with other educational and societal interests a community may legitimately assert." Justice Powell agreed that *Brown* requires school systems in which racial discrimination is neither practiced nor tolerated, and agreed that ethnic and racial diversity in the classroom is a desirable component in the education of children in a country of diverse populations. But he cautioned again, "the question that courts in their single-minded pursuit of racial balance seem to ignore is how best to move toward this goal."[16]

Read closely, the *Dayton* and *Columbus* opinions appear more a revelation of impending danger than a reassurance of unswerving judicial support. They reveal clearly a large gap between the racial balance relief sought by civil rights lawyers and the opposition to that relief now clearly shared by what could easily prove a majority of the Supreme Court in the more difficult school cases likely to come before the Court during the next few years. Late in its third decade, the *Brown* decision remains unfulfilled and in jeopardy. A systematic look at the current status of school desegregation efforts indicates the seriousness of the challenge.

The Problem

Despite the critical role of *Brown* v. *Board* in providing the legal foundation for the whole civil rights movement, its proponents must be concerned that so many minority children have not been touched by that decision's promise of "equal educational opportunity." Though the data evoke more controversy than consensus, Nancy St. John's provocative review (1975) of extant studies leads to the conclusion that many minority students attending desegregated schools have not experienced educational gain. For those who believe that the values of school desegregation are not dependent on achievement-test scores, there is basis for despair in the unarguable statistics indicating that more than one-half of the country's minority children live in the largest twenty to thirty school districts, and that these districts tend to be majority-nonwhite. (See Chapter 1 for statistics on racial percentages in major urban school districts.) Given the lack of support for metropolitan school desegregation evidenced by Congress, the courts, and public opinion polls, it is unlikely that traditional school desegregation remedies will be available to alter these discouraging demographic realities. Indeed, efforts to lessen racial imbalance in large, urban areas through traditional techniques have sometimes decreased the percentage of nonminority children (Armor, 1978).

What Is Being Done?

Government civil rights agencies and nationally recognized civil rights groups have treated these obstacles to full school desegregation as no different from the resistance they have overcome by courageous persistence during the last two decades. In litigation they have continued to press for desegregation plans that maximize racial balance throughout the system. Despite the barriers imposed by the Supreme Court in the *Detroit* case, some lawyers still eye multidistrict remedies for large, predominantly black school districts. And most usually oppose suggestions that they consider alternative plans with less reliance on busing as the remedy for racially isolating schools. This strategy has the virtue of consistency. And there are some smaller districts, or large districts with relatively small minority populations, where this strategy remains appropriate.[17] Yet it becomes clear, particularly in the wake of the Supreme Court's restructuring of traditional school desegregation standards, that judicial support for relief relying on racial balance has been greatly diluted and could disappear entirely. Based on their utterances in recent years, it appears that Chief Justice Burger and Justices Powell and Rehnquist would not be displeased by such a disappearance. Three other justices seem to be moving in this direction, and only Justices Brennan and Thurgood Marshall appear committed to desegregation through the traditional techniques.

The persistence of civil rights groups is both predictable and explainable. Other social reform movements have followed similar sequences, often to their detriment. The quality of strong commitment to the integration ideal that was necessary, even essential, to gain first *Brown* and then any compliance at all during the first decade of bitter resistance is difficult to lay aside when very different circumstances dictate new approaches and tactics.

The movement toward racial balance remedies began in the early 1960s when it became apparent that only through this means could school board recalcitrance and intransigence be revealed. It worked, and the Supreme Court, in effect, adopted the tactic in 1968.[18] By that point it was far more than a tactic for most civil rights veterans who had fought so hard for its recognition. It was a strong, deeply held belief that was not negotiable. No longer the vehicle for reform, racial balance remedies with whatever transportation was required to carry them out became the reform.

But by the mid-1970s this almost religious adherence had become a self-imposed stalling mechanism that created new resistance while rendering desegregation proponents incapable of the much needed rethinking of strategies and goals that the new situations demanded. Rigidity, which had been a virtue, became a disease undermining the movement and breeding intolerance of any view or suggestion that strayed from the accepted integration norm.

Why Change Strategies?

Herbert Wechsler criticized the Supreme Court's decision in *Brown* for failing to weigh the right of white nonassociation against the right of blacks to attend the same public schools as whites (Wechsler, 1959). While many legal scholars have sought to respond to Wechsler's complaint (Pollak, 1959; Black, 1960; Heyman, 1961) it remains true that the Court in *Brown* neither recognized nor evaluated any rights that whites had to sacrifice in order to make school desegregation possible. But in current decisions the Court is both recognizing and evaluating those rights. They are not designated as white rights of nonassociation, but rather as interests in local control, as in *Denver* and *Detroit*, or "local autonomy of school districts"; nor are they denominated a "vital national tradition," as in *Dayton*. Attending a neighborhood school is now a recognized interest that district courts are instructed to balance against relief requiring racially balanced schools.

Although courts will usually enjoin governmental policies whose major purpose is deliberate discrimination against racial minorities, they will not invalidate equally harmful policies that serve a socially acceptable goal or further interests not overtly invidious. This dichotomy in school desegregation litigation is reflected in the Supreme Court's refusal to abandon its de jure-de facto distinction; and it also explains the Court's current insistence that school systems be held accountable for only that degree of racial isolation attributable to board policies intended to have that result. The Fifth Circuit in the *Austin* case,[19] the Eighth Circuit in *Omaha*,[20] and the Sixth Circuit in *Dayton*[21] have responded to Supreme Court demands with decisions reaffirming school board liability under the High Court's strict liability standards. But the Supreme Court is likely trying to communicate, albeit not too coherently, that *whatever* the board's intention, if the result of its actions furthers interests in local school autonomy, then those interests should outweigh the interests of blacks in school desegregation remedies that rely on racial balance and require extensive busing.

In summary, when *Brown* was argued, blacks were able to assert constitutional entitlement to desegregated schools because of the clear harm and stigma attached to requiring their attendance at separate, usually inferior schools solely because of their race. School officials offered arguments based on educational differences, safety, health, and preservation of public peace and order, but they could never explain why not even one black child could ever attend a white school. Their arguments really boiled down to: "Invidious or not, we want segregated schools." The Court decided not even to legitimate the school board position by balancing it against the interests of blacks in desegregation. But today there are no de jure segregated school systems in the overt, pre-1954 sense. In much current school litigation, it is the school board that asserts substantive, educationally rational reasons for not racially balancing their schools, while plaintiffs increasingly must take the position that racial balance is necessary even if expensive, disruptive, educationally nonproductive, and temporary. In effect, plaintiffs are saying: "To hell with the costs, we want integrated schools." A once despised and still subordinated racial minority is not likely to succeed with that argument.

A Viable Alternative Strategy

We tend to forget that the racial separation outlawed in the *Brown* case was but one manifestation of the racism that adversely affected minority children in segregated schools. The real evil was and is the persistent pattern of giving priority to the needs and interests of whites in a school system without regard to whether this policy disadvantages blacks. Racially separate schools facilitated the white priority phenomenon, but its results can be achieved, often with great damage to minority children, within the structure of a desegregated school. Equally damaging are the exclusion of nonwhites from meaningful involvement in school policy making, the exclusion of nonwhite parents from active participation in their children's education on a day-to-day basis, and the inability of nonwhite parents to hold school personnel responsible for effective schooling of their nonwhite children. School remedies, particularly in large urban districts, should be addressed to all aspects of racism, not just separation. Those remedies should focus specifically on techniques intended to improve the educational effectiveness of schools attended by nonwhite children. Such emphasis is appropriate whether or not those schools are predominantly white.

The Supreme Court has indicated in a totally different context that the Constitution does not guarantee quality education.[22] But that decision is irrelevant in litigation involving appropriate remedies for proven racial discrimination. If there were any doubt of this, the Supreme Court removed it with its second decision in the *Detroit* school litigation,[23] approving a Detroit school desegregation plan that rejected much of what racial balance was possible in that 80 percent black district in favor of a number of "educational components." The legal precedent in the *Detroit* case is valuable, but we need not be limited by its rather orthodox ideas regarding educational improvement, most of which were suggested by the Detroit school board.

It is now possible to identify a number of public schools serving poor, nonwhite children, and serving them in an educationally effective fashion. The components of this success—effective leadership, close parental involvement in the educational process, and accountable teachers— clearly indicate the character of educationally oriented relief that should be sought in future judicial decisions.

The challenge for civil rights policy makers is to break free of their rigid adherence to racial balance remedies and develop alternative school desegregation plans containing the educationally oriented components suggested above. Flexibility should be emphasized to enable individual districts to pattern specific provisions to meet local conditions. Detroit and Atlanta show that courts will welcome plans that contain real potential for improving educational opportunities for blacks without the cost and disruption of busing, which has deprived whites of control over where their children go to school without bringing measurably more effective education to blacks.

Minority children need *Brown* today more than ever. The Court promised those children "equal educational opportunity" in 1954, and by focusing future efforts on educational effectiveness, we can utilize the *Brown* decision's still considerable precedential weight to move minority children closer to that goal. The challenge is there. The question is whether school integration advocates will recognize it hunkered down behind the bulwarks of their commitment.

Notes

1. Keyes v. School Dist. No. 1, Denver, 413 U.S. 189, 247-248 (1973) (Powell, J., concurring in part and dissenting in part).
2. Earlier cases included Deal v. Cincinnati Bd. of Educ., 369 F.2d 55 (6th Cir. 1966); Barksdale v. Springfield School Committee, 237 F. Supp. 543 (D. Mass. 1965); Downs v. Board of Educ. of Kansas City, 336 F.2d 988 (10th Cir. 1964); Bell v. School City of Gary, 324 F.2d 209 (7th Cir. 1963).
3. 413 U.S. at 210.
4. The origins and likely motivations for *Brown* and its progeny are discussed in Derrick Bell, "The legacy of W. E. B. DuBois: a rational model for achieving public school equity for America's black children," 11 Creighton L. Rev. 409 (1978).
5. 413 U.S. at 219, 224, 226, 240-242.
6. 413 U.S. at 227, 238, 246.
7. 413 U.S. at 247 (Powell, J., citing Meyer v. Nebraska, 262 U.S. 390 [1923]).
8. 413 U.S. at 247 (Powell, J., quoting Pierce v. Society of Sisters, 268 U.S. 510, 534-535 [1925]).
9. 413 U.S. at 248-250.
10. Milliken v. Bradley (Milliken I), 418 U.S. 717 (1974).
11. Austin Independent School Dist. v. United States, 429 U.S. 990 (1976); Board of School Comm'rs of Indianapolis v. United States, 429 U.S. 1068 (1976); School Dist. of Omaha v. United States, 433 U.S. 667 (1977); Brennan v. Armstrong (Milwaukee), 433 U.S. 672 (1977); Dayton Bd. of Educ. v. Brinkman (Dayton I), 433 U.S. 406 (1977).
12. 429 U.S. at 991-995.
13. Brown v. Board of Educ., 347 U.S. 483 (1954).
14. Swann v. Charlotte-Mecklenburg Bd. of Educ., 402 U.S. 1 (1971). Chief Justice Burger, commenting on a school case decided by a lower court shortly after *Swann*, found it "disturbing" that the court had interpreted his decision as requiring racial balance in each school to be close to that of the school district as a whole. He said that *Swann* had not prescribed the setting of any mathematical formulas. Winston-Salem Board of Educ. v. Scott, 404 U.S. 1221 (Burger, Circuit Justice, 1971), *denying stay to* Adams v. School Dist. #5, 444 F.2d 99 (4th Cir. 1971).
15. Dayton Bd. of Educ., v. Brinkman (Dayton II), 443 U.S. 526 (1979); Columbus Bd. of Educ. v. Penick, 443 U.S. 449 (1979).
16. 443 U.S. at 486 (Powell, J., dissenting).

17. Metropolitan advocates have been successful in Wilmington, Delaware: Evans v. Buchanan, 582 F.2d 750 (3d Cir. 1978), *cert. denied*, 48 U.S.L.W. 3696 (April 29, 1980); and Louisville, Kentucky: Cunningham v. Grayson, 541 F.2d 538 (6th Cir. 1976), *cert. denied*, 429 U.S. 1074 (1977).

18. Green v. County School Board, 391 U.S. 430 (1968).

19. United States v. Texas Educ. Agency, 564 F.2d 162 (5th Cir. 1977).

20. United States v. School Dist. of Omaha, 565 F.2d 127 (8th Cir. 1977).

21. Brinkman v. Gilligan, 583 F.2d 243 (6th Cir. 1978).

22. San Antonio Independent School Dist. v. Rodriguez, 411 U.S. 1 (1973).

23. Milliken v. Bradley (Milliken II), 433 U.S. 267 (1977).

References

Armor, David. 1978. *White Flight, Demographic Transition, and the Future of School Desegregation*. Santa Monica, California: Rand Corporation.

Black, Charles. 1960. The lawfulness of the segregation decisions. *Yale Law Journal* 69:421.

Heyman, A. Michael. 1961. The chief justice, racial desegregation, and the friendly critics. *California Law Review* 49:104.

Pollak, Louis. 1959. Racial discrimination and judicial integrity: a reply to Professor Wechsler. *University of Pennsylvania Law Review* 108:1.

St. John, Nancy H. 1975. *School Desegregation: Outcomes for Children*. New York: Wiley Interscience.

Taylor, William. 1979. Columbus and Dayton: a renewed commitment to equality. *Legal Analysis*, National Project and Task Force on Desegregation Strategies, no. 3.

Wechsler, Herbert. 1959. Toward neutral principles of constitutional law. *Harvard Law Review* 73(15):31-34.

12   Urban School Desegregation from a Black Perspective

BARBARA L. JACKSON

Before public policy can be developed, an issue or problem must be defined. Those in power generally define the issue according to their own values, and from their own perspectives. The assumptions underlying these values will not be questioned unless other groups participate in redefining the issues.

Developing public policy is particularly difficult when it concerns issues that have implications for the distribution of economic benefits and power or that are at the core of the decision makers' value system. Race has been such an issue in America. It has permeated American society since the first Africans were brought to this country. For black Americans, race is all-pervasive—and it is difficult if not impossible for those who are part of the majority to comprehend. Because of the legacy of the peculiar institution of slavery followed by legal segregation, the situation of Blacks and the response of policy makers have been different in kind, not just in degree, from those involving all other immigrant groups. Fundamental value questions as well as economic and political power are at stake.

School desegregation continues to be defined and assessed from changing perspectives. During the battle to eliminate the laws that required segregation, there was a consensus that could be called a black perspective. In the period since the 1954 *Brown* decision, that perspective has changed, primarily in response to the white society's reaction to desegregation. It now seems appropriate to take a realistic look at what has happened to see if there are new policy directions that may emerge from a black perspective—or, as W. E. B. DuBois might say, from "the other side of the veil."

One fact seems clear: the issue of race, with us since the founding of the country, will not easily be resolved. I am convinced, after looking at past efforts to create an integrated society under the rules written by others, that a new approach is needed—one that no longer attempts to erase differences between Blacks, whites, and other ethnic-cultural groups, but accepts them, respects them, and encourages each to perpetuate what is valuable to it.

Education from a Black Perspective

The heritage of slavery and the legal segregation that forced the establishment of parallel and separate institutions, not only in education, but in virtually every phase of life for the freedmen and their progeny, were primarily responsible for creating a black perspective. Perspective is a particular vantage point from which phenomena are viewed, which grows out of the value system and the position of a group in society. A black perspective is a view of a group that has been victimized. It arises not solely from a study of books, but also from "the bones and spirits of those who have stood at the bottom-most point of the pit of humiliation and dehumanization" (Smith, 1976). A black perspective grows out of the historical-cultural heritage of black Americans and their struggle to become citizens. To ignore one's history or to be robbed of it is to lose self-understanding and the roots of one's past so necessary for pride in self and group. A brief review of the significant differences between Blacks and all other immigrant groups will give further meaning to a black perspective.

First, the ancestors of black Americans were forcibly brought to this land of opportunity and subsequently enslaved. As stated by Justice Thurgood Marshall in the *Bakke* decision: "Three hundred and fifty years ago, the Negro was dragged to this country in chains to be sold into slavery. Uprooted from his homeland and thrust into bondage for forced labor, the slave was deprived of all legal rights. It was unlawful to teach him to read; he could be sold away from his family and friends at the whim of his master; and killing or maiming him was not a crime. The system of slavery brutalized and dehumanized both master and slave" (*Regents* v. *Bakke*, 1978).

What made slavery and the segregation that followed so enforceable was the badge of color. Black skins made identification easy and, at the same time, prevented those of African descent from disappearing into the dominant society as other immigrants had done. As time went on, however, the activities of the masters and mistresses became evident in the range of skin colors among the slaves, making identification more difficult and creating a value-laden color consciousness that still exists.

A second factor that contributed to the development of a black perspective was the justification used to perpetuate slavery. Some of the reasons were religious, quasi-scientific, and environmental. But the definition of slaves as property was the most ingenious and has had the most
far-reaching effects. One consequence of this definition was the denial of
any culture and traditions. Only with black folks is there an accusation of
separateness and withdrawal from society when they choose to perpetuate their own customs. Other groups are applauded for still celebrating
their St. Patrick's Day or Columbus Day. In fact, all other immigrant
groups, while being Americanized, were permitted and at times encouraged to keep some of the old-country ways. For them it was recognized as
legitimate that group identity was important in developing individual
identity. Some of these differences in treatment may have been based on
the presumption that the Negro had no culture and, therefore, had nothing to preserve—assimilation into the majority culture was his only
option.

Third, and perhaps most significant in creating a black perspective,
was the process through which the slave, and later the segregated black
American, was enculturated into American society. Because of the slave's
position in the society, he had to adapt to two cultures simultaneously. In
the world of the white master his role as slave was determined by others;
he was forced to develop certain behaviors in order to survive physically
and psychologically. But the slave also lived in the world of his own community, and later in black communities segregated explicitly by law in the
South and subtly by law and custom in the North. It was with his own
group that some sense of humaneness could be nurtured: "The most important aspect of this group identification was that slaves were not solely
dependent on the white man's cultural frames of reference for their ideas
and values . . . the slave's culture bolstered his self-esteem, courage, and
confidence, and served as his defense against personal degradation"
(Blassingame, 1972, p. 76). One result of this heritage, shared by all
whose ancestors came from Africa, is an individual identity based
primarily on group membership in direct conflict with the philosophical
basis on which this country and its democratic form of government were
founded. DuBois defined this phenomenon as a "double consciousness
. . . a sense of always looking at one's self through the eyes of others, of
measuring one's soul by the tape of a world that looks on in amused con-
tempt and pity" (DuBois, 1916, p. 16).

Another outcome of this double life was the way slaves responded to
the white society. Being part of the master's world—working in the big

house—meant access to better food, an easier life in many ways than working in the fields, and at times being treated almost as a human being. It meant exposure to another culture. But it also meant compromise of who they were, especially as they were subject to the ownership prerogative of the masters and mistresses that produced a new species of "coloreds" and the value-laden color consciousness that gave status to light skin. Entering the dominant society today reflects some of these same opportunities, potential benefits, and disadvantages. For now, as then, it is often believed that the only way Blacks can really succeed is not through integration, defined as retaining some differences, but rather through assimilation—giving up all traces of their African heritage and even contact with their own group to be truly acceptable.

One more outcome of this master-slave relationship is the distrust, at times hostility, that prevents honest discourse and impedes progress. A major problem today is finding ways to develop trust among black folks, their leaders, and the larger society. This is not easy because distrust in black communities is so deep-seated, and, unfortunately, conditions have not yet changed enough to make suspicion unnecessary. Other immigrant groups were not faced with the same dilemma—their leaders could retain credibility within the group while trying to gain power and influence in the dominant society.

Finally, the road to citizenship for black Americans was unique—no other immigrant group had to establish its humanness as a condition for citizenship. Blacks were handicapped from the beginning by their status, for not only were they not citizens, they were not even human beings. A civil war, three constitutional amendments (the Thirteenth, Fourteenth, and Fifteenth), and a period of Reconstruction appeared to establish that first condition, and a beginning was made toward securing the right to exercise the privileges associated with citizenship. After Reconstruction, however, advances in the opportunity for Blacks to exercise these rights were blocked by the legislative and executive branches of government. With the 1896 Supreme Court decision in *Plessy* v. *Ferguson*, it appeared that there was no route to gain the rights of citizenship, even through the judiciary. The Supreme Court confirmed the legality of Jim Crow laws that segregated every aspect of life for the Negro in the South. For those who lived in the North, there was also a segregated existence with barriers to participation erected in ways that were more subtle but just as effective in achieving the subjugation of the group and in denying equality of opportunity.

But the Negro was now a citizen. He was no longer defined in law as property, and this was a government of law in which citizens had certain guaranteed rights. As a result of slow but steady pressure, primarily through the courts, the legal barriers created by the other branches of government were eliminated. With the *Brown* decision, an end came to one chapter of race relations—"separate but equal" was no longer the law of the land. A new era in race relations was about to begin.

In the more than twenty-five years since that historic decision progress and change have occurred, but not without continued court action and new modes of protest. In the 1980s a reassessment must be made to permit the development of new policy directions. The moral fervor of the 1960s to right the wrongs of the past seems to have faded. The policies that combined actions of all branches of government, so evident in the 1960s, also seem to have waned. Furthermore, the courts and the dominant society have reacted differently to school segregation not specifically created by legislation, conveniently overlooking all other government action, such as housing policies, that have influenced school-assignment policies. In 1979, with the Ohio cases, however, hope that the original *Brown* decision continued to be the law of the land was rekindled.

Blacks have become disenchanted, though, with the approach that now appears to have been one of assimilation into the dominant culture rather than integration of equal partners. As a result, their ability to sustain constant protest and pressure has diminished. While racial integration of schools in some parts of the South has continued, the student populations in large cities, North and South, have changed so that now most are majority-black. But black educators throughout the country, still few in relative numbers, occupy more positions of authority than ever before. Also, for the first time, the states have taken an active role by creating, through the Commission of the States, a Task Force on Desegregation Strategies.

With these conditions in mind, policy makers need to look specifically at the reasons for the changing population of the cities. As long as those in power believe that Blacks are responsible for "resegregating" the cities, remedial policies will be focused on Blacks. If it is recognized that members of the white, and increasingly the black, middle class are leaving the city because of inadequate services and safety in the city, public policy will take a different direction. If city leaders want to hold middle-class whites and blacks or attract back those who have left, they must now compete with the suburbs in the services and amenities they provide. There is evidence that a few cities, such as Atlanta, San Francisco, Detroit, and Baltimore, recognize this. They have undertaken downtown rebuilding plans in hopes of attracting the middle class back to the cities.

Coincidentally, the energy crisis has had the unanticipated consequence of forcing long-time commuters to rethink the cost of living near trees and grass. The memory of long gas lines and the rising cost of commuting may finally spell the end of the elusive dream of a better life in the suburbs.

But the critical factor for the cities may be the perceived quality of the schools, especially if they are under the direction of Blacks. Will it be possible for black educators (many of whom were prepared at the most prestigious white universities, so their credentials should be acceptable) to change the image of urban schools, particularly if the schools are majority-black?

Urban schools have become majority-black because nonblacks either left the city or enrolled their children in private schools. The Blacks stayed, while those with whom they were being asked to integrate or racially mix left. From a black perspective, to blame the Blacks who stayed for the change in the complexion of the schools is to revert to the practice of blaming the victim instead of addressing the cause. The real problem now is the assumption that once a school system becomes majority-black it must deteriorate. Statistics are always reported with a tone, if not of horror, at least of dismay, reflecting the still prevalent belief that anything black is bad. What seems to be forgotten is that many black people did learn, and learn well, in all-black systems, even without real control of the limited resources. Perhaps the motivation was greater when the barriers to participation were so much clearer. Many black educators are trying to find ways to recapture some of that motivation for black students without returning to separate school systems.

Rather than bemoan the fact of black school systems or look only to busing—even two-way—for solutions, we must look for other ways to achieve the broader goals of a multiracial, multicultural society. There are means by which to bring about the personal contact so necessary to permit communication with those who may be different. One approach that responded to conditions peculiar to Atlanta in 1974 may provide direction to policy makers in other cities in the 1980s. The Atlanta Plan recognized the realities of the city, including the power of a dominant black leadership group. A brief review of the plan follows; further details are given in Jackson, 1978.

The Atlanta Plan

On May 1, 1974, almost twenty years to the day after the Supreme Court's landmark *Brown* v. *Board of Education* decision, Albert J. Hen-

derson, Jr., judge of the U.S. District Court for the Northern District of
Georgia, handed down an equally historic decision in what he termed
"the latest episode in the annual agony of Atlanta." The settlement of
this case, in the courts since 1958, represented a departure from earlier
attempts to attain "the elusive goal of desegregation in the Atlanta
schools." As Judge Henderson stated:

> The Atlanta Public School System presents a situation which is
> unique in the annals of school desegregation litigation following in
> the wake of *Brown* v. *Board of Education*, 347 U.S. 483 (1954).
> During the period of this suit, the system has evolved from one with
> a pupil ratio of approximately 70% white and 30% black to its pre-
> sent state of 17% white and 83% black. From a peak enrollment of
> about 115,000 students, the system has gradually lost about five to
> seven thousand students a year, the great bulk of them white, bring-
> ing it to its present enrollment of approximately 87,900. The admin-
> istration and staff have experienced a similar racial inversion from a
> predominately white composition to a ratio of approximately 68%
> black and 32% white. A majority black Atlanta school board,
> chaired by Dr. Benjamin Mays, a respected black educator and civil
> rights leader, was elected in recent city elections. As noted earlier,
> the administrative staff of the system is over two-thirds black and is
> under the able supervision of Superintendent Alonzo A. Crim, a
> black educator and administrator with an impressive list of creden-
> tials and accomplishments. In short, it would be difficult to attribute
> to those presently charged with the operation of the Atlanta Public
> Schools any intention to discriminate against black students enrolled
> in that system or to continue the effect of past discrimination (*Cal-
> houn* v. *Cook*, 487 F 2nd 680 [1974]).

In 1961 the first step toward dismantling the dual school system of
Atlanta was taken when nine carefully screened black high-school students enrolled in four white schools. The city was congratulated on the
peaceful integration of the schools. Atlanta, like most school systems in
the South through the '60s (and now many in the North), had to be
pushed step by step toward a more fully integrated system. As each step
was taken, more whites left the system—the same pattern evident in
northern cities today. In 1970, with the massive reassignment of teachers,
there was a dramatic decline in the number of white teachers, as well as
of white students. Thus by 1973 the educational and political leadership
of Atlanta was prompted to take a realistic view of the school system and
the city and to propose a different plan.

The Settlement Plan of 1973, approved by the court as an appropriate end to a dual school system, was developed by a coalition of forces representing all segments of the community. The biracial committee, appointed by the judge in 1970, played a dominant role in keeping the parties talking until a plan acceptable to all sides was found. It appeared to those outside Atlanta, as demonstrated by the ouster of the president of the local NAACP by the national organization, that "integration" was being abandoned. What had been gained was more control by Blacks of the administrative and staff assignments. The assumption underlying the plan was that if Blacks were in established positions of authority, the system would be more responsive to what was now the racial majority in the system.

The Settlement Plan has four major components: a student-assignment plan that attempts to maintain in all schools a ratio of no less than 30 percent black students; a staff-desegregation plan that attempts to assign teachers in such a way that each school reflects a percentage similar to that in the whole system; expansion of the majority-to-minority transfer plan whereby a child may transfer to a school in which his racial group is in the minority; and finally, a plan for the central administrative staff. This last component attracted the most attention because the court-approved plan increased the number of administrative positions and then designated which positions would be filled by Blacks and which by whites. It stipulated that the superintendent be Black.

Directions for the Future

Since the Atlanta Settlement Plan was approved by the court, conditions that existed there seem to have emerged in many of the cities now struggling with the desegregation of schools. An identification of some of these factors may suggest new directions for policy makers.

First, the role of the courts was dominant and necessary. In Atlanta, despite the existence of some influential Blacks in the schools and the city, no action to dismantle the dual system was taken until the court order. Pressure had to continue. The court-appointed biracial committee was instrumental in forcing the parties to come together and keep talking. Though the moral commitment, essential to enforce court decisions and to make the work of citizens' advisory committees legitimate and effective, may have declined somewhat since the '60s, the courts are still a powerful and necessary force. What has changed is the way in which schoolpeople want to use the courts. Many black and white educators today want to use the courts to bring about better educational opportunities, in contrast to the recalcitrant boards and administrators of the '60s who resisted any court intervention.

Second is the emergence of black educators. In 1974, the appointment of a black superintendent to a major school system was an unusual occurrence that came about through court action. Today there are many black superintendents, compared in absolute numbers with ten years ago, although they are still only a small percentage of the total. These black educators appear to have a different orientation from their predecessors. They want to make their school systems work for *all* children—urban or rural, black or white. Those still involved with court actions want to use that power to improve the schools; they are determined to provide a model of educational excellence and to demand effective performance on the part of students and faculty alike.

There is some evidence in Atlanta that the black leadership is beginning to make a difference. Achievement-test scores have risen. There has been an emphasis on staff development, and attention to reading is a high priority. But one objective of the plan, to achieve some degree of racial balance in the schools, is more and more difficult to accomplish as there are fewer and fewer schools that black children can attend in which they would be in the minority.

A third factor that may have been more significant in the South, especially in Atlanta because of prior legal segregation, is the political influence of Blacks. The existence of a black middle class whose economic position came from banking, insurance, and construction, as well as higher education, had created a leadership group comfortable with the white economic and political leaders. Within the confines of legal segregation, the Blacks did exercise some influence and had a measure of power unlike those in most northern cities, at least at that time. Some of this influence was evident even before their numbers consituted a majority, and before they occupied official positions of power in the schools or the city.

Both the political and economic power holders now recognize that schools are essential to the health and continued growth of the city. This may be true in many cities, especially where rebuilding of the downtown area and bringing in employees (especially executives) from the suburbs are priorities. In the early 1960s it may have seemed to Atlanta's small group of white business leaders, who were instrumental in building "their" city according to "their economic self-interest," that they could ignore (or at least pay little attention to) the schools. By the mid-1970s it was clear that the schools mattered. And as the years progressed the need for a quality school system—even if majority-black and dominated by black leadership—was recognized.

Now the Atlanta Chamber of Commerce is more interested than ever in the schools. In his acceptance speech in 1978, the newly elected Chamber president, Robert W. Scherer, listed better schools as a top priority for his organization. He pointed out that "the quality of public education in a community plays 'a major role' in the decisions by corporate executives over where they will locate, expand, or invest in plants or offices." He continued, "Presently, we have designed and are seeking funding from various sources for a major eighteen month effort which would allow us to expand our commitment to public education . . . We hope to hire a full-time coordinator to implement new programs and to increase the reach of our already successful programs, like 'Schools Without Walls' and 'Adopt a School' " (*Atlanta Journal*, December 15, 1978). It is clear that the economic power bloc must support public schools if they are to survive.

This recognition by the political and economic leaders of the role of schools in protecting their investment, and the future viability of the city, has helped encourage another trend in Atlanta, as well as other cities—the return of white families, especially young ones, to the central city. In two Atlanta neighborhoods major renovation has occurred, with very large old homes being restored to their former grandeur—some at high cost, some through a do-it-yourself approach. Many of the families in these neighborhoods want to send their children to the public schools. The cost of commuting in time, money, and energy is being reexamined, especially in light of recent gasoline shortages and higher prices. A white middle-class group, the Northside Parents for Public Schools, is also encouraging white parents to return their children to the public schools. They have had some success, even though the numbers are still only a small proportion of the total enrollment. This movement may indicate that whites believe that their children can learn even in schools with black children—indeed, that they may learn certain things as a result of being with black children.

The group in Atlanta—and apparently in other major cities —that has not responded to the support of public schools is the black middle class. Even with black administrative control in some cities, too may black middle-class parents who could have an influence have not been willing to keep their children in public schools. More research is needed to verify the extent of this trend and to suggest strategies to reverse it.

The conditions that appeared unique to Atlanta in 1973, and that made it possible for the school desegregation case that had been in the courts for fifteen years to arrive at what some have called a "compromise" rather than a "settlement" plan, are now emerging in many northern cities. This suggests that decision makers should reassess their current plans to face the realities of the cities in the 1980s. The conditions that parallel the Atlanta situation in 1973 are a majority-black student population in most large cities, making numerical balance in every school a virtual impossibility; an increasing number of black educators in positions of authority and power whose commitment to excellence for all children, but especially the black children in their system, is paramount; the increasing number and influence of black political officeholders; and recognition by economic leaders that cities cannot remain viable and attract and hold business interests unless the school system provides quality education. To provide an equal opportunity and access to the goods and services of society for all citizens—especially those who have been denied, whether by law or by fact—new plans are needed.

Conclusion

The question now is, What policy implications can be drawn from these conditions and trends? And that brings me back to where I started. How does the issue of school desegregation look from at least one black person's perspective early in the 1980s?

Remember that perspective means defining the world in ways that are understood and accepted by all those who share that point of view. In fact, what often gives a particular group its power is its ability to define the world and consequently control the issues that are the basis of public policy. The power brokers often turn to the social scientists for help because part of their job is to provide a rationale for action. But how a problem is perceived will often dictate the policy choices.

Before the *Brown* decision there was little disagreement about the meaning of *segregation* in white and black communities. Segregation was not just any kind of separation; it was a special kind that was imposed, forced by various governmental units through a variety of legal sanctions against the will of the subjected groups. It was specifically aimed at Negroes—those who were socially defined (certainly not by physical appearance) as being descendants of slaves. These laws were quite explicit in the seventeen southern states and the District of Columbia; in the North the approach was more devious but just as effective—remember the restrictive covenants, policies of the Federal Housing Administration, and zoning laws?

What made segregation so devastating was that it branded a whole group inferior—it determined the status in society of all the descendants of former slaves. It was imperative that these legal shackles be removed. And this is exactly what the *Brown* decision did—it said that coerced, forced separation by government solely on the basis of race was no longer the law of the land.

But somehow in the years since 1954 black Americans seem to have strayed from the real goal being sought in the removal of those legal restrictions. These words of W. E. B. DuBois, written in 1960, state so well, as his words usually do, where black Americans should be going.

> What we must now ask ourselves is when we become equal American citizens what will be our aims and ideals and what will we have to do in selecting these aims and ideals. Are we to assume that we will simply adopt the ideals of Americans and become what they are or want to be and that we will have in the process no ideals of our own?
>
> That would mean that we would cease to be Negroes as such and become white in action if not completely in color. We would take on the culture of white Americans doing as they do and thinking as they think.
>
> Manifestly this would not be satisfactory. Physically it would mean that we would be integrated with Americans losing, first of all, the physical evidence of color and hair and racial type. We would lose our memory of Negro history and of racial peculiarities which have long been associated with being Negro. We would cease to acknowledge any greater tie with Africa than England and Germany. We would not try to develop Negro Music and Art and Literature as distinctive and different, but allow them to be further degraded as is the case today. We would always, if possible, marry lighter-hued people so as to have children who are not identified with the Negro, and thus solve our problem in America by committing racial suicide . . .
>
> I repeat I am not fighting to settle the question of racial equality . . . by getting rid of the Negro race . . . forgetting the slave trade and slavery, and the struggle for emancipation; of forgetting abolition and especially of ignoring the whole cultural history of Africans in the world. No! What I have been fighting for . . . is the possibility of black folk and their cultural patterns existing in America without discrimination; and on terms of equality. If we take this attitude we have got to do so consciously and deliberately (1973, pp. 149-150).

References

Blassingame, John. 1972. *The Slave Community*. New York: Oxford University Press.

DuBois, W. E. B. 1916. *The Souls of Black Folk* (original printing 1903). Greenwich, Connecticut: Fawcett.

————. 1973. Whither now and why. In *The Education of Black People*, ed. Herbert Aptheker. New York: Monthly Review Press.

Jackson, Barbara. 1978. Desegregation: Atlanta style. *Theory into Practice* 17: 43-53.

Regents of the University of California v. *Allan Bakke*, No. 76-811, June 28, 1978.

Smith, Cooper. 1976. Quoting Caroline Jackson in Toward a theory and a place for the arts and the humanities in the public schools. Doctoral dissertation, Atlanta University.

13   Bilingual Education
and School Desegregation

LINDA HANTEN

In many communities conflict has arisen between proponents of desegregation and proponents of bilingual education, giving rise to the impression that these two methods of seeking equal educational opportunity for minority students are necessarily incompatible. Hispanics are currently the second largest minority enrolled in the nation's public schools.[1] Many Hispanic parents see bilingual-bicultural education as the principal means of overcoming discrimination against their children in the educational process, and in many Hispanic communities desegregation is seen only as a means for black students to achieve equality of opportunity. Its supposed benefits to the Hispanic community are viewed with skepticism. In fact, when it threatens the existence of hard-won bilingual educational progress, desegregation is viewed as a hindrance to achievement of Hispanic goals.

A blanket statement that Hispanics oppose desegregation cannot be made. Many Hispanic communities have in fact instituted court action to stop patterns of de jure segregation. Seven years before the Supreme Court decision in *Brown*[2] provided a basis for ending de jure segregation of blacks, Chicano plaintiffs successfully challenged a policy of segregation in a California community.[3] In recent years Chicano communities throughout the Southwest have sought desegregation,[4] and the battle continues in many communities. It is true, however, that some Hispanic communities and some advocates of bilingual education oppose the dispersal of Hispanic students and the removal of bilingual programs from barrio schools. Whether correctly or not, they fear that through integration assimilationist sentiment will destroy bilingual programs and dissipate Hispanic influence; in some cases, therefore, they favor the segregated status quo.[5]

This situation is most likely to arise as classic black-white desegregation cases spread to the Southwest and the North, into areas where sizable Hispanic communities have not initiated the action or attempted to participate in it until a reassignment plan is contemplated, or even implemented. Both the underlying constitutional violation and the reassignment plan are apt to be viewed by the parties involved and the court in black-white terms only, and Hispanic concerns are likely to be ignored. Thus, Hispanics see reassignment as a threat to their own educational objectives.

Despite the experiences and fears of many Hispanic communities throughout the country, including those affected by desegregation cases filed and litigated on behalf of blacks only, there need be no irresolvable and inevitable conflict between bilingual education and desegregation. This chapter examines the right to bilingual education, or linguistically different education for linguistically different students, as a federal right of equal status with the right to be free from de jure segregation. Further, it explores ways in which Hispanics have participated and can continue to participate in desegregation litigation to preserve bilingual programs and to ensure that the rights of all students to equal educational opportunity are protected.

Much of the feeling that bilingual education is necessarily in conflict with desegregation and that desegregation must take precedence in judicial proceedings is derived from the Tenth Circuit Court of Appeals decision in *Keyes* v. *School District No. 1*,[6] the first decision to address the apparent conflict. The district court, having found "education . . . in the minority schools . . . to be inferior"[7] as well as segregated, permitted the Congress of Hispanic Educators (CHE) to intervene and present a plan on behalf of Chicano students in Denver.

Faced with a situation in which Chicanos were being expelled from school or retained in grades and special-education classes at excessive rates and few were being included in remedial English programs, CHE focused on bilingual education rather than desegregation as a means of remedying inferior education for Chicano students. In response to the intervenors' proposal, the district court ordered the school district to develop a comprehensive pilot bilingual-bicultural educational program in several schools. Acknowledging that Chicanos opposed dispersal if it interfered with these comprehensive programs, the court held desegregation not to be in the best interests of the Chicano community and excluded the pilot schools from its pupil-reassignment plan.[8]

On appeal the Tenth Circuit reversed this part of the district court's order, observing: "Bilingual education . . . is not a substitute for desegregation. Although bilingual instruction may be required to prevent the isolation of minority students in a predominantly Anglo school system . . . such instruction must be subordinate to a plan of school desegregation. We therefore remand this portion of the case for a determination whether the continued segregation of students at the [pilot] schools may be justified on grounds other than the institution and development of bilingual-bicultural programs at the schools."[9] The Tenth Circuit opinion, however, did not ban the development of bilingual programs in Denver, only the type of programs requiring segregation of an entire school.

The major problem with the court's approach to bilingual education in *Keyes* is the failure to recognize the right to bilingual education as a distinct right derived from statute, regulation, and case law. Plans for bilingual education, as a right, must be developed in conjunction with desegregation plans where appropriate. While bilingual education is not a substitute for desegregation, neither is it necessarily subordinate. The statement that "bilingual education . . . must be subordinate to . . . desegregation" assumes that of the two protected rights, the former is inferior, and that the relationship between the two is antagonistic. Both of these assumptions are misconceived.

Bilingual education is mandated by federal as well as state laws, and violation of those laws should not be the product of a desegregation decree designed to enforce other rights. Many provisions of federal law require that the large numbers of non-English-speaking and limited-English-speaking children[10] receive suitable specialized instruction. The major statutory sources of the right to bilingual programming are in Title VI of the 1964 Civil Rights Act; they have been further clarified by regulations, interpretive guidelines, and court decisions. The essence of this body of law is that each limited-English-speaking student is entitled to an educational program in a language he or she understands, taught by a teacher who is competent in that language. Native-language instruction does not, as some critics suggest, draw students out of the educational mainstream; rather it allows them to effectively enter it by progressing on a course of substantive instruction while learning English.

Title VI bans discrimination by recipients of federal funds, and thus by virtually all school districts, "on the grounds of race, color, or national origin." Regulations issued by the Department of Health, Education, and Welfare (HEW) pursuant to Title VI prohibit recipients of such funds from "restrict[ing] an individual in any way in the enjoyment of an advantage or privilege enjoyed by others receiving any service, financial aid, or other benefit under the program."[11] Nor may such recipients "utilize criteria or methods of administration which have the effect of subjecting individuals to discrimination" or "of defeating or substantially impairing accomplishment of the objective of the program as respects individuals of a particular race, color, or national origin."[12]

On May 25, 1970, HEW issued clarifying guidelines based on these regulations. The May 25 Memorandum, as this document has come to be called, construes the mandate of the statute and regulations to encompass an obligation by school districts to meet the needs of limited-English-speaking students and states, "Where inability to speak and understand the English language excludes national origin minority group children from effective participation in the educational program offered by a school district, the district must take affirmative steps to rectify the language deficiency in order to open its instructional programs to these students.[13]

In 1974, in *Lau* v. *Nichols*, a unanimous Supreme Court sustained HEW's authority to promulgate the May 25 Memorandum and agreed that Title VI required special assistance for students lacking basic English-language skills.[14] As the majority opinion pointed out: "Basic English skills are at the very core of what these public schools teach. Imposition of a requirement that, before a child can effectively participate in the educational program, he must already have acquired those basic skills is to make a mockery of public education. We know that those who do not understand English are certain to find their classroom experiences incomprehensible and in no way meaningful.[15] It is notable that the court did not distinguish between segregated and nonsegregated classrooms in finding that education in a language the student does not understand is meaningless.

Subsequent to *Lau* v. *Nichols*, Congress incorporated into law the concepts set out in that decision and in the HEW guidelines. Legislation passed in 1974 makes actionable the failure by an educational agency to take appropriate steps to overcome language barriers that impede equal participation by its students in its instructional programs.[16] Congress made no distinction between language barriers occurring in segregated and integrated settings. A violation of this provision of the Equal Educational Opportunities Act could clearly occur in a segregated setting, but several courts have indicated that the existence of an unconstitutional dual school system is not a prerequisite for finding that a violation has occurred.[17] The right of limited-English-speaking ability (LESA) students to some form of language assistance has been decisively established by federal guidelines, case law, and legislation.[18]

Though neither *Lau* nor the Equal Educational Opportunities Act expressly responded to the English-language problems of LESA students, further guidelines promulgated by HEW and subsequent legislation and court opinions have made it clear that native-language instruction must be part of the response. The legislative recognition of the effectiveness of bilingual instruction is found in the Federal Bilingual Education Act,[19] the preamble to which states: "Congress declares it to be the policy of the United States . . . to encourage the establishment and operation, where appropriate, of educational policies using bilingual educational practices, techniques, and methods.[20]

The House, in reporting out the bill, articulated its understanding of bilingual education as being "the use of two languages, one of which is English, as a media [*sic*] of instruction in a comprehensive school program. There is evidence that the use of the child's mother tongue as a medium of instruction concurrent with an effort to strengthen his command of English acts to prevent retardation in academic skills and performance. The program is also intended to develop the child's self-esteem and a legitimate pride in both cultures. Accordingly, bilingual education normally includes a study of the history and culture associated with the mother tongue."[21]

A recent federal district court decision in New York, relying on this congressional declaration of policy, as well as on Title VI, *Lau* v. *Nichols*, and the "suggestion" of the *Lau Remedies*, discussed below, held that the defendant school district was required to provide a program of bilingual-bicultural education for LESA students.[22] The New York court cited with approval the Tenth Circuit's opinion in *Serna* v. *Portales Municipal Schools*, which discussed the psychological trauma suffered by non-English-speaking students who are taught in English.[23]

In the summer of 1975 HEW convened a number of experts to advise them on how to respond to the *Lau* mandate. From that gathering evolved a document informally known as the *Lau Remedies*,[24] which constitutes the core of HEW's policy. This document establishes standards for identifying LESA students, for assessing their language ability, for diagnosing their educational needs, and for prescribing a program to meet those needs. For the elementary student, at least, whose predominant language is one other than English, native-language instruction must be provided.[25] The document has been construed to require native-language instruction in core subjects at the secondary level, except under extraordinary circumstances. The *Lau Remedies* further prescribe that those teaching the LESA students must be linguistically and culturally familiar with the background of the students involved.

Two recent cases have incorporated the commonsense notion set forth in the *Lau Remedies* that equal educational opportunity can only be provided by ensuring that all children attend classes conducted in a language they understand. In *Cintron v. Brentwood Union Free School District*, the New York case discussed above, the court relied on the *Lau Remedies* and other authorities, ruling that LESA students had a federal right to a bilingual-bicultural program with bilingual teachers. A second New York decision, *Rios v. Read*,[26] relied on the same authorities to reach the same result.

Rather than attempting to strike a compromise between the approach to equal educational opportunity of bilingual programming and that of desegregation, parents, educators, and courts often escalate tension between these concepts to irreconcilable conflict. The tension results from the fact that a desegregation decree seeks to break up racially or ethnically identifiable schools by dispersing their students throughout the system. On the other hand, the need to cluster students of similar ethnic and linguistic backgrounds in order to achieve the fundamental objectives of bilingual education is inescapable. To be effective, bilingual programs require a critical mass of students.[27] Unless there are adequate numbers of bilingual children at each grade level, each class must accommodate students of different ages, as well as disparate needs, abilities, and language proficiencies. Moreover, a viable program needs to span several consecutive grades at the same school. Finally, qualified teachers are in exceedingly short supply and great demand and cannot be spread any thinner than they are already.[28]

Serious problems arise when children in need of bilingual programming are arbitrarily dispersed without taking that need into consideration. It is unlikely that in most communities there are sufficient numbers of children in any one school or area to justify separate classes, so random dispersal cannot ensure the opportunity for bilingual education. In addition, the shortage of trained bilingual teachers and instructional material would make the existence even of "watered-down" programs for many of the randomly dispersed children unlikely. But there is no need for random, insensitive dispersal of LESA children, even in black-white desegregation cases. The Boston desegregation decree[29] serves as a model for dealing with Hispanic LESA students in an otherwise black-white case. The *Morgan v. Kerrigan* court sought to resolve the tension between bilingual education and desegregation by attempting to accommodate both interests in its pupil-reassignment plan.

First the court determined the percentage of minority and nonminority students who should be in each school. For example, a school might be required to have 40 percent minority students. The court then determined that three consecutive bilingual classes with a total of at least sixty students was the minimum necessary for effective bilingual programming. If the sixty students brought the minority percentage of the school to 20 percent, there was then space available for 20 percent black students. The order of procedure was that first LESA students had to be identified, then the minimally acceptable number of such students for effective bilingual instruction had to be determined, and finally (only after LESA students had been assigned) the other minority students and the Anglo students were to be assigned.[30] This approach has been followed by courts implementing desegregation decrees in Wilmington[31] and Buffalo[32] in an effort to accommodate the diverse interests of bilingual education and desegregation.

The Tenth Circuit's ruling in *Keyes* that retention of entirely segregated schools cannot be justified in the name of bilingual education need not pose a threat to ethnically identifiable bilingual classrooms in otherwise desegregated settings. Courts and districts faced with the competing interests of bilingual education and desegregation have many options for ensuring that effective bilingual programs neither maintain unlawful segregation nor create resegregation.

To follow the approach set out by the *Morgan* court, districts should identify those Hispanic children who are actually in need of bilingual instruction. These students can then be retained in their current school or reassigned to a school where a bilingual teacher and program can follow them, or they can be reassigned along with LESA students from other schools to a school where adequate new programming can be efficiently developed. The school can then be desegregated around these bilingual clusters. There is no need to exclude large segments of the Hispanic student population from pupil reassignment in order to facilitate bilingual education, as was attempted in Denver. Nor is random assignment of LESA students necessary to achieve ethnic balance. The need to cluster LESA students of a particular ethnic background does not, then, require the creation or maintenance of minority schools, since non-LESA students of that ethnic background need not remain in or be assigned to the school. Judge W. Arthur Garrity, for example, reduced the Hispanic population in Boston's Hernandez School by 30 percent while ensuring that a sufficient number would remain for the bilingual program to flourish.[33]

Furthermore, a school with a concentration of bilingual students need

not run segregated bilingual programs. Although the Supreme Court implied in *Lau* v. *Nichols*[34] that in certain limited circumstances separate
classes for bilingual education may be appropriate,[35] many urban districts have sought to integrate their bilingual classrooms while maintain-
ing the educational components essential to high-quality programs.[36]
Where bilingual programs of instruction are provided for LESA students,
districts can[37]—and in fact may be obligated to—include non-LESA
children in the classroom, thus combining the concepts of bilingual education and desegregation. In a case challenging the unlawful segregation
of Chicano children in a south Texas school district, the district court
ordered San Felipe del Rio to institute *integrated* bilingual classrooms,
utilizing open classrooms and innovative curricular change, as part of the
remedy.[38]

Legislation at both the federal and state levels has either encouraged[39]
or mandated[40] the inclusion of non-LESA children in bilingual classrooms. Nearly every bilingual statute provides for voluntary inclusion of
non-LESA children. An explanation of the desirability of inclusion of
such students was given by the then special assistant to the director, and
later, director, of the Office for Civil Rights, who observed that "to meet
the needs of ethnically isolated children . . . participation of Anglo children in the bicultural/bilingual programs is essential."[41] Thus, while the
primary focus of bilingual education is remedying the LESA students'
language deficiency, there is still an obligation to provide this specialized
education in the most integrated setting possible.[42]

It is clear that by pairing bilingual and nonbilingual classrooms, by inclusion of non-LESA students in bilingual programs, and by the creative
use of space and nonacademic time, schools can ensure that bilingual
programs operate in integrated environments. One court has specifically
ordered that they do so. The *Cintron* court recently held that a bilingual-
bicultural program that segregated Spanish-speaking students from the
rest of the student body except for physical education and lunch was in
violation of federal law.[43] Keeping these students in separate classes for
music and art was seen as violative of the *Lau* guidelines,[44] and the court
ordered increased contact between English- and non-English-speaking
children in all but subject-matter instruction.[45]

There is no inherent conflict between the goals of bilingual education and
desegregation, but it is likely that bilingual educational programs will
suffer at the remedial stage of black-white desegregation cases when the

constituents of the program are not before the court to make their interests known. An overview of four cases provides some insight into the dynamics of this situation.

These cases involve the cities of Boston,[46] Wilmington,[47] Denver,[48] and Milwaukee,[49] where during the late 1960s and the early 1970s bilingual-bicultural programs emerged, largely as a result of pressure from the Hispanic community. Concurrently, black parents in each city initiated and litigated successful school desegregation lawsuits. Prior to a finding of unlawful segregation of black students in these communities, the issue of language-minority education was not raised.

When it became apparent in each community that neither the plaintiffs nor the school districts would adequately account for the needs of bilingual students in their proposed desegregation plans, Hispanic groups intervened. The relief requested by the intervenors was a variation on one primary theme: the preservation of bilingual programs and the concentration of students necessary for such programs. In Boston the court was also asked to make provision in the reassignment plan for the concentration of students that would be required if the district were to meet its full obligation regarding bilingual education. (Massachusetts had mandatory state bilingual legislation.) The Denver intervenors asked the court to take general jurisdiction over the issue of the adequacy of minority education. In Wilmington, Boston, and Denver the trial courts granted the requested relief, although, as mentioned earlier, the specific remedy allowed in Denver was later rejected on appeal.

In Milwaukee the district court denied the petition for intervention, but stated that its own refusal to preserve existing bilingual programs should not be construed as prohibiting the school district from doing so subsequent to desegregation.[50] Because the school district had once established bilingual programs, the district court may have expected that these programs would be reestablished after desegregation. Apparently the court felt the district had acted in good faith regarding bilingual education and was not antagonistic to Hispanic interests. Whether the court's faith would have been vindicated and whether the district would have been able to reestablish programs after the random dispersal of students is a matter of speculation because the desegregation decree was reversed by the Supreme Court.[51]

The failure to permit intervention in this case is significant. Without the status of intervenor, the language-minority community has no guarantee that its legal interests will be raised, advocated, considered, or protected. The Milwaukee court is not the only court to deny intervention to

Hispanic students with legitimate interests in remedial action in a desegregation lawsuit. On September 1, 1978, the Federal District Court denied a Latino motion to intervene at the remedial stage of the Detroit
desegregation case.[52] The intervention attempt was prompted by the district judge's concerns—expressed in a hearing on April 24, 1978, on further student and teacher reassignment[53] in region 2 of the school district
—about the possibly segregative effects of placing clusters of LESA students in bilingual programs.[54] At this point in the protracted litigation it
became clear that the judge was contemplating a reassignment plan that
would strongly affect Hispanic students in region 2 bilingual programs
and thus affect the programs themselves. On August 7, before acting on
the Hispanic motion to intervene, the district court ordered further desegregation of region 1 of the school district by means of a plan that
would include transferring nonblack students from region 2 to the overwhelmingly black neighboring region 1.

After the order to reassign Hispanic students, the court denied these
students' motion to intervene on two grounds: first, that the motion was
untimely, and second, that their interests were adequately represented by
the school district. The court's action showed a misunderstanding of the
intervenors' motives. Contrary to the court's fears, the Hispanic intervenors had no interest in relitigating issues of liability or in establishing
the principle of law that Hispanics are exempt from reassignment in desegregation cases. Their primary purpose was to ensure that there would
be enough LESA children in some schools to preserve bilingual programs, and to ensure that children needing bilingual programs were assigned to these schools rather than randomly dispersed. Their goal was
not to prevent all dispersal of Hispanic students.[55]

As in the Milwaukee case, the adequacy of school representation of
Hispanic interests in the Detroit case is a matter of speculation. In its
order of September 1, 1978, the court appeared to emphasize the fact
that the district had implemented bilingual programs and seemed willing
to trust the district to continue such programming after reassignment.
The court instructed that "[any reassignment] plan make provisions for
bilingual-bicultural programs consistent with state law and the prior orders of this court; where pupil reassignment materially affects current
bilingual-bicultural programs, the Detroit board shall create new programs to maintain the current level of bilingual-bicultural offerings."[56]
Nevertheless, the district did not refer to bilingual students or programs
in its initial plan submitted to the court.

Intervention of right under Federal Rule of Civil Procedure 24(a)[57] is appropriate in the Milwaukee and Detroit desegregation cases because Hispanic LESA children have a substantial interest in any remedial student- or teacher-reassignment plans that may be implemented. For that matter, non-LESA Hispanic children have a right to be adequately represented in desegregation litigation, because a number of courts have found that they are a distinct ethnic group with a history of discrimination similar to that suffered by blacks and are entitled to protection under the Fourteenth Amendment.[58] When three distinct groups are involved, as is the case in most northern and western urban desegregation cases, "[no] remedy for the dual school system can be acceptable if it operates to deprive members of a third ethnic group of the benefits of equal educational opportunity."[59] This situation can occur if LESA Hispanic students are deprived of bilingual programming or if non-LESA Hispanic students are forced to bear a greater burden of desegregation efforts than other ethnic groups.[60]

Intervention in these situations is appropriate also because it cannot be assumed that the school district will adequately represent the interests of LESA children as did the courts in Milwaukee and Detroit.[61] Even assuming the district in good faith wanted to continue effective bilingual programs, it might be unable to do so if dispersal of LESA children occurred without regard to their linguistic needs. After reassignment the district might find that there were not sufficient clusters of LESA children in any schools to allow for meaningful programming, that the bilingual teachers were in schools without LESA children, or that the LESA children were too widely dispersed to allow existing staff to serve even a portion of them meaningfully.

Finally, intervention should not be denied as untimely even if the attempt occurs some time after the initiation of the lawsuit. As in Detroit, remedial action may take place a number of years after the filing of a lawsuit, a finding of liability, and numerous appeals, because that may be the first time that the rights of LESA students are directly at issue. In school desegregation cases that involve time-consuming litigation, the courts have overwhelmingly decided in favor of allowing intervention not intended to impede desegregation.[62] In these cases LESA students sought not to impede desegregation, but to protect their own interests under any reassignment plan. If courts are unwilling to allow intervention by Hispanic LESA students at the remedial stage of desegregation litigation, these students can preserve their rights by filing separate lawsuits to compel the district to meet federal, and perhaps state, requirements by providing adequate bilingual programming. Such actions may focus a court's energy in a manner that yields more comprehensive relief for LESA students than intervention in a desegregation suit. But because student and teacher assignments will be crucial in both bilingual and desegregation suits, motions for consolidation may be appropriate.

In summary, there is no fundamental antagonism between the right to bilingual education and the right to be free from de jure segregation. Bilingual programming and desegregation are both legitimate means to the end of equal educational opportunity. Conflict results when one method is pursued without consideration of the other, and it can be avoided if the rights of LESA students are considered in pupil-reassignment plans and if reassignment is made in other than a random manner.

Notes

1. U.S. Department of Health, Education, and Welfare, Office for Civil Rights, Directory of Public Elementary and Secondary School Districts: Enrollment and Staff by Racial and Ethnic Group (1972), p. vii.
2. Brown v. Board of Education, 347 U.S. 483 (1954).
3. Mendez v. Westminster School Dist., 64 F. Supp. 544 (S.D. Cal. 1946).
4. See, for example, Soria v. Oxnard School District, 386 F. Supp. 539 (D.C. Cal. 1974); Alvarado v. El Paso Independent School Dist., 326 F. Supp. 674 (W.D. Tex. 1971); Cisneros v. Corpus Christi Independent School District, 324 F. Supp. 599 (S.D. Tex. 1970).
5. See Peter Roos, "Bilingual education: the Hispanic response to unequal educational opportunity," *Law and Contemporary Problems* 42 (1978): 111-140.
6. Keyes v. School Dist. No. 1, Denver, 521 F. 2d 465 (10th Cir. 1975).
7. Keyes v. School Dist. No. 1, Denver, 380 F. Supp. 673, 682 (D. Colo. 1974).
8. Id. at 692.
9. 521 F.2d at 480.
10. Non-English-speaking and limited-English-speaking children are present in large numbers throughout the United States. A study commissioned by the Department of Health, Education, and Welfare found that 13 percent of the U.S. population aged four or older (approximately 25,000,000 people) live in households in which languages other than English are spoken. Of these, approximately 8.2 million are Spanish speaking. Thirty-five percent of the Spanish speakers are under eighteen (Dorothy Waggoner, *Language and Demographic Characteristics of the U.S. Population with Potential Need for Bilingual and Other Special Educational Programs, July 1975*, National Center for Education Statistics, 1978).
11. 45 CFR 80.3(b)(1).
12. 45 CFR 80.3(b)(2).
13. May 25 Memorandum, 35 Federal Register 11595 (July 18, 1970).

14. Lau v. Nichols, 414 U.S. 563 (1974).

15. Id. at 566.

16. 20 U.S.C. §1703(f).

17. See, for example, Martin Luther King Jr. Elementary School Children v. Michigan Bd. of Educ., 451 F. Supp. 1324 (E.D. Mich., 1978); Evans v. Buchanan, 416 F. Supp. 328, 339 (D. Del. 1976).

18. A number of states have also addressed the right to bilingual instruction. Since Massachusetts passed the first bilingual legislation in 1972, at least eleven states have followed suit. While some state legislation may exceed federal requirements, it typically covers only certain grades or is permissive. An example of the mandatory and specific statute in California's recently enacted legislation is the Chacon-Mascone Bilingual and Bicultural Education Act of 1976. The Chacon-Mascone bill requires that each district K-12 in California must conduct a yearly survey in October to ascertain the number of limited-English-speaking and non-English-speaking students. The census is to be an individual, actual count, not an estimate or sampling. Cal. Ed. Code §52164. Three specific bilingual education models must be offered in any school having ten or more limited-English-speaking students with the same primary language enrolled at any grade level K-6 inclusive. Other students must receive an individual learning program. Cal. Ed. Code §52165. Teachers in bilingual programs must hold bilingual cross-cultural credentials. Waiver of the credential requirement is allowed if the teacher is enrolled in an educational program leading to the credential and the district can demonstrate that a credentialed teacher is unavailable. Cal. Ed. Code §52166.

19. 20 U.S.C. §880 b.

20. H.R. 805, 93d Cong., 2d Sess., *reprinted in* 3 U.S. Code Cong. and Ad. News 4093, 4148 (1974).

21. Cintron v. Brentwood Union Free School Dist., Bd. of Educ., (E.D.N.Y., 1978). 455 F. Supp. 57, 64.

22. Id. at 62, quoting Serna v. Portales Municipal Schools, 449 F. 2d 1147, 1150 (10th Cir. 1974).

23. The full title of this document is "Task force findings specifying remedies available for eliminating past educational practices ruled unlawful under *Lau v. Nichols*" (Summer 1975) [hereinafter cited as Lau Remedies].

24. Lau Remedies at 7, 10.

25. Rios v. Read 480 F. Supp. 14 (E.D.N.Y., 1978).

26. See Center for Law and Education, "Bilingual-bicultural education: a handbook for attorneys and community workers," Cambridge, Massachusetts, 1975, pp. 203-205.

27. In California, as in other states, the educational needs of only a portion of limited-English-speaking students are being met, and it is projected that in the years ahead a smaller, rather than greater, percentage of these students will be served (G. Lopez, California State Board of Education Report, *Education for Limited-English-Speaking and Non-English-Speaking Students, Part II,* July 1978). Incomplete data for 1977 showed 256,000 such students in California (id. at p. 9). This is recognized to be an undercount by the California State Department of Education because, at the time of release of these data, those from the Los Angeles Unified School District, largest in the state and heavily Hispanic,

were not complete. The department projects that in 1982 there will be approximately 400,000 limited-English-speaking students in California, and in 1990 approximately 500,000 (id. at 10). Districts failing to meet the special educational needs of non-English-speaking and limited-English-speaking children, and thus their federal and local mandate, uniformly cite the shortage of qualified teachers as the reason for their failure. In recognition of the shortage, California's Bilingual Education Act sets out a provision by which the credential requirement may be waived in certain instances (see note 18). As of June 30, 1978, the State Board of Education had granted 2,418 teacher waivers to 150 school districts. Pending were requests for twenty-one additional school districts for 2,223 teacher waivers (Lopez, p. 19).

28. Morgan v. Kerrigan, 401 F. Supp. 216 (D. Mass. 1975).

29. Id. at 216, 242, 252.

30. Evans v. Buchanan, 416 F. Supp. at 359.

31. Arthur v. Nyquist, 415 F. Supp. 904 (W.D. N.Y. 1976).

32. Information provided by Ernest J. Mazzone, director, Massachusetts Bureau of Transitional Bilingual Education.

33. 414. U.S. at 568.

34. The court made this implication by its express reference to the following HEW regulation: "Any ability grouping or tracking system employed by the school system to deal with the special language skill needs of national origin-minority group children must be designed to meet such language skill needs as soon as possible and must not operate as an educational deadend or permanent track." 35 Federal Register 11595 (1970).

Regulations promulgated under the Emergency School Aid Act, 20 U.S.C. 1601-1619, allow classes to be ethnically segregated for less than 25 percent of the school day, 45 CFR 185.43(c), or for longer periods if they can be shown to be in accord with standard pedagogical practices. It is clear that the prohibition against ethnically identified ability grouping, 45 CFR 185.43(c)(1), is not directed toward progress of bilingual instruction. The harm the regulation sought to address was the disproportionate assignment of language-minority students to classes for the retarded or nonacademic tracks based on English-language tests. See Roos, p. 138.

35. These cities include Boston; New York; Redwood City and San Bernardino, California. See Bruce Cohen, "The co-existence of bilingual-bicultural programs with school desegregation decrees" (unpublished paper prepared for the American Academy of Arts and Sciences, 1978), pp. 18-19.

36. The shortage of teachers and materials and the fact that only one-ninth of the LESA students currently receive bilingual education create an economic pressure to exclude nonminority children from bilingual programs, however.

37. United States v. Texas, 342 F. Supp. 24 (E.D. Tex. 1971).

38. See, for example, 20 U.S.C. §880 b - 1(a) (4) (B). N.J. Rev. Stat. §18A: 35-20; Colo. Rev. Stat. §22-24-112(6).

39. See, for example, Ind. Code §20-10.1-5.5-3; Gen. Laws of R. I. §16-54-5b.

40. M. Gerry, "Cultural freedom in the schools: the right of Mexican-American children to succeed" (unpublished paper for the Office for Civil Rights, U.S. Department of Health, Education, and Welfare, 1971).

41. The regulations implementing the Bilingual Education Act, however, require that priority for placement in bilingual programs be given to LESA students, and that the number of non-language-minority students be limited. See 45 CFR §123.02(g) (2) (i). Two courts, in pre-*Lau* decisions, in ordering bilingual-bicultural instruction for Chicanos, also required Anglo students to be included. See Serna v. Portales Municipal Schools, 499 F.2d at 1151; United States v. Texas, 342 F. Supp. at 28. See also José A. Cardenas, "Bilingual education, segregation, and a third alternative," *Inequality in Education* 19:19-22.

42. 455 F. Supp. at 60, 63.

43. Id. at 63 and n.9.

44. Id. at 64.

45. Morgan v. Kerrigan, 401 F. Supp. 216 (D. Mass. 1975).

46. Evans v. Buchanan, 416 F. Supp. 328 (D. Del. 1976).

47. Keyes v. School Dist. No. 1, Denver, 380 F. Supp. 673 (D. Colo. 1974).

48. Amos v. Board of School Directors, 408 F. Supp. 765 (E.D. Wis. 1976).

49. Armstrong v. O'Connell, 427 F. Supp. 1377, 1380 (E.D. Wis. 1977).

50. Brennen v. Armstrong, 433 U.S. 672 (1977).

51. Bradley v. Milliken, 460 Supp. 320 (E.D. Mich. 1978).

52. The hearing was prompted by the 6th Circuit remand of this case, 540 F.2d 229 (6th Cir. 1976).

53. The Detroit school district is divided into eight regions. The overwhelming majority of Hispanic students reside in region 2, and all of the Spanish-English bilingual programs conducted by the district in the academic year 1977-78 and fall 1978 were conducted at schools within that region.

54. See Intervenors Lulac Council No. 11054, et al.'s Memorandum in Support of Motion to Intervene filed July 21, 1978, Bradley v. Milliken, 460 F. Supp. 320 (E.D. Mich. 1978).

55. Bradley v. Milliken, Civil Action No. 35257 (E.D. Mich., August 7, 1978) (unreported order). See Bradley v. Milliken, 460 F. Supp. 299 (E.D. Mich. 1978).

56. Federal Rule of Civil Procedure 24(a) provides: "*Intervention of Right.* Upon timely application anyone shall be permitted to intervene in an action . . . (2) when the appliant claims an interest relating to the property or transaction which is the subject of the action and he is so situated that the disposition of the action may, as a practical matter, impair or impede his ability to protect that interest, unless the applicant's interest is adequately represented by existing parties."

57. Keyes v. School District No. 1, Denver, 413 U.S. 189 (1973); United States v. Texas Education Agency (Austin Independent School Dist.), 467 F.2d 848, (5th Cir. 1972) en banc. See also Castaneda v. Partida, 430 U.S. 482, 495 (1977).

58. 467 F.2d at 869, quoted in Ross v. Eckels, 468 F.2d 649, 650 (5th Cir. 1972).

59. Courts have frequently struck down reassignment plans that place an unfair burden on one particular group of minority students. See, for example, Arvizu v. Waco Independent School Dist., 495 F.2d 499, 504 (5th Cir. 1974); Felder v. Harnett County Bd. of Educ., 409 F.2d 1070 (4th Cir. 1969); Brice v. Landis, 314 F. Supp. 974 (N.D. Cal. 1969).

60. Intervenors do not have the burden of demonstrating actual inadequacy of representation by existing parties: "The requirement of the Rule is satisfied if the applicant shows that representation of his interest *may be* inadequate; and the *burden of making that showing should be treated as minimal.*" (Emphasis added.) Trbovich v. United Mine Workers, 404 U.S. 528, 538 n.10 (1972).

61. See, for example, United States v. Jefferson County Bd. of Educ., 372 F. 2d 836, 896 (5th Cir. 1966) (intervention timely after school board submitted plan in compliance with court decree); Keyes v. School Dist. No. 1, Denver, 380 F. Supp. at 673-694 (intervention by Mexican Americans allowed eight years after original filing, and following numerous court decrees, including an appeal to the Tenth Circuit and the Supreme Court); Pate v. Dade County School Bd., 303 F. Supp. 1068 (S.D. Fla. 1969) (intervention allowed to reopen school deseg-regation suit nine years after original court decree); Robinson v. Shelby County Bd. of Educ., 330 F. Supp. 837 (W.D. Tenn. 1971) (dicta) (intervention would have been timely after two district court and one appellate court decisions).

Since most school desegregation cases involve relief of an injunctive nature, which must prove its efficacy over a period of time, the timeliness requirement for intervention in these cases must be one of *substantive* timeliness. As was stated by the Tenth Circuit in a *per curiam* opinion: "Proceedings of this nature [school desegregation] which continue over such an extended period of time are unique in respect to the timing of the arrival and departure of parties. In our opinion intervention and withdrawal should be freely granted so long as it does not seriously interfere with the actual hearings." Dowell v. Board of Educ., 430 F.2d 865, 868 (10th Cir. 1979). Thus, timeliness is not to be perfunctorily rejected because of time elapsed, but is to be guided by the established rule that "timeli-ness is to be determined from all the circumstances." NAACP v. New York, 413 U.S. 345, 366 (1973).

14 Inexplicitness as Racial Policy in Britain and the United States

DAVID L. KIRP

Since 1950 Great Britain has acquired a sizable nonwhite population, with the proportion of nonwhites—predominantly Indian, Pakistani, African, Asian, and West Indian—rising from 0.7 percent to almost 3 percent.[1] A similar increase has occurred in the school-age population, now 4 percent nonwhite. Britain's response to this influx is noteworthy for two reasons: that country has consistently minimized the issue of race (and, somewhat less clearly, ethnicity) with respect to social policy generally and educational policy specifically; and it has also demonstrated a reluctance to treat the issue as having a significant legal dimension. In both respects, Britain has followed a policy course at deliberate variance with that pursued by the United States, which at least since *Brown* has treated racial issues in explicit, and primarily constitutional, terms.

This chapter briefly describes the workings of an educational policy of racial inexplicitness, focusing both on the general strategy and on an apparent and conspicuous exception to the overall policy, busing. It then identifies the sources of that policy, relating racial inexplicitness to a general preference for universalistic social policy and consensual decision making in the public domain and to widely shared private suspicions of claims that there is a racial "problem" deserving serious attention. The final section contrasts the quite different British and American approaches to race and education. The situation in the two countries is, of course, far from identical—differences with respect to history, demography, institutional responsiveness, and the like are substantial—but there are comparisons to be drawn between the policy experience of the two nations. Britain does not offer lessons in race relations to the United States, but it does permit one to consider seriously the question, Is a less

The research on which this chapter is based was supported by a Ford Foundation traveling fellowship.

explicit, and less legalistic, racial policy a plausible possibility for the
United States?

The Educational Policy Context

The nonwhites who came to Britain during the past quarter-century entered an educational system struggling with two related issues. Substantive tension existed between the tugs of egalitarianism and elitism, and
between diversity and uniformity, both issues in the protracted political
dispute over comprehensive schooling. Also detectable was a structural
tension between the long-dominant tradition of localism in education
and the hesitant claims of the Department of Education and Science
(DES) for national policy-making authority in certain areas. Although
none of these educational policy questions were directly related to race,
both the structural and substantive conflicts helped shape the educational
system's response to its new clientele; these matters are treated briefly
below. The appearance of nonwhites also trailed in its wake many issues
that have come to be associated with the American race and schooling experience; the relationship between these issues and the reception accorded racial and ethnic minorities in Britain is more fully explored in a
subsequent section.

Inegalitarianism and Localism

Until recently, the British educational system was structured along social-
class lines, providing very different education to rich children and poor
children. Indeed, the presumption of that system was inequality of opportunity. This was especially the case with respect to secondary schooling. Until the passage of the 1944 Education Act, such schooling was
effectively reserved for the middle and upper classes; even after its passage, the maintenance of grammar schools as one of three "options"—
college preparatory, general, and vocational—substituted selection by
differentiation for selection by elimination. By the time the nonwhites
arrived, however, differentiation that effectively distinguished along social-class lines had come under sharp attack; "comprehensive schools"
were, by Labour Party edict, replacing the tripartite arrangement. Nonwhites who needed some special assistance and who eventually began to
claim a right to equal treatment had somehow to be fit into this larger
debate.

Comprehensive schooling was, and remains, a controversial proposition among those who fear that its impact would be the absorption of

grammar schools, generally considered institutions of excellence, into a larger system widely regarded as mediocre. That the central government was insisting upon the shift also provoked unease among those who perceived a special source of strength in the localist tradition of British school management.

Both the debate over the wisdom of comprehensive schooling and the disputes between central and local authorities over final say in the matter affected educational policy concerning nonwhite students. It was hard to argue simultaneously for commonality of educational experience, the educational predicate for comprehensive schooling, and for the necessity of paying special heed to nonwhites. Were nonwhite students different from white students, aside from the matter of language, in a way that secondary modern students and grammar students were not different from one another? Why should race, but not social class or measured intelligence, be treated as relevant to policy? The wisdom—even the political possibility—of substantial educational policy initiatives with respect to nonwhites was limited by the debate over comprehensive schooling, which occupied center stage throughout the 1960s and early 1970s.

The Relevance of Race and Ethnicity

Britain's nonwhite school population is concentrated in relatively few educational authorities (school districts). A majority of nonwhites attend school in the London metropolitan area; a great many of the rest are in the industrial Midlands. In a half-dozen of Britain's 146 educational authorities, one in every five students was nonwhite in 1970 (the last year for which statistics are available); in just 217 schools did nonwhite enrollment exceed 50 percent.

Although racial concentration may not be inherently problem creating, related factors have contributed to a sense of social unease. In the political arena, hostility has been epitomized by the growth of the fascist National Front and the antagonism toward immigrants displayed by Prime Minister Margaret Thatcher and the Conservative Party. Opinion surveys and school-yard violence directed against nonwhites have revealed the same antagonisms at the individual level. At the same time, such reports of nonwhite achievement as are available (as of 1978) indicate relatively weak performance: in London, from which the best data come, more than half the West Indian students and nearly half the Indian and Pakistani students performed in the lowest quartile on mathematics and reading achievement tests. The educational careers of nonwhites appear to mirror their test performance: disproportionately few nonwhites pursue postsecondary education, and disproportionately large numbers of nonwhites, particularly West Indians, are enrolled in classes for the mildly retarded.

The institutions concerned with race policy have not been unaware of this situation. The Race Relations Board (now the Commission for Racial Equality), charged with rectifying discrimination—through court action, if necessary—has reviewed a number of complaints alleging discrimination in education. Liberal groups have been concerned with several aspects of race relations, and a parliamentary select committee undertook three relevant inquiries between 1969 and 1977.

Despite all this, race as such has had only modest impact on British educational policy. Little attention has been paid to nonwhite underachievement. Discrimination against nonwhites in school, the touchstone of American legal intervention, has until recently been presumed irrelevant in Britain. The aim of British policy has been, on the one hand, to stress the infinitely diverse needs of individual students and, on the other, to suffuse race or ethnicity with some broader concern, such as educational disadvantage. This deemphasis of race and ethnicity does not constitute nonpolicy, a lapse of governmental attention. Quite the contrary: inexplicitness has been the policy goal.

Educational Policy in Operation

Throughout the 1960s the chief policy response to the increase in the proportion of nonwhites in British public schools was to define this group in nonracial terms, the most important of which were linguistic and cultural. Attention focused on the newcomers' (except the West Indians') unfamiliarity with the English language and innocence concerning British customs. In subsequent years the educational disadvantage that this group shared with others, notably urban dwellers and the poor, became most salient. That these were nonwhite students mattered not at all.

Language

The nonwhite as non-English-speaking attracted initial and sustained policy attention. Uniquely in the realm of race and schooling policy, the central government offered both guidance and money (50 percent and later 75 percent of teaching-staff salaries) to assure instruction in English; teacher training, new curricula, and support for "industrial language centers" have also been part of this effort. Consistent with strongly localist educational tradition, however, implementation of the language instruction program was left largely to local authorities, and as a result efforts have varied widely from community to community: there is, for example, a fiftyfold range in per-pupil expenditure. Yet in many instances something is being done to address what is perceived as a concrete pedagogical task—language acquisition—within the competence of the school.

The focus on English-language acquisition relates to an undeniable need. But the attractiveness of this manageable task—as compared with, say, the quicksand characteristics of institutional concern for human or community or race relations—has encouraged DES to define educational problems in terms of language, even when this diagnosis does not fit the case at hand. DES's belated insistence that West Indians were afflicted with language problems akin to those that had more obviously beset Indian students, even at a time when the Creole dialect was no longer being spoken as a primary language by British West Indians, illustrates the phenomenon.

Custom

The development of an appropriate policy response to the ethnic or cultural differences between nonwhites and native Britons proved more problematic than efforts to overcome language deficiencies. The government's initial aspiration was straightforward: to render the newcomers at ease with their surroundings by making them into Britons. The educational task, as DES saw it, involved the "successful assimilation of immigrant children" (DES, 1965).

The rhetoric of assimilation was ultimately too inconsistent with presumed British tolerance of diversity. In 1966 Home Secretary Roy Jenkins announced a different aspiration: "not a flattening process of assimilation but an equal opportunity accompanied by cultural diversity" (Deakin, 1970, p. 23). Local practice, however, changed less than national rhetoric. The presence of nonwhites tested the schools' commitment to a particular British conformity—the permissibility of Moslem girls' wearing *shalwars*, rather than the usually required skirt, or of Sikh boys' carrying the ceremonial dagger, for instance—but did not deeply affect the perceived mission of the schools. Instruction in the native language and culture was resisted at both national and local levels; proposals for black studies met with a cool reception.

Urban Blight and Educational Disadvantage

Identification of the nonwhites as newcomers presumes that their educational problems will disappear over time. To some extent this has been the case: the proportion of students experiencing language problems dropped from one in four to one in six during the early 1970s; nonwhites educated wholly in British schools did better than later arrivals, although not nearly so well as the national average. As educational problems (or the perception of problems) persisted despite the dramatic decline in the number of newcomers, new categories of need were required. The terms chosen were pointedly nonracial. The 1968 Urban Program focused the concern of authorities on "special social needs," race being just one of these needs. DES subsequently rejected a parliamentary select committee proposal that it earmark funds for "the special needs of immigrant children" (DES, 1973, p. 57). Instead, the department established a modestly funded independent center to consider educational disadvantage generally.

In fact, any label other than the racial one has found favor with DES. The most dramatic illustration of this has been the fate of DES-collected statistics on race and immigration. When in 1971 the utility of such data was questioned by the parliamentary select committee, DES ceased collecting the statistics, and though there have been proposals to revive them, nothing has happened. No longer having a statistically identifiable group about which to talk has undeniably made it harder to focus attention on that group's particular needs. Conceivably it has also helped to avert or at least postpone an overtly racial battle over the ends of schooling.

Dispersal Policy: An Apparent Exception

In 1963, years before *busing* became a scare word in the American political lexicon, nonwhite students in Britain were being "dispersed," or bused, by several local authorities. This DES-approved policy was explicitly racial. Whatever DES or local authorities might now say, students were being bused primarily on the basis of color. The eventual abandonment of official support for the policy by DES and a challenge to the legality of dispersal by a liberal Race Relations Board lend weight to the characterization of British efforts as minimizing the relevance of race.

Busing in Britain was not a developed response to well-understood and fully anticipated events. At least initially, it represented very hasty reaction to a widely regretted circumstance: the concentration of sizable numbers of nonwhite students in a handful of educational authorities. At no time were more than a minority—perhaps 10 percent—of nonwhites ever dispersed. Nor did busing have deep ideological roots. It was not thought essential to secure racial justice, but rather was seen as the commonsense way to cope with a perceived racial crisis in a manner consistent with Britain's reputation for tolerance of differences.

Racial antagonism toward Indian children in a single school, which had become preponderantly nonwhite, precipitated national dispersal policy. As the education minister stated in Parliament in 1963: "I must regretfully tell the House that *one school* must be regarded now as irretrievably an immigrant school. The important thing is to prevent this happening elsewhere" (*Hansard*, 1963). That was what dispersal was designed to achieve. The policy of distributing nonwhites "thinner and wider" was intended to allay white fears that the academic standards and, more nebulously but no less importantly, the character of their schools would be altered by the minority presence; busing would minimize the numbers and thus the significance of that presence in any one school. Dispersal was also thought to benefit nonwhites, and indeed the nation as a whole. It immersed those who came to school knowing no English in an English-speaking environment (following rudimentary language instruction in special classes), thus presumably easing language acquisition and making relatively painless assimilation possible. It was also believed that to bring nonwhite and white children together in the same schools could only improve the racial climate, and so strengthen British society as a whole.

These considerations led a number of educational authorities to adopt dispersal. But the policy was controversial almost from its inception. Dispersal was problematic because, as a result of DES action, it became a national policy pronouncement, and as such appeared to intrude upon local initiative. Administrative difficulties of a more mundane sort—arranging bus routes and student assignments, and mollifying irate parents—provoked concern, as did the considerable expense of busing. Taken together, these factors led some educators and politicians to see the policy as simply too much trouble.

Educationally rooted objections were just as important. The deliberate separation of home and school caused by busing was at odds with the prevailing British educational wisdom that a school should forge close links with the neighborhood it served. Of at least equal significance was the perceived curtailing of parents' educational choice—also a strong tradition in British education. That this restriction was based on race was especially troubling. Defenses of busing were not persuasive for a people long attentive to individual liberties, distrustful of basing policy on group characteristics, and dubious about the benefits that might flow from the practice. Finally, the very fact that dispersal was an explicit policy proved disturbing. It was one thing "naturally" to disperse students through reshaping school attendance zones and new school construction, but quite something else to call attention to a matter better left undiscussed.

Over time, these factors—as well as absence of the arguments for integration based on pedagogical reasons or principles of justice and equality that have dominated discussion of the issue in the United States—produced a shift in the political consensus. By 1969, DES was hedging its support for dispersal; by 1973, it was treating the matter as wholly within the province of the local authorities. The parliamentary select committee concerned with race relations engaged in an even more dramatic volte-face. It moved from enthusiasm to downright hostility toward the policy.

The Race Relations Board went even further. In a most uncharacteristic action it brought suit against a local authority, charging that its dispersal program discriminated on racial grounds. Ironically, the community that was haled into court in 1976 was the very city whose unhappiness over racial concentrations produced a national dispersal policy in the first place; more important, the challenged dispersal effort, whether judged in terms of programmatic quality or reduction of racial tension, was exemplary. Nevertheless the authority agreed not to assign newcomers to the program on the basis of race, and to phase it out by 1981. Consequently, as an explicit policy, busing is dead. Even though in some respects dispersal "worked," it is difficult to locate a defender of the practice. Efforts persist to secure effective dispersal in education and public housing of nonwhite immigrants—but without having to acknowledge formally that any deliberate policy of dispersal has ever been decided upon. Local authorities are still doing what they can to promote racial mixing. Now, however, they follow the maxim "Do good by stealth."

The Roots of Inexplicitness: Private and Public Policy

Several related factors, cited earlier, help to explain Britain's reliance on inexplicitness as a predicate for policy in this domain: the unwillingness of Britons to perceive race as a social-policy issue; a preference, in public policy, for consensual decision making; and a commitment to universalism as a public-policy norm. Each deserves some attention.

Private Policy: What Racial Problem?
Although the British had long experience with nonwhites through the years of empire, that history did not prepare them for the strains of a multiracial society. Quite the contrary: as the nineteenth-century British historian Goldwin Smith observed in 1878, British insularity precluded "not only fusion, but also sympathy and almost intercourse with the sub-

ject races" (Bolt, 1971, p. 214). Strong subconscious resentment at the loss of imperial grandeur was directed against the nonwhite arrivals, themselves tangible evidence of Britain's altered international status. In a 1967 poll more than three-fifths of all Britons regarded themselves as superior to Africans and Asians; the relative lack of education and cultural differences of the newcomers were the stated causes of this feeling of superiority. The persistence of such views rendered the British most ambivalent hosts.

Yet the British have a rather different sense of the matter. They see themselves as an extremely tolerant people vigorously opposed to racism. Sociologist Michael Banton, writing in the 1950s, detected a widely suffused norm of tolerance; only 2 percent of the British, he concluded, could be described as strongly prejudiced (Banton, 1959). In subsequent surveys, the "untalented tenth" of the population was singled out as problem causing. Unlike the United States, Britain has no deep and scarring history of racial exploitation at home; the colonies were far away and very different from Britain itself. Though there is a British counterpart to the "American dilemma" in the gap between a self-image of tolerance and the reality of the shabby treatment accorded to those viewed as racial (or social-class) inferiors, this has not been widely appreciated. "The English people," as Ann Dummett writes, "are accustomed to thinking of racism as a Bad Thing, but they are convinced that it is always happening somewhere else" (Dummett, 1972, p. 14).

This British self-image has profound significance for policy. Change is most likely when there exists consensus that the status quo can no longer be endured. Change comes hardest when present arrangements seem perfectly acceptable. In Britain there has not been much sense of a racial "problem"; hence there has been little enthusiasm for developing remedies. Cures involving the British themselves—antidiscrimination legislation, conciliation efforts, or redistribution of resources from whites to nonwhites—were seen as at best unnecessary, at worst harmful to good race relations. If anything was needed, the typical Briton noted, it was time. According to one observer, "British people are very fair: if the newspapers would only stop [harping on race] we would get on very quietly with living together" (Dummett, 1972, p. 88). Such a view hardly constitutes a mandate for aggressive public intervention in racial issues.

Public Policy: Consensual Decison Making and Universalist Ideology
Inexplicitness with respect to the racial aspects of educational policy is also consistent with a pronounced political and bureaucratic preference

for consensual, incremental decision making; that preference is threatened by the confrontationist, potentially revolutionary, nature of a racial orientation. It is also traceable to a deep-seated ideological commitment to universalism in social services, and consequent allergy to group labeling for even allegedly benign governmental purposes.

Thus, when confronted by demands that it undertake almost anything, the typical DES response is to stress its own institutional powerlessness. In fact, the operant statutes render ambiguous DES's authority—although if DES were interested, it could seek broader powers from Parliament. Of greater importance are the department's preference for government by partnership and its consultation with almost every would-be stakeholder in the educational-policy arena. Rule making intended to alter the behavior of local authorities is simply uncongenial to the enterprise, whose goal is consensus, not mandate. This preference, reinforced as a practical matter by the failure of the 1965 initiative of the national government to command general adherence, has effectively limited race-specific policy initiatives.

The desire for consensus concerning policy substance is matched by a desire to minimize conflict in the negotiation of policies, and this too has affected DES's willingness to address racial questions. As the department declared to a team of Organization for Economic Cooperation and Development (OECD) evaluators: "When it comes to planning leading to policy decisions . . . informal methods . . . are superior to highly structured formal procedures which invite half-baked and politically sectarian battles, and encourage demagogy, confrontation, and publicity" (OECD, 1975, p. 30). These limits placed on the negotiation process have tended to exclude race as a focus of consultation. From DES's point of view, attending to race might have been calculated to produce bile, not balm.

The tension between race specificity and universalism is also relevant in understanding Britain's policy in these matters. As Catherine Jones notes in *Immigration and Social Policy in Britain:* "The whole philosophy of the Welfare State . . . had hitherto seemed to centre around the idea of catering for certain categories of social need irrespective of 'extraneous' social, cultural, or economic personal characteristics. To treat, or even to record, coloured immigrants differently, for no other reason than because they were coloured immigrants, seemed to strike at the heart of this philosophy, and to constitute a form of discrimination which, whether it was intended to be positive or negative in the first instance, seemed a highly dangerous and unwelcome precedent'' (Jones, 1977, p. 193).

Universalism has never been the basis for coherent policy; it is more a slogan for an exuberantly romantic socialism. As long as individual demands exceed the collective willingness to share resources, some selectivity is required. Nor do universalists forget that certain social categories broadly deserve to benefit from "positive discrimination"; to ignore poverty, for instance, only produces formal equality while in fact preserving inequity. Yet for the universalist the question remains, How can government prefer some (and which categories of "some"), even as it serves all? As Richard Titmuss, the most passionate and persuasive advocate of universalism, framed the issue: "What particular infrastructure of universalist services is needed in order to provide a framework of values and opportunity within and around which can be developed socially acceptable selective services aiming to discriminate positively, with the minimum risk of stigma, in favour of those whose needs are greatest?" (Titmuss, 1968, pp. 113-114). That concern underlies, for instance, the British preference for an approach to special treatment that considers a neighborhood, rather than a particular individual, as eligible for assistance.

The press for a race-specific educational policy is, in these terms, highly problematic. Special attention would predictably arouse antagonism, for there is little sense in Britain that nonwhites are more deserving than the poor generally. For that reason local authorities have often been willing to aid nonwhites only when white residents were, so to speak, looking the other way. Nor is stigmatization easily avoided: aiding racial minorities might just reinforce the long-standing British perception that these groups are, after all, innately inferior.

Even if these objections could be set aside, there remains a further problem: What constitutes an intelligent and positive race-specific policy? The real possibility exists that any race-specific approach (focusing on West Indians' special achievement difficulties, for instance) would be of little use to the very group it is intended to benefit. Far better, or so it has been thought in Britain, to define educational needs in terms of language or poverty. Better also, according to DES policy, to stress the "shared educational disadvantages associated with an impoverished environment," in the expectation that the benefits flowing to the large and amorphous group identified by that phrase would simultaneously reach the smaller, more visible, more vulnerable racial minority. It follows from this view of the world that one helps nonwhites by not favoring them explicitly. If race goes officially unnoticed, even against the weight of the evidence, its relevance might just disappear over time.

Appraising Inexplicitness

Most policy decisions involve not the happy discovery of a social panacea, but rather the less happy task of choosing between the disagreeable and the intolerable. That caution is usefully borne in mind in assessing the British and American policy records with respect to race.

Policy Constraint and Policy Choice
The most stunningly obvious facts bearing on the racial situations in the United States and Britain speak to what is distinctive about each. Noting the differences concerning demography, history, and decision-making style helps to fix the bounds of policy choice open to the two nations.

The nonwhite population of Britain is, proportionately, only a quarter as large as that of the United States. Moreover, the major cities of the United States either have sizable nonwhite minorities or nonwhite majorities, while in Britain in no city of any size does the nonwhite population exceed 15 percent. These differences are reflected, in exaggerated form, in the schools. In 1970, for example, the ten biggest American school systems each enrolled more than 20 percent black students; four of the ten were majority-black. By contrast, in the same year, just 6 of Britain's more than 500 authorities, none of them among the largest, were more than 20 percent nonwhite. Demography bespeaks policy. A minority population of 5 or 10 percent can remain politically invisible, but a substantially larger nonwhite population necessarily influences a range of urban policies and thus cannot be ignored.

Nor are the nonwhite populations of the two countries alike in terms of background. In America, blacks—who make up more than 60 percent of the minority population—share a cultural and historical heritage; in Britain, differences stemming from region of origin, urban or rural background, and status remain profound. There exists a positive black American culture; by contrast, the only common experience of Britain's nonwhite consists in white Britons' treatment of them. These cultural differences have policy relevance. American blacks do constitute a legitimate group; Britain's nonwhites sometimes seem less a single group than a categorical artifact, rather like redheads.

The different histories of American blacks and British nonwhites are the best-known distinctions between the two groups. Blacks came to America as slaves; even when freed, they were victims of officially sanctioned discrimination until the passage of the 1964 Civil Rights Act. They have only begun to participate as formal equals in American political, economic, and social life. Britain's nonwhites came very recently and willingly to a country that offered a valued set of social ideals and the prospect of economic advancement. The discrimination they suffered was never officially sanctioned: John Bull did not learn from Jim Crow. This history also bears on the present. A good deal of America's racial policy, especially as crafted by the judiciary, takes the sins of the past as its warrant for present-day intervention. The shared realization that as a nation America has ill-treated blacks has provided a vital impetus for government action. In Britain no readily detectable residue of social guilt exists, and policy initiatives with respect to race derive from other sources.

Less familiar but equally important in explaining the policy differences between the United States and Britain is what might be termed the customary style of decision making in the two nations. American policy decisions are often made directly, as either/or propositions, in visible, formal, adversarial settings. The legalist influence prevails, both in the relatively greater reliance on the judiciary as a problem solver and in the emulation of the judicial approach by administrative agencies. The British style, in decided contrast, is nonconfrontational, nonformal, and nonlegal.

This distinction applies especially to the issue of race relations, which in America has been conceptualized largely in terms of rules, legal *dos* and *don'ts*. For the past decade the management of antidiscrimination efforts with respect to schools has been almost exclusively the province of American courts. Desegregation, the policy task, has become a matter of rule-mindedness, obedience to (or defiance of) court decisions. School districts that obey the law by not discriminating against black students are impervious to legal challenge; those that break the rules are ordered to behave differently. This legalist regime, which emerged at a time when undoing segregation was first mandated by law, persisted in the 1970s under circumstances in which neither legal nor moral right and wrong were so clear-cut.

The British situation is almost wholly different. The considerably greater reticence of the British judiciary to rule on racial issues is partly attributable to the absolute supremacy of Parliament and the nonavailability of judicial review of parliamentary actions on constitutional grounds. Even when the propriety of judicial review is unquestioned, the inclination of the British courts is to narrow the issue at hand, minimizing its policy implications. Nor do British administrative agencies behave as if they were courts. DES has not been inclined to adopt lawlike modes of responding to alleged racial discrimination even when authorized to do so, as under the 1976 Race Relations Act; the department's preference has been for informal inquiry and ad hoc solutions, not definitive statements of right. This distinction between the adversarial and legalist, on the one hand, and the nonconfrontationist and nonformal, on the other, shapes the range of substantive policies available in each country.

The Possibility of Policy Learning

If there are profound differences between the American and British experiences, nascent common themes also exist, making it possible for one nation to learn from the experiences of the other.

With respect to racial issues, the present situation in the United States and Britain reveals far more likenesses than has the past. Discrimination in both countries has become more a furtive and private matter, rather than open and public. Overt racial discrimination in America now seems of less policy moment than even a decade ago. Disadvantage more nebulously linked to race, more clearly tied to economic circumstance, appears newly significant.

The distinguished black sociologist William Julius Wilson comments in *The Declining Significance of Race:* "The systematic efforts of whites to suppress blacks . . . do not provide meaningful explanation of the life chances of black Americans today." The past decade has witnessed a "progressive transition from racial inequalities to class inequalities" (Wilson, 1978, pp. 1, 2, 153). For talented and highly educated blacks, nondiscrimination has become largely a reality, while poorly trained inner-city blacks—like their unskilled white counterparts—seem destined to endure perpetually marginal economic and social status.

This observation must be qualified by the realization that in certain spheres, such as access to housing, widespread racial discrimination persists in America. Yet white Americans now overwhelmingly believe that race per se has a diminishing impact on one's life chances. If blacks are worse off, the cause is thought not to be discrimination; thus the preferred remedy is catch-up assistance, not preferential treatment. Racial inexplicitness, in the form of compensation for all those needing special help, commands majority enthusiasm.

American debates over two vital racial-policy issues—court-ordered busing and racially preferential treatment—also reveal support for remedies less racially explicit than has been the policy rule since the 1954 *Brown* decision.

With respect to busing the definition of "deliberate," and hence properly proscribable, segregation has broadened considerably as the courts have shifted their focus to the behavior of school districts that never mandated separate schools. The wrong committed by northern districts has grown harder for the average American to comprehend. Moreover, the nexus between alleged discrimination and the sweeping remedy of reassigning students throughout a city's public-school system appears remote, at least to the popular mind, and hence arbitrary. It is not surprising, then, that this judicially mandated development has provoked spirited critiques rooted in concern for freedom of educational choice as well as for the constitutionally appropriate allocation of power between the political and judicial branches of the federal government. Both sources of concern stem from dissatisfaction with an explicitly racial policy, student busing.

Even more dramatic are the divisions in the once unified civil rights coalition over the wisdom of explicit preferential treatment of nonwhites. On one side stand those who insist that the appropriate measure of nondiscrimination is full partnership in the social, political, and economic order; that full partnership can be defined only in outcome terms, as proportionate participation; that past participation justifies this remedy; that less rigorous measures are unresponsive to the demand for equality; and that, at least as a temporary expedient, racial preference is appropriate. On the other side stand those who believe that it is improper and illegal to single out racial groups for any purpose, and who consequently oppose reliance on race as a policy criterion even for ostensibly good causes—especially where others, themselves innocent of any wrongdoing, are hurt as a result.

Unlike the historic efforts to combat discrimination, the dispute over the rightness of preferential treatment cannot be depicted as a struggle between good and evil; it is rather a choice between two concepts of good. The principled partisans in this fray each advance a definition of equality, one group centered and the other individual centered, one outcome oriented and the other process oriented, one insisting upon racial explicitness and the other resistant to using race as a predicate for special treatment.

The point is not that the appropriateness of court-ordered busing or preferential treatment is in any way resolved by mechanical reference to the principle of racial inexplicitness; the issues are far too complex, the values at issue far too deep. It is rather that, in recognizing that racial questions are no longer the matters of simple justice that they once were, and that their explicit resolution is not necessarily the appropriate course, America may be verging closer to the long-standing British position.

Britain and the United States confront different but complementary policy challenges. The American policy task, succinctly stated, is to link a well-developed legalist understanding of racial fairness with the emerging possibility of a sense of justice, at once more finely tuned and ad hoc, less clearly defined and generalizable, that can develop through the political process. This aspiration calls for a minimalist judicial role, with courts serving as guarantors of basic rights rather than as detailed policy shapers (see Kirp, 1977). Can this objective be achieved? In the United States racial politics—particularly at the state and local levels—has frequently operated to frustrate legitimate minority aspirations; whether it can give a fuller reckoning to those aspirations is still untested. Furthermore, the American judiciary has become habituated to an activist stance, preferring clarity to compromise, legal principle to politics. Can one imagine the issue of busing or preferential treatment ultimately being resolved by other than a Supreme Court decision?

For Britain the situation is quite different. The need, briefly put, is to couple considerable virtues of inexplicitness with a recognition that discrimination—unequal treatment based on race—deserves more serious public-policy attention than it has thus far received. Discrimination ought to be anathema in a country that values personal liberty so highly. Nondiscrimination represents the embodiment of respect for the individual, the formal guarantee that a given group identity will not denigrate the person. It involves undoing explicitly disadvantaging rules and practices, as well as attending to practices that—although not overtly racial— in fact operate to discriminate against racial minorities. This undertaking does not equate differences between the minority and majority as necessarily disadvantaging. It does argue for the need for sensitive appraisal of the nature and invidiousness of those differences.

The point bears directly on British educational policy. The nondiscrimination principle suggests that, at the least, claims by nonwhites who have been victimized on account of race receive an attentive hearing, and that, in addition, certain practices that disadvantage nonwhites as a group be subject to careful review. Beyond effectively assuring nondiscrimination, particular matters are probably best resolved in the particular, not by general pronouncement: that is true for the United States as well as Britain. As Philip Mason has framed the challenge: "What we have to do . . . is to direct our whole educational system toward the treatment of other groups and people as autonomous persons with their own values and yet achieve this within a system of authority and unity of values. But it must be an adult system of values, that is, one which each constituent accepts as its own. At the same time, there is the insoluble dilemma that, violent as is our need, we cannot literally 'direct' our system of education into any channel without doing violence to our own beliefs about intellectual freedom" (Mason, 1964, pp. 123-124).

The ultimate hope for both Britain and the United States is much the same. What is needed is a public policy that neither becomes officious meddling nor degenerates into mere neglect, with the result that race slowly disappears as a policy problem. As to the likelihood of that eventually happening in either nation, it is far too soon even to hazard a prediction.

References

Banton, Michael. 1959. *White and Coloured*. London: Cape.

Bolt, Christine. 1971. *Victorian Attitudes to Race*. London: Routledge and Kegan Paul.

Deakin, Nicholas. 1970. *Colour, Citizenship and British Society*. London: Panther.

Department of Education and Science. 1965. The education of immigrants. (Circular 7/65 to local authorities.)

———. 1973. *Education*. London: HMSO.

Dummett, Ann. 1972. *A Portrait of English Racism*. Harmondsworth: Penguin.

Hansard, vol. 685, cols. 433-444, November 27, 1963 (emphasis added).

Jones, Catherine. 1977. *Immigration and Social Policy in Britain*. London: Tavistock.

Kirp, David. 1977. School desegregation and the limits of legalism. *Public Interest* 47:101-128.

———. 1979. *Doing Good by Doing Little: Race and Schooling in Britain*. Berkeley: University of California Press.

Mason, Philip. 1964. *Prospero's Magic*. London: Oxford University Press.

Organization for Economic Cooperation and Development. 1975. *Education Development Strategy of England and Wales*. Paris: OECD.

Titmuss, Richard. 1968. *Commitment to Welfare*. London: Allen and Unwin.

Wilson, William Julius. 1978. *The Declining Significance of Race*. Chicago: University of Chicago Press.

PART FOUR

An Overview

15 Constitutional Values and Public Education

LANCE LIEBMAN

America's natal ideology was grounded on the Enlightenment faith that social institutions could remake human nature while limiting it. The physical circumstances of the New World had already created an especially independent and progressive personality; the right rules for the political process would assure the improvement of that personality, at the same time curbing its tendencies to excess. The conception was subtle. It included a deep sense of man's defects, his passions and weaknesses. While it did not assert man's perfectibility, it did claim his capacity for improvement in an institutional environment designed in the light of practical reason.

From early days, the Montesquieued structure created to implement this faith included a constitutional judiciary: officers not responsible to the electorate, whose task was to apply the state's written first principles as they adjudicated disputes over the allocation of limited power. In particular, the judges were expected to identify the bounds imposed by the Constitution on the authority of the popular institutions to respond to temporary passion and preference.

The logic of the system was that the judges were to be teachers as well as arbitrators: they were to reason from written principle and show citizens how to live with freedom; to demonstrate to them that their better nature does not want what mere interest dictates; and to make them understand, especially by institutional mechanisms commanding pause and reconsideration, that the Constitution's evolving applications represent their own best values. That is why the function can be performed only by an institution that hears argument, that gives reasons, and that honors precedent, or at least by one that is obliged to consider the relationship between what it does today and what it did yesterday.

Over a century ago constitutional jurisprudence (and political accommodation too) failed the test of slavery, leaving only war. This volume asks, among many difficult and important questions, whether the performance of the courts during the past twenty-five years in dealing with issues of school desegregation—graded so highly not very long ago—has in fact served the country well.

For the struggle to desegregate, and to overcome the century of caste that followed two hundred years of slavery, has been in significant part a constitutional revolution. Black assertiveness was essential. But blacks, as Thurgood Marshall and Martin Luther King, Jr., repeatedly said, did not have the numbers or the weapons to win freedom without help. They could not succeed like the workers of England or the masses of India. It was essential, and it happened, that white opinion regard segregation as wrong and unconstitutional—as in violation of values, and of values backed by formal authority. Only the courts could express basic social values in the necessary way. So while presidents moved, hesitantly, against certain manifestations of the system of segregation, and while a few legislatures (but not the national one) acted, the Supreme Court took apart Jim Crow.

For all Americans who were not benighted, and for many persons overseas who were coping with similar issues of anticolonialism and national identity at the same time, *Brown* v. *Board of Education* was a great and wonderful development; the cause of desegregation was noble and essential; and every judicial and legislative assault on the fabric of discrimination was valid. From today's perspective all these sentiments were completely correct. Yet antisegregation is not the same thing, or not necessarily the same thing, as integration, much less the same thing as equality. Intellectually and practically, the cause of equality developed rapidly, in ambiguous relation to the desegregation movement from which it sprang. Developing so quickly, in historical circumstances of such flux and drama, and in a country without traditions of overt ideological dispute, certain theoretical ambiguities were inevitably obscured. Among them were these.

(a) *Federalism:* To what extent were we ready to substitute national authority in a realm—public education—heretofore under predominantly local influence?

(b) *Opportunity:* Were we seeking a defensible, race-blind system of allocating preferential positions, or seeking to lessen inequality in final status, or seeking to distribute blacks throughout the economic and social system (and if the last, in what relation to their total number)?

(c) *Compensation:* If, as Chief Justice Warren Burger was to write, no fair race can be run with one group of contestants crippled from past mistreatment, what would we do to even the odds?

(d) *Togetherness:* If the main goal was to achieve social harmony and good relations among people of different races, ought not young people be placed in environments where they relate across racial barriers?

(e) *Other deprived groups:* What categories beyond black and white were relevant to these issues? What ought to be done for other deprived groups—Chicanos, Puerto Ricans, Native Americans, Estonians, women, the physically handicapped, the poor, illegitimates, and so forth?

Had we attacked racism through politics, these issues might have been dealt with gradually, by compromise, as we picked our way among contradictory principles from one temporarily supportive foothold to another. Our constitutional jurisprudence is hardly an engine of logic, but it is held to a higher degree of coherence than is required by the world of legislation and of political negotiation. Thus it was necessary for judges to find assertions they could bring themselves to utter, to face one another's (and the profession's) scrutiny, and to listen today to the arguments invited by the propositions expressed yesterday. Meanwhile, of course, the same Supreme Court was playing the leading role in one of the grandest and most fundamental political rearrangements ever accomplished with so little force; and the inferior courts (chiefly but not entirely federal courts) found themselves obliged to become something quite different from deciders of cases—they were obliged to become implementers of complex remedial plans and managers of large public agencies.

This book tells the story of a twenty-five year judicial assault on segregated public education. In part, it is a story of legal doctrine. First, active efforts to segregate were held invalid. Next, in *Brown II*, the "remedy" opinion, "deliberate speed" was established as the ambiguous pace for moving from here to there. This raised two types of problems. One was practical. Implementation was in the hands of the local wielders of power. They and their constituents wanted no change, or as little and as slow as possible. Inevitably movement occurred only when adequate artillery was assembled. Meanwhile all the attention was on departing from "here," and little occurred to shape the constitutional definition of "there." Deliberate speed caused a second, subtler problem, as Justice Hugo Black expressed in his end-of-career television interview with Eric Sevareid. In the public perception judges tell what is right and what is wrong. If segregation is wrong, a court should say so and require that it be stopped. Weighing the exigencies of remedy, and especially weighing them with as many relevant factors as are encompassed in "deliberate speed'' (availability of buildings, need to change bus routes, but also community attitudes, teacher perceptions, and student preparation for particular programs), makes the final judgment inherently unjudicial, brings the courts to the level of political traders, and so forfeits some of their scanty capital. (It also encourages, by rewarding, every sort of hindrance. This is a parallel to the new research finding that lead time in busing plans increases white flight.)

At this juncture the courts looked like pointy-headed bureaucrats, not to mention do-good social planners. They were not declaring that any student had a right to an integrated (or otherwise describable) education; nor that any school board was necessarily obligated to behave in a particular way. There was a clear charge to school boards not to seek segregation. That was comprehensible and the public came with some speed to accept it. Was there a further charge to school boards to go beyond, to seek affirmatively to put black and white pupils together? Over time we got an odd answer to that question from the courts: there was no such duty, and where housing patterns or educational background merged with assignment policies of plausible educational justification to create segregated, or substantially segregated, schools, the Constitution was not violated. Where violations had occurred—where segregation had been unlawfully sought by responsible officials—the remedy for the misdeed could be a positive duty imposed upon them or their successors to integrate the local schools. Violations of nearly any sort led to root-and-branch remedies, often large programs of rearranged attendance zones publicly seen as "busing." But only in some cities: those that had been segregated once by law, or had sinned since; those where adequately funded plaintiffs were willing to bring a case; those where accidents of evidence made it possible to prove what everyone knows happened nearly everywhere; those where certain judges happened to sit.

Judge-made school assignment policy created one boundary that was not random or capricious. I remember teaching the school cases to first-year law students in the spring of 1973 and predicting confidently that the one outcome not even the courts could give the country was broad integration remedies stopping arbitrarily at the boundary of city and suburb. Yet after the Court divided evenly in the *Richmond* case, that is exactly the answer it gave us, 5-4 to be sure, in *Detroit*. In a country where well-off whites have left the cities since World War II, it is certainly extraordinary to impose a requirement of integration in the old cities, while leaving suburbanites free to make voluntary political decisions about minor (but sometimes controversial) ventures in which junior high-schoolers go bowling with their in-city neighbors on Tuesday afternoons.

Detroit, and reversal by the U.S. Supreme Court of the local judge's cross-district, metropolis-wide integration order, marked the end of the *Brown* period and the intellectual and political bankruptcy of the *Green-Swann* approach. Why should Boston and Los Angeles be integrated, while Atlanta and Chicago and Miami are not? Because plaintiffs in Boston and Los Angeles proved positive efforts by officials to preserve segregation and wanted the busing remedy. (Who wanted it? By decision of what constituency?) Fine, even if we know that it is difficult to make the distinction seem legitimate to the individual white parent who perceives that his child's schooling is being disrupted. Now add the degree of perceived unfairness provided when the suburban residents near Boston and Los Angeles are exempt. Who caused the segregation? The suburbanites who fled the city, whose legislators refused state funds to the city, whose zoning policies kept blacks out of their towns, who consume the city's jobs and culture and widgets but not its public schools? Integration might have been salable as a positive constitutional duty of citizens and their representatives. It has been ordered instead on a fault theory, a remedy theory, a punishment theory.

Law traditionally determines wrongs and requires that they be righted. Here, however, the attenuations are too great: that child C be bused because politician P once offended; that parents F + M have their lives altered even though they did not vote for politician P, did not know P was misbehaving, did not themselves specifically benefit; all while other cities, and friends and relatives who had just enough money or initiative to move to the suburbs during the great migration, are spared. Society might accept (and, in nontrivial ways, this one *has* accepted) a duty to make good its centuries of evil treatment of blacks. That would be different from asserting that certain families should pay a price, when they cannot be shown why it is fair that only they pay.

And of course, the payment theory is all wrong, educationally and socially. Is it a burden to attend school with blacks? Is it a joyous benefit for blacks to attend school in South Boston? Are we in fact in favor of integration? If so, why aren't we pursuing it more broadly, and why the immobility of all those citizens who could take steps toward it? Only the theory of integration-as-a-present-punishment-to-remedy-past-evil-deeds explains what has happened, and that theory requires a connection between misdeed and punishment that does not exist in these circumstances.

The school integration story, as Alexander Bickel perceived a decade ago, shows constitutional courts dragged beyond their ken, in part because the reactions of the judges' peers was so positive to the earlier, far more justifiable interventions they had made. It is a constitutional proposition when the Supreme Court says separate education cannot be an application of the equal protection of the laws. It could be a constitutional proposition were the Court to require integrated schools, or efforts to integrate, or achievement of integration where there are no significant impediments. It is not a constitutional proposition that certain school districts be integrated, but not others whose history, overall, is not different—and even those only to the gates of the suburbs.

The chapters of this book silently reflect approximately this view of the constitutional significance of integration. Desegregation was, is, and will be a constitutional principle in this country. Integration was such a principle at certain points, but it is not so today and appears unlikely to be so in the near future. The authors of these chapters are hardly a cross-section of Americans, but surely on this issue they are not far from the common belief. Equality, by some definition or other and some measure or other, is important. So is harmony among the groups inhabiting the country. It may well be that neither is achievable without racially mixed public schools. Therefore, the pursuit of mixed schools is a value, and a significant value—one worth pursuing in one's daily life and in one's political activities in the community. But it is not a *constitutional* value, one that must prevail against other important considerations, even against such ordinary values as economy, reduced transportation time, and neighborhood autonomy, and certainly not when perceived to be in conflict with the effectiveness of the educational process itself.

If this view is correct, constitutional consideration of the significance of race in school assignments will now focus on three groups of issues:

(a) *Can the fault-remedy investigation be restricted or closed down altogether?* If it is not right to order large efforts to integrate in arbitrarily selected cities, is there any way to retreat from the Supreme Court's busing doctrines with explanations that show a sense that evolving judicial doctrine bears some relation to a conception of law? Justice Lewis Powell, a former leader of the Richmond school board, has seemed sensitive to this need. We should probably expect that integration will be ordered only when there is a clear connection between acts of segregation and the resulting racial separation. Certain cases would have to be explicitly overturned, not a happy prospect for the Court, but the dubious doctrine that integration is constitutionally necessary only as remedy for specific political acts, and not as remedy for the large forces of history, would be preserved and merely redefined.

(b) *How should we define the no-segregation principle?* Consider Andrew Jackson High School, in southeastern Queens, New York City.

Over the last twenty years Andrew Jackson moved with its neighborhood from being a predominantly white school to being a school without a single white student. (The school's attendance area runs up to the Nassau County line; Valley Stream, just over the line, is 93 percent white, but that is another story.) The city school board, desiring (and legally obligated) to pursue integration, offered Jackson pupils the option of attending other high schools in Queens, but sought to cushion the impact on those other schools (in an effort, surely, to discourage so-called white flight from those schools) by limiting Jackson transfers to schools more than 50 percent white and also limiting the number of Jackson blacks who could transfer to a particular school in a single year. A distinguished judge found the restrictions unconstitutional, saying they restricted minority pupils' access "because of their race." The judge did not pause to note that the school board was going out of its way to grant transfer opportunities only because of their race.

The Andrew Jackson case is important in part because it is not so special; many like it are decided each year. They are cases which repeatedly demonstrate that we are dealing with a public service—education—the relevant significance of which depends on the group of people with whom one consumes it. Therefore, almost necessarily, the racial composition of that group is important to us. Yet when a society accepts a responsibility for that composition, especially given other constraints such as student freedom to switch to private schools and parent freedom to move to Valley Stream, it almost inevitably acts in ways that achieve the goal to different extents for different subpopulations, and that seem constitutionally questionable judged from the perspective of some individual or group. "Behave without consideration of race" might be an implementable standard, although it would be a strange rule in a society as race conscious as ours. "Seek integration" would be another manageable rule. "Don't discriminate," or even "Don't discriminate against any nonwhites," is a difficult standard with which to comply, given the various other considerations and goals that we declare to be legitimate or even mandatory.

(c) *To what extent will we develop a satisfactory conception of constitutional rights lodged in groups of citizens?* Conventional legal doctrine assumes an individual who has rights against the state and obligations to the state. Yet desegregation and integration have never been rights of an individual pupil. The earliest plaintiffs in school cases received for their victories only the consolation that at a "deliberate" speed, based on a unique range of equitable considerations, a judge would gradually alter the mechanism of school assignment and eventually disestablish the dual system. The clearest example of the evolving concept of a group right was the Atlanta litigation, where it was assumed that plaintiffs could obtain an order for community-wide busing; yet some black leaders negotiated a settlement of the case changing school assignment very little but obtaining instead other political goals, including especially leadership jobs for blacks in the school system.

Who authorized the black negotiators to speak for individual black children whose parents might have preferred integration, or for the hypothetical white pupil who might have preferred integration to jobs for blacks? The courts that approved the negotiated settlement were accepting a view of a right to an integration remedy resting in the black community as a whole, negotiable by representatives legitimated by the court itself. The "realism" quotient is high: an awareness that persons perceived these issues in terms of blacks and whites as separate groups, and that forcing the groups to deal as collective entities advances relatively acceptable accommodation. Nevertheless, the challenge to ordinary notions of law and of constitutional rights is significant.

If the analysis of this chapter is correct, and the years ahead will see a restriction of city-wide transportation remedies, difficulty determining what is unacceptable racial discrimination, and confusion over the integration threat as a political bargaining weapon for nonwhite groups, an important conclusion follows. There will not be a substantial increase in racially integrated elementary and secondary education in the United States in the next twenty years. We have desegregated the schools, but not the cities or the suburbs. Integration may come when black gains in employment, if and when accompanied by effective assaults on housing segregation *and* by a diminution in citizen desire to live among persons of one's own race, result in economically homogeneous but racially heterogeneous schools. That time is likely to be in the twenty-first century. Meanwhile it is necessary to explore whether the country ought to formulate constitutional propositions governing public education. After all, integration is not the only basic value relevant to education. Desegregation attracted so much of the nation's constitutional attention because dual schools were such an abomination. Now, if we desegregate but will not integrate, we must ask whether education is just another public service, to be organized, packaged, and delivered however local political and bureaucratic processes determine, or whether those processes should be constrained by national commitments derived from the basic charter of the country—the Constitution; and, if so, whether those national commitments should be defined and applied by the judiciary.

This discussion has relevance only if we first agree that education is important, indeed fundamental, and fundamental in a constitutional sense. Education is not, as *Brown* v. *Board of Education* understood but certain later cases ignored, just another public service, like a swimming pool or a paved street. Education is the official means of socialization, civilization, and "citizenization." It is the common shared experience (no matter how many more hours are spent collectively watching television). Its credentials are the prime determinant in the distribution of jobs and thus of status. It is also the hub activity around which other public affairs revolve. The American system has not been convinced that it should treat integrated education as a basic goal. Yet Americans are ready to be convinced, if the case is put to them properly, that education itself does matter in a fundamental way, a way crudely categorizable as having aspects of both the minimum and the equal.

Must there be schools? No case has said so, but no case (save certain closings to avoid integration, which the courts managed to resolve while asserting they did not need to face the larger issue) has had to, which is more important. We dispute the age at which public responsibility begins (must there be day care?) and the age at which it ends (alone among advanced countries, we ration significant sectors of higher education by financial ability to pay—plus willingness and ability to borrow). But from age six to sixteen, and often from five to twenty-five, we provide the service, frequently by state constitutional command. If we raised education above the level of streets and sewers, we would have to confront explicitly the question of its content as a fundamental right of the individual and duty of the collectivity, and our confrontation of that issue would pose questions of individual entitlement and of fair decentralization.

Constitutionally Adequate Education

The period since World War II has witnessed a vast expansion in the commitment of resources to education in this country. Especially since enactment of the Elementary and Secondary Education Act of 1965, the share of resources raised locally has diminished. With steadily greater funding from Washington, and from the states as well, the federal and state governments have assumed more and more authority to prescribe the nature and content of public education. I remember as a high-school debater in the 1950s dismissing as clumsy the formulation "He who pays the piper calls the tune." From today's perspective on American education, the proposition certainly looks defensible.

Yet an educational policy imposed from Washington by the Department of Education is inherently different from a policy made by a professionally advised school board in a suburb of 50,000 residents, or even by a large city's educational apparatus. Washington is not Paris. It does not prescribe textbooks and curricula, imposing a single educational system on the country. It is not even London, requiring local education authorities to establish "comprehensive" secondary schools. Traditionally, Washington has intervened in public education in two ways. First, it reinforces professional views of the appropriate way to do things. This is often the function of extra, or supplementary, or innovative expenditures. Washington pays for consultants and conferences and training and development of materials. It is thus an agent of momentum, of transmission of ideas, of certifying the legitimacy of those ideas. Federal resources increase the effectiveness of those participants on the local scene —whether parents or teachers or administrators—who share the national, the progressive, the enlightened position. Second, Washington underwrites certain specific services. Much national expenditure has been aimed at expanding particular subcategories of the package of educational services provided locally: hot breakfasts, vocational training, science labs, bilingual instruction. In taking the funds, local school systems accept a formal responsibility to spend the money in prescribed ways. Consumers frequently are poorly situated to discover, much less enforce, such promises. To the extent of its inspectional resources, its credible sanctions, and its willingness to speak for interests that are by definition locally weak, Washington can enforce its own rules.

Gradually, however, the piper's payer has broadened his focus from tunes to programs, instrumentation, and audience. Without seeking (indeed, aware it could not sustain, politically or administratively) effective operational authority over education, Washington nonetheless was driven by a range of entirely legitimate national concerns to require that local processes meet certain national standards of sufficiency and equity. In part, the Office of Education and the Justice Department have pursued compliance with nondiscrimination principles, as discussed above. In another part, they have sought geographic and other definitions of equity in distribution of school resources, as discussed below. Most interestingly, they have acted to direct resources (sometimes, but not always, federal resources) toward particular consumers of educational services. The Elementary and Secondary Education Act itself sought increased resources for children from poor families. Other federal initiatives have been focused on the physically and medically handicapped; on students from non-English-speaking households; on students whose parents are federal employees.

Considered one at a time, these are traditional congressional responses to perceived problems, to needs easy to dramatize at hearings. Seen whole, however, as they appeared at the meetings that spawned this volume, they now appear as something more: as an incomplete but nonetheless significant statement, by accumulation of official national actions, that local government is obliged to meet the educational needs of all young residents. These laws were passed and funded in the same period when the Supreme Court, by a 5-4 vote, refused to find education sufficiently "fundamental," in a particular constitutional context, to require judicial scrutiny of its adequacy. Perhaps we do now have something very close to a national right to education, enforceable by a deprived citizen against the local school authority, based on federal statute.

We certainly have such rights for two groups often previously neglected by local processes for allocating resources: the handicapped, whose needs can be so great and from whom society traditionally averts its eyes; and those who do not speak English, whose needs are also great and whose effectiveness in local political processes has been restricted. One might soon expect an additional federal initiative on behalf of the educational needs of immigrants, especially unlawful ones, whose presence can easily be described as a matter of federal responsibility and whose children surely present a strong prudential claim for educational resources. More generally, one might expect codification of a right to education, within established federal parameters, with ultimate resort to the courts for determinations of relevant facts and laws. The concept is hardly without ambiguities and tensions. Consider an example:

What happens when the claim for educational adequacy is pressed on behalf of the purportedly "gifted," or the admittedly "average," child, who asserts that attention to the Finnish-speaking or the mentally retarded or the culturally deprived classmate is depriving him or her of all the education that would have been available were these other children not in the classroom? Nationalizing some part of the determination of educational needs and priorities does not assure easy solutions to difficult choices. Still, to some extent we have come, and to an additional extent we may soon come, to feel more comfortable removing some portion of these issues from local determination.

Are there limits to our willingness to commit resources? States with statutory entitlements for students presenting "special needs" have sometimes been obliged to spend very large amounts on particular children. Is the country willing to commit unlimited resources, or capable of defining fairly the limits to its commitment?

What happens when one student's maximum development is costly to the progress, or the convenience, of other students? At least sometimes, it must happen that a handicapped student will do best in a classroom with nonhandicapped students, but that his or her presence is detrimental to them. Can we work out a calculus for deciding such cases? Who in fact ultimately decides what is best for a child? Parents? The child? Local teachers? Bureaucrats? Judges?

Would such a right begin at age five or six (no day care?) and run to eighteen? Or would it inevitably affect our arrangements for distributing child care for preschool children, and for distributing and financing higher education and adult education as well?

What is the relationship between this commitment to developing the capacities of all young people and other social undertakings? It would be an unusual society that sought to take all twenty-one-year-olds to their maximum potential, and then offered them an economy grievously short of opportunities to do what they had been prepared to do and a general physical environment they had been educated to despise. Thinking about education in terms of rights is likely to be an infectious experience.

We are considering, of course, fundamental alterations in the processes of allocating opportunity, status, fulfillment, and respect. My point is that steps taken already have moved significantly in these directions, without clear acknowledgment of their implications. Only basic commitments can justify, guide, and legitimize the incredibly complex matrix of national, state, and local legislative processes, of administrative mechanisms at all those levels, of many different institutional arrangements for deciding relevant budget matters, of the tortuous and often conflicting progression of educational and other social-service professional considerations, and of the infinitely varied capacities of parents to pursue their own definition of their child's interests.

Without imposing silly rigidity on these social systems, but given the extent to which we are already committing vast resources and the extent to which we have already legislated in pursuit of selected aspects of the general goal, we could surface some of the more important questions, raise them to a level of debate and consideration, and reach clearer and more honest answers. For ultimately, suppressing the issues among the maze of competitive institutional structures and avoiding broad consideration of the most general questions is a recipe for fat bureaucrats, poorly served customers, and unfair benefits for those consumers able to play the system's complexities. If education is fundamental, we must organize ourselves to face the large issues it poses.

Constitutional Delegation to School Districts

The previous section has treated education as a public service (and a public good) delivered by government to individual consumers. That is one correct way to understand education. Individuals seek it, they believe it meets their needs, they want different sorts of it at different times in their lives, and government supplies it according to official determinations of eligibility, entitlement, and appropriateness. The U.S. Constitution has not been interpreted as compelling the federal government or the states to supply any particular quantum or type of educational service to individuals, but various federal and state statutes (and interpretations of state constitutions) have moved significantly toward an assured right of individuals to educational services minimally appropriate for fulfilling their potential to use education effectively.

Nevertheless, education is not a service consumed individually, like a seat on the log with Mark Hopkins, or in a car listening to a cassette lecture on property law; or like consumption of renal dialysis or food stamps or pure air or a golf course or safety from nuclear attack. Public education as we know it is inherently communal. What my children get depends on the teacher and the blackboard and the library and the films, but it also depends greatly on the children sharing the work table and the block corner. Children learn from one another. The content of the experience for those who receive public education is significantly determined by the group of students in the class, in the school, and in the community. A fact about American society is that neighborhoods are formed by cultural dispositions regulated by economic and racial constraints; thus individual children receive an education whose nature is formed by the interaction of parental choice of neighborhood with the simultaneous choices of thousands of others, all bounded by such realities as income, housing costs, policies of lending institutions, and racial discrimination. We see the process functioning; we know it could not accurately be labeled either a process of choice or a process without choice; we observe its fundamental significance for mobility, opportunity, socialization, and acculturation; and we struggle to decide whether the process as it functions is or is not compatible with our best and deepest—our constitutional—commitments.

These issues have appeared in a litigational contest most explicitly in the school finance cases, known to lawyers as *Serrano* (California), *Rodriguez* (Texas), and *Robinson* v. *Cahill* (New Jersey). In each version the issue is whether the state can supply education by a system of delegation to geographic districts plus substantial local property tax funding, with the result that some districts can raise a large sum per pupil with a low tax rate, while other districts must levy more onerous property taxes to generate smaller per-pupil school funds. The stereotype of rich suburbs and poor cities is not entirely accurate; some cities have substantial taxable commercial and industrial property from which school budgets benefit. But it is not wrong to visualize the constitutional issue as arising when Alamo Heights Independent School District, near San Antonio, could raise $333 per pupil with a tax rate of $8.50 per $1,000 of assessed valuation, while nearby Edgewood needed a tax rate of $10.50 to generate only $26 per pupil.

What these figures show is that for education, as for other public services, demand (or need) and supply (or capacity to pay) depend on political jurisdictions. All Americans benefit from living in a wealthy country that can supply elaborate public services without levying heavy taxes. In America one's taxes-and-services situation depends on one's neighbors; on whether they have many children who attend public schools and whether they put a lot of trash out at the curb; on whether they vote to have government provide desired services; on the tax arrangements they select; and on whether they insist on efficient institutional arrangements for providing services. To a degree, individuals can choose places of residence according to these criteria, which often are as relevant as the climate or the view. To a degree, land prices reflect the attractiveness of neighborhoods to prospective residents. The school finance cases are based on an assumption that individual preferences about services and taxes, combined with differences in individual needs and capacity, all mediated through political and economic markets, are a more or less satisfactory way of taking account of "neighborhood effects," but are not acceptable when they determine the nature and quality of the public education program. The stated or unstated assumption is that education is unique among public services because it makes the future, because its impact is on children who did not choose their circumstances in life, and because its availability under satisfactory arrangements is essential to our intellectual structure for justifying other social arrangements.

In the school finance context, the problem can be solved. The property tax is a poor revenue device in any event, and a trend to other taxes not presenting these problems is under way. Even California's Proposition

13 is part of that trend. Or, retaining the property tax, states can devise redistributive arrangements so that the economic capacity of a district to pay for schools no longer determines the price of the education provided to its children.

The issue seriously posed in the finance cases does not vanish when state constitutional provisions reform systems of paying for public education. For even if the same amount were spent on every schoolchild, the impact of geography would hardly disappear. First, some children arguably need more education because they start behind others, or because they will do more with it. That is the issue of asserted individual needs, a justification for some current expenditures and a matter discussed earlier. Second, and more important, the school has a major impact in establishing a young person's identity: his or her goals, attitudes, assumptions, plans, and behavior patterns. Other children have this impact as much as teachers, and much more than the wage per child paid to a teacher.

Yet seeing society's impact, seeing involvement by government as provider of education in the socialization processes of which schooling forms a central part, is not the same as identifying an occasion for the prescription of neutrality or equality as a constitutional rule. Arranging education by political subdivision—and delegating significant discretion in the provision of education to the states and, beyond them, to their subordinate school districts—is not only convenient. It also responds to genuine diversity, encourages citizen involvement, and fosters fraternity. Decentralization is a necessary, if of course an insufficient, ingredient of a meaningful local politics of education.

Thus it is possible to describe an institutional structure that leaves education to local communities (accepting as a result that an individual child's schooling will be importantly affected by whether the child lives in community A or community B) and yet requires the state to close most or all of the gap in the economic capacity of communities to provide this fundamental public good. The economic multiplier effect—the geometrically intensified fiscal burden resulting when the poor are forced to live together and are denied the resources to provide for their children what the broader society perceives as quality education—of state arrangements is easy, and so necessary, to correct. But the general force of social and cultural impact, more significant to be sure, is an inevitable consequence of human relations that are not computerized and homogenized, and therefore should be permitted, indeed encouraged.

A stronger argument is available too. Assume significant geographic communities within the large society, even a larger society that energetically seeks openness, opportunity, and choice. If those communities have resources—because federal intervention assures adequate individualized minimum educational standards and adequate resources to provide education meeting locally influenced needs—then local communities will have the capacity and incentives to choose their priorities and meet their needs and desires. This reads like a recipe for a responsible local politics of education, with substantial matters at stake, the sort of local politics that contributes to effective participation in the wider society.

Are these predictions of constitutional advance—toward the right of an individual child to an appropriate education and the right of a municipality to adequate resources to serve the educational needs of its children —plausible, given the constitutional story of school integration as recounted in this chapter and elsewhere in this book?

Start with the right to education, and consider it in light of our current dilemma: unlimited demand for public services and dissatisfaction with the nature, quality, and price of those services. Education is public and free, the professionals do their own thing, and warring subgroups of the citizenry compete to shape the content of the service. Compared to Europe and Japan, our scandal is that university education is not available free to whoever meets the entrance criteria. Yet our universities are better than theirs, perhaps because—to a degree, at least—ours must satisfy market demand.

Our problems in delivering public goods overlap with our problems of unconstrained demand. A right to education sounds fine when one thinks of human potential receiving the maximum nurture. But society does not place that value above all others, as John Rawls convincingly shows. And while all education announces itself as development and investment, some is luxurious present consumption. In the end, truths of political economy argue against severing education from market controls on quality and quantity. To the extent that externalities and distributional considerations require public and/or free distribution, day-to-day political controls—with all their limitations—are all we have, and they should not be constrained by overriding constitutional commitments.

Now consider community rights. Again, education is necessity and frill, fundamental requirements and optional consumption. The net flows of local revenue—taking into account the variety of taxation devices and spending programs—are difficult to estimate and in some instances not disadvantageous to large cities or to poor communities. Crude constitutional rules of resource distribution among political subdivisions might interfere significantly with political flexibility for small gains in the general income distribution or in the distribution of education opportunity.

With respect to both educational services as an individual's right and the equal opportunity to spend on education as a community's right, the real question is institutional: would we be happier with heavy judicial involvement in decisions so evanescent, so technical, so unresolvable by reason, so little given to absolute—or even lexically orderable—truths? The question is not rhetorical. Although it is possible to argue that we should invite the courts into these matters, court participation in rearranging school assignments in the past dozen years is hardly an irrefutable argument for such an invitation.

The underlying consideration for new constitutional commitments to education is the same as it is and has been for desegregation. Is the country near enough to agreement, or near enough to being persuadable, that the rights and duties in question are basic, fundamental, necessary? Can such rights be stated in terms that command assent, and then be formulated in enough detail to permit implementation that appears fair and necessary, and not just a judge's disagreement with a school board's decision about how much education to provide or a legislature's decision allocating financial burdens among the subdivisions of the state?

The participants in the 1978 American Academy of Arts and Sciences meetings on desegregation were—many of them—ready to have the country make new commitments to educational quality and equality, and to have those commitments replace integration as our most fundamental educational obligation. Even after the meetings, however, few of those participants were ready to argue that the new duties should be formulated and implemented judicially. Those issues, then, remain our unfinished business as we pursue into its second quarter-century the great goals described by Chief Justice Earl Warren in his *Brown* opinion.

Contributors

Derrick Bell, Dean of the University of Oregon School of Law, has spent his professional career in civil rights litigation, teaching, and writing. In the mid-1960s he supervised school desegregation litigation as a staff attorney with the NAACP Legal Defense Fund, and from 1965 to 1967 he served as Deputy Director of the Office for Civil Rights, U.S. Department of Health, Education, and Welfare.

James S. Coleman is Professor of Sociology, University of Chicago. He was principal author of *Equality of Educational Opportunity*, prepared in response to the Civil Rights Act of 1964. He writes and lectures on education and desegregation, as well as on other aspects of social organization and social change.

Nathan Glazer is Professor of Education and Sociology at Harvard University and coeditor of the journal *The Public Interest*. He is author of *Affirmative Discrimination: Ethnic Inequality and Public Policy*, coauthor (with Daniel P. Moynihan) of *Beyond the Melting Pot*, and coeditor (with William Gorham) of *The Urban Predicament*. The main subjects on which he lectures and writes are urban and ethnic problems and policies.

Frank Goodman is Professor of Law, University of Pennsylvania. He teaches constitutional law and writes on school desegregation and other questions. He has served with the Solicitor General of the United States and is a consultant to several government agencies.

Linda Hanten is Deputy General Counsel, Legal Services Corporation, Washington, D.C. Formerly staff attorney for the Mexican-American Legal Defense and Educational Fund, she has specialized in cases involving school desegregation, voting rights, and discrimination in education and employment, especially with reference to Mexican-American women.

Willis D. Hawley is Director of the Center for Education and Human Development Policy and Professor of Political Science at Vanderbilt University. He heads the Education Policy Development Center—Desegregation, which advises the U.S. Department of Education, and has been cochairman of the National Review Panel on School Desegregation Research. His areas of professional interest are school desegregation, organization of schools, urban politics, and political behavior.

Harold R. Isaacs, Professor Emeritus of Political Science at the Massachusetts Institute of Technology, has written extensively about politics and human behavior. His works include *Idols of the Tribe: Group Identity and Political Change, India's Ex-Untouchables, The New World of Negro Americans*, and, most recently, *Power and Identity: Tribalism in World Politics*.

Barbara L. Jackson is Dean, School of Education, Morgan State University (Baltimore). She has taught at Atlanta University, worked with the National Urban League and the Boston Model Cities Administration, and served as a consultant and on the boards of educational and community organizations.

David L. Kirp is Professor in the Graduate School of Public Policy and and Lecturer in the School of Law, University of California, Berkeley. He has written on problems of race and education. His most recent book is *Doing Good by Doing Little: Race and Schooling in Britain*.

Lance Liebman is Professor of Law at Harvard University. He was a law clerk to Supreme Court Justice Byron White and from 1968 to 1970 served as an assistant to Mayor John Lindsay of New York. His teaching and writings concentrate on social welfare law and urban problems.

Gary Orfield is Professor of Political Science and a member of the Institute of Government and Public Affairs at the University of Illinois. In March 1980 he was appointed by the federal district court in St. Louis as its expert in the development of a plan for school desegregation in that city. Among his publications are *Must We Bus? Law, Segregated Schools, and National Policy* and *The Reconstruction of Southern Education: The Schools and the 1964 Civil Rights Act*.

Thomas F. Pettigrew is Professor of Social Psychology, University of California, Santa Cruz. Author of *A Profile of the Negro American* and *Racially Separate or Together?* and editor of *Racial Discrimination in the United States* and *The Sociology of Race Relations: Reflection and Reform*, he has been involved in the development of several school desegregation plans.

Diane Ravitch is Associate Professor of History and Education at Teachers College, Columbia University. She is author of *The Great School Wars: New York City, 1805-1973* and *The Revisionists Revised: A Critique of the Radical Attack on the Schools*, as well as of many articles and reviews.

Nancy H. St. John has been primarily concerned with the sociology of education. In addition to journal articles, her writings include two books, *Social Class and the Urban School* (with Robert Herriott) and *School Desegregation: Outcomes for Children*. Active in community organizations, she is especially involved in working with Maine Indians.

Corinne S. Schelling is Assistant Executive Officer, American Academy of Arts and Sciences, Boston. Coeditor of several books and reports, including *When Values Conflict: Essays on Environmental Analysis, Discourse, and Decision*, she has participated in Academy studies on poverty, ethnicity, the environment, and other social science and public policy problems.

Charles V. Willie is Professor of Education and Urban Studies, Harvard Graduate School of Education. He has been a court-appointed master in the Boston school desegregation case, an expert witness in the Dallas school desegregation case, and a consultant to the Illinois Department of Education in evaluating the Chicago school desegregation plan. His recent books are *The Sociology of Urban Education* and *Community Politics and Educational Change*.

Adam Yarmolinsky practices law in Washington, D.C. and has held government and academic positions. Arms control, urban problems and policy, and health care have been his principal areas of professional interest. His publications include many articles on domestic and international affairs.

Index

and school, 3, 39, 56-65, 75-76, 78n37;
Supreme Court distinction between de
facto and de jure, 45-49, 194-195; prob-
lem of remedy, 49-71; causation, 51-65;
prevalence in housing patterns, 130-131,
136-142, 185; black perspective, 206, 214-
215. *See also* Desegregation; Racial balance; Supreme Court
Segregation academies, southern, 32
Self-concept/esteem, effects of desegregation, 91-92, 152-153
Serge, Victor, 109
Serna v. *Portales Municipal Schools*, 221
Sklare, Marshall, 140
Slavery: black perspective, 205-207; caste
system following, 254
Slavin, Robert E., 96-97, 149
Social action: by racial minorities, 131-133;
minority and majority responsibility for,
133-134
Southern States: resistance to desegrega-
tion, 11, 12, 30; school desegregation, 24-
44; cities compared with northern, 28, 38;
prevalence of metropolitan approaches,
179n2
Stability, and metropolitan approaches to
desegregation, 170, 173-174
Staff development programs, for successful
desegregation, 156
State governments, role in desegregation,
176-177
Stewart, Potter, 165
Student body, maintenance of stability, 156
Suburbanization trend, 16-19, 38-39, 136-
142. *See also* White flight
Supreme Court: *1954* decision on desegregation (*Brown*), 1-4, 84, 108, 124, 182-
183; on southern desegregation, 13-14,
29-30; decisions after *1976*, 21-22, 35-37;
on northern desegregation, 35-37, 39,
194; de facto/de jure distinction, 45-49,
194-195; theory underlying remedial decisions, 49-71; on problem of multidistrict
desegregation, 71-77; and urban school
cases, 194-203; constitutional aspects of
decisions, 254, 255. *See also* Judiciary;
and specific decisions, such as *Brown*,
Dayton, *Keyes*

Swann v. *Charlotte-Mecklenburg*, 13, 30,
31-32, 37, 50, 51, 257

Taeuber, Karl E. and Alma F., 131, 165
Teachers, role in effective desegregation,
95-96, 155, 156, 157
Thurmond, Strom, 26
Title VI (Civil Rights Act of *1964*), 11, 12,
219-221
Titmuss, Richard, 243
Tracking, effect on race relations, 149-150,
155
Transportation, *see* Busing
Truman, Harry S, 108

Urban demography, 3, 16-19, 21, 38-39,
198; and prognosis for ghettoized education, 39-41; and educational reform, 126-
135; as requiring metropolitan approaches, 163-166; and Supreme Court
decisions since *1973*, 194-203; of Great
Britain, 244. *See also* Cities; Metropolitan approaches; White flight

Values: of equality and of community, 10-
11, 14-16, 21, 22-23; and public educa-
tion, 28; constitutional, 253-269
Veroff, Joseph, 91
Voting Rights Act (*1965*), 14, 28, 40, 108
Voucher plans, 192

Wallace, George, 26
Warren, Earl, 84
Washington v. *Davis*, 21, 74
Wechsler, Herbert, 199
Weinberg, Meyer, 88
White flight, 16-19, 21, 22, 38-39, 75, 147,
157-159, 166-169, 256
Wilcox, Preston, 15
Willie, Charles V., 4, 95, 126-135
Wilmington, Delaware, 73-74
Wilson, William J., 126, 129, 246
Wisconsin, desegregation in, *see* Milwaukee

Yarmolinsky, Adam, vii-ix